"As the word itself indicates, theology's most essential task is to speak about God. To do this responsibly requires close collaboration between systematic and biblical theology. Regarding the theme of God's incomprehensibility, which has already been addressed in systematic theology, this book makes an important contribution from biblical-theological perspectives. It provides clear and original exegetical analyses that offer further insight into this highly significant topic."

—**H.G.L. Peels**
Emeritus Professor of Old Testament Studies, Theologische Universiteit Apeldoorn, The Netherlands

"*Deus semper major*: God is always greater . . . a fundamental principle in Reformed theology. This book reveals how this confession weaves consistently through both the Old and New Testaments. It is surprising to discover how, from various biblical passages, one clear and relevant message emerges. Though we cannot fully comprehend God, what we do know is reliable—adequate to foster trust, guide our walk with him, and lead us to worship."

—**Michael C. Mulder**
Assistant Professor of New Testament and Judaism, Theological University Apeldoorn, The Netherlands

"One fact that is important to comprehend in biblical theology is the incomprehensibility of God within the biblical corpus. Indeed, the hiddenness of God in the First and Second Testaments reminds us of the transformative power of the Divine Presence and the human necessity of God's saving-revealing work. In this fine international collection gathered by Francois Viljoen and Albert Coetsee of NWU Potchefstroom, readers will become reacquainted with holy mysteries in biblical times, as well as today. A must-read for Bible readers and theologians alike!"

—**Paul N. Anderson**
Author of *The Christology of the Fourth Gospel*

"The (in-)comprehensibility of God is a problem commonly discussed in systematic theology. Here, biblical scholars from both the Old and the New Testament address this issue from various biblical passages, applying multiple approaches. Six contributions are from the Old Testament and four are from the New Testament. Larger units like the narrative parts of the Old Testament, books (Job), and different passages from the Bible are investigated. The variety of passages, as well as the different approaches followed, make for interesting reading, aiding the reader in a more nuanced understanding of the incomprehensibility of God."

—**S. D. (Fanie) Snyman**
Research Associate for Old and New Testament Studies, University of the Free State, South Africa

"The authors who contributed to this seminal publication are all well-known scholars in the field of biblical studies. Under the meticulous editorial supervision of the South African theologians Francois Viljoen and Albert Coetsee, who authored as well, these scholars ventured a thesis on the incomprehensibility of God. It is indeed an achievement because the theme was in the past mainly debated by systematic theologians. However sound systematic theology stands on the shoulders of well-researched biblical theology, and in this respect the publication succeeds in illuminating core aspects of God's incomprehensibility and could serve the cause of further engagement with the topic within the ambit of other theological disciplines."

—**Jakobus M. (Koos) Vorster**
Faculty of Theology, North-West University, South Africa

Biblical Theological Investigations into the Incomprehensibility of God

Biblical Theological Investigations into the Incomprehensibility of God

Edited by
FRANCOIS P. VILJOEN
& ALBERT J. COETSEE

WIPF & STOCK · Eugene, Oregon

BIBLICAL THEOLOGICAL INVESTIGATIONS INTO THE INCOMPREHENSIBILITY OF GOD

Copyright © 2025 Wipf and Stock Publishers. All rights reserved. Except for brief quotations in critical publications or reviews, no part of this book may be reproduced in any manner without prior written permission from the publisher. Write: Permissions, Wipf and Stock Publishers, 199 W. 8th Ave., Suite 3, Eugene, OR 97401.

Wipf & Stock
An Imprint of Wipf and Stock Publishers
199 W. 8th Ave., Suite 3
Eugene, OR 97401

www.wipfandstock.com

PAPERBACK ISBN: 979-8-3852-4356-3
HARDCOVER ISBN: 979-8-3852-4357-0
EBOOK ISBN: 979-8-3852-4358-7

VERSION NUMBER 102325

Contents

Lists of Tables and Figures | ix
Research Justification | xi
Notes on Contributors | xiii
Preface | xix
Abbreviations | xxv

Chapter 1

The Incomprehensibility of God in the Old Testament Narratives: The Mystery of God "Changing His Mind" | 1

—P. PAUL KRÜGER

    Abstract | 1
    Introduction | 2
    The Concept of Incomprehensibility | 3
    The Notion of Divine Attributes | 6
    Types of Incomprehensibility in Narratives | 8
    Divine Reversals | 11
    Conclusion | 17
    Bibliography | 18

Chapter 2

Divine Incomprehensibility Fostering Human Responsibility: The Structure and Rhetorical Aim of Deuteronomy 10:12–22 | 20

—ALBERT J. COETSEE

    Abstract | 20
    Introduction | 20
    Previous analyses of the structure of Deuteronomy 10:12–22 | 21
    A verse-by-verse overview of the content and form of Deuteronomy 10:12–22 | 28

A new suggestion of the structure of Deuteronomy 10:12–22 | 39
Conclusion: The rhetorical function of Deuteronomy 10:12–22 | 41
Bibliography | 43

Chapter 3

Ways the Lord Makes Himself Known in the Book of Job | 45
—Robin Gallaher Branch

Abstract | 45
Introduction | 46
Other Views on the Book of Job's Theme | 48
Methodology | 48
Two Inclusions Frame the Book of Job | 49
Aspects of the Lord's Character in the Book of Job | 51
Conclusion: The Joy of Knowing You, Lord | 66
Bibliography | 68

Chapter 4

Incomprehensibility of God as Zest of Life: Proverbs 30 | 70
—Frédérique D. Dantonel

Abstract | 70
Introduction | 70
"Discerning," "understanding," and "comprehending" in the book of Proverbs | 72
Examples of key junctions | 75
"Understanding" and Proverbs 30 | 80
Conclusion | 83
Bibliography | 84

Chapter 5

The Incomprehensibility of God in LXX Psalm 102 | 85
—Gert J. Steyn

Abstract | 85
Introduction | 86
The LORD's Divine Attributes in LXX Psalm 102 | 87
Clustering and Systemizing the Divine Attributes in LXX Psalm 102 | 94
Conclusion | 99
Bibliography | 100

Chapter 6

The (In)comprehensibility of God and His Works: A Re-education of Judah in Isaiah 40:12–31 | 102

—P. CHRIS VAN DER WALT

   Abstract | 102
   Introduction | 103
   Background to Isaiah 40 | 104
   Structure of Isaiah 40 | 104
   Isaiah 40:12–31 | 105
   Key concepts | 109
   Conclusion | 112
   Bibliography | 113

Chapter 7

Jesus Reveals the Incomprehensible God by Sharing Exclusive Knowledge with Humble Followers: A Biblical Theological Investigation into Matthew 11:25–30 and Luke 10:21–22 | 115

—FRANCOIS P. VILJOEN

   Abstract | 115
   Introduction | 116
   Narrative context of Jesus's utterances | 119
   Jesus's praise | 128
   Conclusion | 133
   Bibliography | 135

Chapter 8

The Unknowability of God in John's Gospel | 136

—PAUL J. CREEVEY

   Abstract | 136
   Introduction | 137
   Paul: Unknowability of God | 138
   John: Making God Known? | 141
   Conclusion | 151
   Bibliography | 151

Chapter 9

"Tightrope Acts": Interpretive Tension, Incomprehensibility and Divine Directive in Acts 1:6–8 | 153

—MATTHEW W. WATSON

- Abstract | 153
- Introduction | 154
- The structure of Acts 1:6–8 | 155
- Contextualizing the query: Israel's restoration in Luke and Acts | 157
- It is not for you to know: Deliberate incomprehensibility | 159
- It is for you to be witnesses: the refocusing power of divine directive | 161
- Luke's vision for Israel's future: management of expectations or ironic reinterpretation? | 162
- A visual metaphor: The "tightrope" of human response to divine directive and incomprehensibility | 166
- Conclusion: Acts 1:6–8 and a biblical theology of divine incomprehensibility | 168
- *Bibliography* | 169

Chapter 10

The Relation Between Spiritual Intelligence and Understanding God: Reading 1 Corinthians 2:6–16 | 172

—ELMA M. CORNELIUS

- Abstract | 172
- Introduction | 173
- Socio-historical background to 1 Corinthians, relevant for an interpretation of 1 Corinthians 2:6–16 | 175
- The place of verses 6–16 in the letter structure of 1 Corinthians 2 | 176
- An outline of the argument in 1 Corinthians 2:1–16 | 177
- The power of contrast in 1 Corinthians 2:6—3:4 | 179
- Persuasion strategies in 1 Corinthians 2:1–16 | 182
- Theological analysis | 185
- Conclusion: What is the relation between spiritual intelligence and understanding God? | 190
- *Bibliography* | 192

Lists of Tables and Figures

TABLES

Table 1: Block's view of Deuteronomy 10:12—11:1 | 26
Table 2: Distribution of the lexemes ןיב, הניב and הנובת in the 915 verses of the Book of Proverbs | 73
Table 3: The parallel between Matthew's and Luke's versions of Jesus's revelations about God | 117
Table 4: Jesus's praise | 128
Table 5: Jesus's thanks to the Father | 129
Table 6: Gnosis resides in Jesus | 131
Table 7: Jesus's invitation | 132
Table 8: The contrast between Ψυχικὸς and πνευματικὸς | 180

FIGURES

Figure 1: A visual overview of the structure of Deuteronomy 10:12–22 | 39
Figure 2: The syntactical correspondence within Acts 1:6–8 | 156
Figure 3: A visual metaphor of human comprehension and divine incomprehensibility | 167

Research Justification

The incomprehensibility of God is a divine attribute found either explicitly or implicitly in the text of the Old and New Testament. While God can be known as far as he reveals himself, the text of both the Old and the New Testament bears witness to the fact that his nature and work is ultimately unfathomable. In the Old Testament, for example, the psalms attest that God's knowledge is too wonderful (Ps 139:6) and his greatness unsearchable (Ps 145:3); Job declares that no one can understand the thunder of God's power (Job 26:14); in Isaiah, God's thoughts and ways are described as much higher than the thoughts of human beings (Isa 55:8–9). In the New Testament, Paul reflects that no one truly comprehends the thoughts of God except the Spirit of God (1 Cor 2:10–11), that God dwells in unapproachable light (1 Tim 6:16), and that God in his wisdom is ultimately incomprehensible (Rom 11:33–36).

Systematic theology has long since engaged with this concept. Fewer studies, however, are devoted to investigating God's incomprehensibility from a biblical theological perspective. This is exactly what this publication aims to do: it provides several exegetical investigations into the attribute of God's incomprehensibility by investigating specific verses, chapters, and corpora from Scripture and indicating how these portray God's incomprehensibility as part of the developing, unfolding and progressive story line of the text. This includes research of topics that have not been adequately explored in the past.

Each chapter included in this volume originated as a paper of the research unit *Biblical Theological Investigations into the Attributes of God* which were presented at the annual conference of the *European Association of Biblical Studies* (EABS), July 15–18, 2024, at Sofia University St. Kliment Ohridski in Bulgaria. The research unit *Biblical Theological Investigations into the Attributes of God* explores how biblical texts from the First and Second Testaments depict attributes of God, tracing their development and progression throughout Scripture's unfolding narrative. For the 2024 edition of this conference, scholars were invited to submit papers on biblical texts with explicit or implicit references to the incomprehensibility of God in its rich diversity, and to investigate these texts from a biblical theological perspective. Following the conference, contributors refined and expanded their papers into the chapters featured in this volume.

No empirical research was conducted, and the various chapters do not pose ethical risks. The chapters contained in this volume are written by Old and New Testament scholars, and the target audience is fellow Old and New Testament scholars and scholars interested in God's attributes. All chapters are original investigations with original results. No part of the volume has been published elsewhere before.

Francois P. Viljoen
Albert J. Coetsee

Notes on Contributors

Robin Gallaher Branch
Department Religion & Philosophy, Christian Brothers University Memphis, Tennessee, USA, and Unit for Reformational Theology and the Development of the South African Society, Faculty of Theology, North-West University, Potchefstroom, South Africa
Email address: rbranch3@cbu.edu
ORCiD: https://orcid.org/0000-0002-7574-1028
Keywords of chapter: The Lord as administrator, teacher, listener, tour guide, one with good manners, one who restores and promotes
Robin Gallaher Branch has a PhD in Hebrew Studies from the University of Texas at Austin, 2000. She was a Fulbright Scholar to South Africa, 2002-2003, and has kept her affiliation with North-West University. She has published three books: (1) *Six Biblical Plays for Contemporary Audiences* (Eugene, Oregon: Cascade Books, 2016); (2) *Jeroboam's Wife: The Enduring Contributions of the Old Testament's Least-Known Women* (Baker Academic, 2009; reprint edition, Wipf & Stock, 2018); and (3) *Only in Zaire* (Atlanta: Presbyterian Church, USA, 1981). She plays her flute regularly in various venues. She serves her church as a teacher and as what she fondly calls "a rocker and stroller of the little ones in the house of the Lord."

Albert J. Coetsee
Unit for Reformational Theology and the Development of the South African Society, Faculty of Theology, North-West University, Potchefstroom, South Africa
Email address: albert.coetsee@nwu.ac.za
ORCiD: https://orcid.org/0000-0002-5549-2474
Keywords of chapter: Deuteronomy 10:12-22, structure, rhetorical aim, divine incomprehensibility, human responsibility, transcendence, immanence

Albert J. Coetsee studied theology at the North-West University. From 2011 to 2016, he was the minister of the Reformed Church Uitschot. During these years, he completed his PhD in New Testament, investigating the theme of God's speech in the book of Hebrews. Since 2017, he has been an Old Testament lecturer at the North-West University, and an associate professor since 2023. He serves as Sub-Programme Leader of the group Bibliological Perspectives. He is the author and co-author of thirty-one articles and book chapters and the co-editor of six scholarly books. His academic interests include the book of Deuteronomy, the book of Hebrews, the use of the book of Deuteronomy in Hebrews and hermeneutics.

Elma M. Cornelius
Research Focus Area: Ancient Texts: Text, Context, and Reception, Faculty of Theology, North-West University, Potchefstroom, South Africa
Email address: elma.cornelius@nwu.ac.za
ORCiD: https://orcid.org/0000-0001-5420-0647
Keywords of chapter: Spiritual intelligence, understanding God, 1 Corinthians 2:6–16, incomprehensibility, comprehension of God
Elma M. Cornelius is associate professor in New Testament Studies in the Faculty of Theology on the Vanderbijlpark campus of the North-West University in South Africa. She has a DPhil in Religious studies from the University of Stellenbosch in South Africa. Before Stellenbosch, she earned her Master of Fine Arts degree from the Potchefstroom University in Greek. From 1993–2003 she taught Greek at the PU for CHE, from 1998 as head of the subject group of Greek. In 2002, she became associate professor in the Faculty of Theology at the PU for CHE. From 2004–2018, she taught New Testament part-time in the Faculty of Humanities on the Vanderbijlpark campus of the North-West University. Since 2019 she taught New Testament full-time in the Faculty of Theology of the North-West University. She has supervised four Master studies and co-supervised one Masters and one PhD study. She has published forty articles in national journals and three chapters in books.

Paul J. Creevey
Department of Biblical Studies, University of Divinity, Melbourne, Australia
Email address: paul.creevey@ctc.edu.au / paul.creevey@marists.org.au
ORCiD: https://orcid.org/0009-0005-8744-648X
Keywords of chapter: John, incomprehensibility, incarnation, self-revelation of Jesus, divine pneuma, agency of Jesus, loved by God

Paul J. Creevey is a lecturer in Biblical Studies and Languages as well as Systematic Theology at the University of Divinity in Melbourne. At Catholic Theological College, he is the program director for the faith formation of teachers in Catholic Schools. At Yarra Theological College, Paul is the director of higher research applications. He has a recent monograph, *In the Garden There Was a New Tomb* (2024), that provides a new structural analysis of John 19:38–20:29.

Frédérique D. Dantonel
Goethe Universität Frankfurt am Main, Germany
Email address: frederiquedantonel@outlook.de
ORCiD: https://orcid.org/0009-0009-3301-6176
Keywords of chapter: Understanding, knowledge, responsibility, wisdom, God

Frédérique Dantonel is a doctoral candidate at the Goethe University in Frankfurt am Main, Germany. She studied the German language and literature in Paris and Berlin, as well as Protestant theology at the Humboldt University of Berlin. Her recent publications include the following: "Alexei Anatoljewitsch Nawalny" in *Biographisch-Bibliographisches Kirchenlexikon*, Verlag Traugott Bautz: Nordhausen, 2024, and "How are Spaces and Places of Experiences accessible? Song of Songs and Proverbs" in *Song of Songs in Sense, Sound and Space*, ed. by Gavin Fernandes, Stefan Fischer and Annette Potgieter, (Hebrew Bible Monographs 112), Sheffield Phoenix Press: Sheffield 2024.

P. Paul Krüger
Unit for Reformational Theology and the Development of the South African Society, Faculty of Theology, North-West University, Potchefstroom, South Africa
Email address: biblio.akad@gmail.com
ORCiD: https://orcid.org/0000-0002-0847-6527
Keywords of chapter: Divine attributes, incomprehensibility, inapprehensibility, ineffability, incongruency, impassibility, divine reversals, נחם, פלא, אֵין חֵקֶר

P. Paul Krüger is a research fellow affiliated with the Faculty of Theology at the Potchefstroom Campus of the North-West University. From 2000 to 2016, he served as associate professor in Old Testament Studies at the same faculty. During this time, he was also affiliated with the Theological School in Potchefstroom and the training of ministers. He holds a master's degree in Semitic Languages and a ThD in Old Testament Studies. His doctoral dissertation focuses on coherence relations as an exegetical tool, illustrated in texts from the Pentateuch. His primary research interests include Biblical Theology and the methodology of exegesis, particularly with regard to the Pentateuch and the Former Prophets.

Gert J. Steyn
Theologische Hochschule Ewersbach, Germany and Extraordinary Professor of the Faculty of Theology and Religion, University of Pretoria, South Africa
Email address: gert.steyn@the.feg.de
ORCiD: https://orcid.org/0000-0002-0261-1652
Keywords of chapter: Psalm 103(102), Septuagint, healer, redeemer, ruler, righteous judge, majestic king, creator and sustainer, wisdom teacher

Gert J. Steyn holds doctorates in Theology (DD, Pretoria) and Ancient Greek (DLitt, Stellenbosch). He lectured since 1987 at Unisa and the Federal Theological Seminary; since 2001 as professor at the Universities of Johannesburg and Pretoria; since 2017 as professor at the Theologische Hochschule Ewersbach (Germany). He was principal of T.E.E. College and departmental head at the University of Pretoria. Specializing in early Judaism (LXX; Philo) and early Christianity (Hebrews; Luke-Acts), he authored 200+ scholarly publications. He is a founding member of the LXXSA, former president and secretary of the NTSSA, member of the SNTS, IOSCS, SBL, EABS, AfeT, external reviewer for Theological Institutions across Africa and Europe, and reviewer for research projects of the European Science Foundation, DFG, and Von Humboldt Stiftung. Research awards include the Alexander von Humboldt Fellowship, D.A.A.D., NRF, and UP Exceptional Academic Achiever's Award.

P. Chris van der Walt
Unit for Reformational Theology and the Development of the South African Society, Faculty of Theology, North-West University, Potchefstroom, South Africa
Email address: chris.vanderwalt@nwu.ac.za
ORCiD: https://orcid.org/0000-0001-9889-0280
Keywords of chapter: Babylonian exile, eternal, comfort, Isaiah 40:12–31, (in)comprehensibility, omniscience, prophetic perspective, righteous

After being a minister for twenty-one years, P. Chris van der Walt was appointed by the NWU in 2011 to teach Old Testament and specifically the prophets. His PhD dealt with the identity of God's people in the book of

Isaiah, and since then, some articles and book chapters have been written about Isaiah. He loves nature and is also involved in eco-theology.

Francois P. Viljoen
Unit for Reformational Theology and the Development of the South African Society, Faculty of Theology, North-West University, Potchefstroom, South Africa
Email address: viljoen.francois@nwu.ac.za
ORCiD: https://orcid.org/0000-0001-8251-4539
Keywords of chapter: Incomprehensibility, divine revelation, wisdom, eschatological knowledge, christological revelation, humility, revelation and concealment, acceptance and confession, Matthew 11:25-30, Luke 10:21-22.

Francois P. Viljoen is a professor of New Testament at the Faculty of Theology at North-West University (NWU) in South Africa and at the Theological School of the Reformed Churches in Southern Africa. Holding both a PhD (Nijmegen) and a ThD (Potchefstroom), he is a C2-rated researcher by the National Research Foundation (NRF). His expertise lies in New Testament studies, with a particular focus on Synoptic Gospels, Matthew, and Hermeneutics. He has authored numerous publications inter alia on Jesus's teachings, identity formation in Matthew, the interpretation of the Torah in Matthew, and the attributes of God. He has served as editor and co-editor of several academic publications.

Matthew W. Watson
Instituto Bíblico Português (Portuguese Bible Institute), Portugal
Email address: m.watson.portugal@gmail.com
ORCiD: https://orcid.org/0000-0002-0809-3729
Keywords of chapter: Biblical theology, hermeneutics, attributes of God, incomprehensibility of God, knowability of God, eschatology, Luke-Acts, Acts 1:6-8

Matthew W. Watson currently serves as the vice director and academic dean of the Instituto Bíblico Português, an interdenominational seminary outside Lisbon, Portugal, where he lectures in hermeneutics and exegesis, research methodology, and the New Testament. He completed his MTh with distinction at the North-West University of South Africa in 2023, focusing on the hermeneutical and rhetorical aims of Luke's gospel. He has published a number of articles on the intersection of Luke-Acts, biblical theology, social dynamics, and the communicative strategies of the first century and has also worked on the textual criticism of Bible revision projects in Portuguese. He aims to inspire the next generation of thinkers across the Lusophone world to engage with the Scriptures and the contemporary world with rigor, grace, humility, empathy, and practical impact.

Preface

INTRODUCTION

The aim of this publication is to provide several exegetical investigations into the attribute of God's incomprehensibility by investigating specific verses, chapters and corpora from Scripture and indicating how these portray God's incomprehensibility as part of the developing, unfolding and progressive story line of the text.

The publication consists of two sections, of which the first contains investigations of God's incomprehensibility in the Old Testament and the second God's incomprehensibility in the New Testament.

GOD'S INCOMPREHENSIBILITY IN THE OLD TESTAMENT

In his article "The incomprehensibility of God in the Old Testament narratives: The mystery of God 'changing his mind,'" Paul Krüger examines the divine attribute of God's incomprehensibility in the narrative texts of the Old Testament, with a particular focus on the so-called Henneateuch. He first investigates what the notion of incomprehensibility involves before focusing on two types of divine incomprehensibility in these narratives, namely references to God's incomprehensibility due to the magnitude of his attributes and deeds, and references to incomprehensibility of incongruency (instances where God's attributes appear contradictory). Subsequently, he turns to investigating divine reversals in the Old Testament narratives, reflecting on instances where God relents from the impending doom he has announced and instances where God reverses a positive situation due to unacceptable human behavior. He concludes that instead of offering various explanations, we must accept that God remains incomprehensible to humankind simply because he is God and God alone.

Noting the lack of scholarly consensus concerning the structure of Deut 10:12–22, Albert J. Coetsee investigates the structure and rhetorical aim of the passage anew. He did this by providing an overview of previous analyses of the structure of the passage and examining Deut 10:12–22 on a verse-by-verse basis in order to identify aspects of the passage that influence and contribute to its structure. Based on this, he provides a new proposal for the structure of the passage, followed by reflection on its rhetorical aim. His chapter found that the passage contains exhortations that are supported by motivations that focus on divine transcendence and immanence, and that the passage has a deliberate and consistent alternation between human responsibility and divine incomprehensibility, highlighting the latter in order to foster the former.

Robin Gallaher Branch investigates the ways in which the Lord makes himself known in the book of Job. She takes issue with the view that God is inscrutable and difficult to understand and demonstrates how the book of Job indicates that God can and wants to be known. Her chapter investigates several character traits the Lord reveals about himself in the book of Job. She argues that the book of Job should be read from the Lord's viewpoint, and that the primary theme of the book is correct knowledge of God.

Frédérique D. Dantonel's chapter, "Incomprehensibility of God as zest of life: Proverbs 30," contributes to the debate on how "understanding" should be interpreted within the book of Proverbs. Since "understanding" is a prerequisite for knowledge, she argues that the difference between the different Hebrew terms for "understanding" and "comprehending" can be explained by the modern distinction between propositional and perspectival knowledge. She consequently starts by discussing this distinction. Next, she identifies occurrences of the concept of "understanding" in the book of Proverbs and then examines key passages in light of her findings to indicate how "understanding" can be interpreted in the book. She concludes that human beings are gifted not only with propositional but also with perspectival "understanding." To this end, human beings should learn to behave ethically and morally responsible toward their fellow human beings, other living beings and God.

Gert J. Steyn's chapter investigates the incomprehensibility of God in LXX Ps 102. His attention is exclusively focused on the ancient Greek translation of the Psalm (Ps 102 in the LXX; Ps 103 in the MT) as a version in its own right. He starts by providing an overview of the Lord's divine attributes in LXX Ps 102 according to the three strophes of the song. The survey reveals that LXX Ps 102 presents a high density of divine attributes that are linked to the Lord God of Israel, and that the image of the Lord clearly differentiates itself from the numerous idols within a multi-religious context.

Especially four categories of divine attributes can be identified from LXX Ps 102: God as Divine Creator and Sustainer, the Great and Majestic King, a Righteous Judge, and a Wisdom Teacher. Steyn concludes that LXX Ps 102 portrays an exclusive picture of an incomprehensible Lord (ὁ κύριος) who is Holy, Creator, Sustainer, Ruler, Revealer, Healer, Redeemer, Reconciler, Consoler, Compassionate Father, Merciful, and Righteous.

Chris van der Walt explores the complex theological discourse in Isa 40:12–31, where the prophet confronts misconceptions regarding the comprehensibility of God and his actions in history. In response to Judah's doubts following the capture of Jerusalem and their exile, the prophet re-educates the people on Yahweh's sovereignty, challenging their flawed beliefs tied to land and temple. While God's nature is incomparable and beyond full human understanding, he reveals himself through prophets, shaping perspectives on his character and works. The prophet's role is pivotal in transforming lament into praise, emphasizing divine revelation as the foundation for Judah's hope. This study sheds light on the tension between human comprehension and God's vast existence, offering theological insight into Israel's reformation.

GOD'S INCOMPREHENSIBILITY IN THE NEW TESTAMENT

The study by Francois P. Viljoen delves into Jesus' role in revealing the incomprehensible God by sharing exclusive knowledge with humble followers, focusing on Matt 11:25–30 and Luke 10:21–22. Despite rejection by unrepentant cities, Jesus thanks God for revealing divine truths to the humble while concealing them from the wise. The investigation explores what these "hidden things" are and their relation to God's incomprehensibility. Jesus, possessing unique knowledge due to his sonship, invites the weary to find rest by taking his yoke, symbolizing obedience to his teachings. This yoke, unlike Pharisaic burdens, provides guidance and relief. Jesus' ministry, marked by rejection and acceptance, highlights the dynamic of divine revelation and concealment, emphasizing humility as the key to receiving God's wisdom. Through Jesus, the divine nature becomes accessible, underscoring the transformative impact of his message.

Paul J. Creevey's analysis in "The Unknowability of God in John's Gospel" examines the theological paradox of knowing God through the lens of John's Gospel and Pauline texts. The study highlights the apophatic tradition, emphasizing God's incomprehensibility, while acknowledging the Incarnation as a revelation of God's nature through Jesus Christ. John's Gospel asserts that Jesus, as the divine Logos, makes God known, yet God's essence remains ultimately mysterious. Paul's writings reinforce this by suggesting that true knowledge of God comes through the divine Spirit. The chapter argues that while God's essence is unknowable, through Jesus' life, death, and resurrection, humanity is invited into a relationship with God, understanding that they are known and loved by God. This duality encompasses both the unknowability and the revealed presence of God.

Matthew W. Watson's chapter "Tightrope Acts" explores the theological tension between divine incomprehensibility and knowability in Acts 1:6–8. The apostles' query about the restoration of Israel and Jesus' response illustrate this tension. Jesus redirects the apostles' focus from eschatological concerns to a mission enabled by the Holy Spirit, emphasizing the incomprehensibility of divine plans within God's authority. Watson examines the structure and content of the text, the literary context of Luke's Gospel, and the implications for understanding God's plan. He argues that the apostles' mission highlights the balance between human comprehension and divine mystery, underscoring the need for humility and reliance on the Holy Spirit in interpreting and acting upon divine directives.

Elma M. Cornelius's chapter delves into the relationship between spiritual intelligence and understanding God, particularly through an analysis of 1 Cor 2:6–16. Cornelius highlights the incomprehensibility of God, emphasizing that divine wisdom and knowledge are revealed through the Spirit, which only believers possessing spiritual intelligence can comprehend. The chapter explores Paul's distinction between worldly wisdom and God's wisdom, underscoring that true spiritual maturity involves receiving the Spirit and having the mind of Christ. Cornelius argues that while God's plans and actions are not fully understandable, spiritual intelligence enables believers to grasp the essence of divine wisdom, fostering a deeper relationship with God and a transformative understanding of His revelation.

Throughout this publication, scholars explore the incomprehensibility of God as a theological theme across both Old and New Testament texts. Each investigation illuminates how human limitation intersects with divine mystery. The studies demonstrate that while God's essence remains beyond full human grasp, his self-revelation through Scripture enables believers to encounter and engage with his wisdom. In tracing these themes, the publication contributes to ongoing theological discourse, encouraging a deeper reflection on the boundaries of human knowledge and the gracious invitation to divine insight through faith and revelation.

In conclusion, we extend our sincere gratitude to each author for their valuable contribution to the exploration of the incomprehensibility of God.

Furthermore, we express our heartfelt appreciation to Mrs. Bertha Oberholzer for her assistance in preparing the document for publication.

Francois P. Viljoen

Albert J. Coetsee

Abbreviations

BBET	Beiträge zur biblischen Exegese und Theologie
BibInt	*Biblical Interpretation*
BZAW	Beihefte zur Zeitschrift für die alttestamentliche Wissenschaft
CBQ	*Catholic Biblical Quarterly*
DBLH	Dictionary of Biblical Languages with Semantic Domains: Hebrew Old Testament
ESV	English Standard Version
HALOT	Hebrew and Aramaic Lexicon of the Old Testament
JSJSup	Supplements to Journal for the Study of Judaism
KJV	King James Version
LTPM	Louvain Theological & Pastoral Monographs
LXX	Septuagint
MT	Masoretic Text
NETS	New English Translation of the Septuagint
NICOT	New International Commentary on the Old Testament
NIDOTTE	New International Dictionary of Old Testament Theology and Exegesis
NIV	New International Version
NKJV	New King James Version
NRSV	New Revised Standard Version
NTS	New Testament Studies
SBL	Society of Biblical Literature
TDOT	Theological Dictionary of the Old Testament
TLOT	Theological Lexicon of the Old Testament
TWOT	Theological Wordbook of the Old Testament

VTSup	Supplements to Vetus Testamentum
WBC	Word Biblical Commentary
WUNT	Wissenschaftliche Untersuchungen zum Neuen Testament

Chapter 1

The Incomprehensibility of God in the Old Testament Narratives: The Mystery of God "Changing His Mind"

—P. Paul Krüger

Unit for Reformational Theology and the Development of the South African Society, Faculty of Theology, North-West University, Potchefstroom, South Africa

ABSTRACT

The concept of God's incomprehensibility is primarily discussed in descriptive and expository texts, often employing poetic language to evoke a sense of awe and wonder. This chapter examines how this divine attribute is also reflected in the narrative texts of the Hebrew Bible. The study begins by addressing the notion of divine incomprehensibility, noting that the Hebrew Bible does not contain a specific term or phrase that directly conveys this concept. It is argued that incomprehensibility should not be understood as an inherent or absolute attribute of God; rather, it arises from the limitations of created beings, who are unable to fully grasp the magnitude of divine attributes such as omnipotence and wisdom. Moreover, God's attributes frequently appear incongruent—mercy and anger, for example—thereby challenging human logic. A notable instance of such apparent incongruity occurs when God, who is described as righteous—meaning consistent in his actions, life-giving promises, and warnings—appears to change his mind in response to human behavior. These so-called "divine repentance" passages confront the reader with a depiction of God whose attributes seem to be in tension with one another.

INTRODUCTION

This chapter examines the divine attribute of God's incomprehensibility in the narrative texts of the Old Testament, with a particular focus on the so-called Henneateuch (comprising the Pentateuch and the Former Prophets), which constitutes the core of Israel's grand narrative. In addition, this chapter explores references to this attribute in texts embedded within these narratives.

The notion of God's incomprehensibility as a divine attribute has made its way into doctrinal statements and systematic theology, where it is explicitly stated alongside other divine attributes to indicate the unique nature of God as portrayed in Scripture. For the first time, incomprehensibility as an attribute of God was included in a creed in the first canon of the Fourth Lateran Council in 1215.[1] Since then, it has been reflected in many other creeds, including most of the Reformed confessions of faith from the sixteenth and seventeenth centuries.[2] The Reformed scholar Herman Bavinck commences his *Locus de Deo* with a chapter on the incomprehensibility of God.[3] In doing so, he establishes a standard for the significance of this divine attribute, at least within Reformed theology.

The meaning of the terms "incomprehensibility" and "divine attributes" must be extrapolated from the biblical text, as these terms do not occur in the Bible. The broad concept of God's incomprehensible nature is attested in a few texts of a descriptive and expository nature, but not explicitly in narratives. This chapter thus relies on texts in other genres for the definition of God's incomprehensibility before considering Old Testament narratives.

Before turning to the implicit references to God's incomprehensibility in Old Testament narratives, it is crucial first to gain a clear understanding of what the notion of *incomprehensibility* involves and to consider the notion of *divine attributes*.

---

1. Klooster, *Incomprehensibility of God*, 79–80; Fourth Lateran Council, *Confession of Faith* (1215), in *Enchiridion Symbolorum* (DS 800).

2. For example: *Belgic Confession*, article 2, with reference to Rom 11:33; Westminster Assembly, *Westminster Confession of Faith*, article 2.1, with reference to Ps 145; and Westminster Assembly, *Larger Catechism*, Q&A 7, with reference to 1 Kgs 8:27.

3. Bavinck, *Gereformeerde Dogmatiek*, 1–29.

THE CONCEPT OF INCOMPREHENSIBILITY

The Latin word *comprehendere* carries meanings such as "to grasp firmly," "to seize," or "to catch."[4] While in a figurative sense it can refer to superficial awareness or apprehension, it is more commonly used to denote thorough, exhaustive, and complete knowledge or understanding.[5] Similarly, the English word *comprehend* typically means to grasp (i.e., to understand) the meaning, nature, or significance of something.[6] The notion of taking hold of something, grasping, or catching is also evident in Germanic languages such as German (*begreifen*), Dutch (*begrijpen*), and Afrikaans (*begryp*), where the idea of physically catching something is retained in terms that denote real or genuine understanding.

Conversely, *incomprehension* or *incomprehensible* means that it is impossible—or extremely difficult—to grasp or understand something. The object in question is unintelligible, unfathomable, impenetrable, inexplicable, or inconceivable.[7] *Incomprehensibility*, then, is the state or characteristic of being beyond understanding or difficult to be grasped. This means that the subject has some awareness of the object, but the scope, depth, or implications of what is known exceeds—or largely exceeds—the subject's capacity to fully comprehend it. In this sense, incomprehensibility presupposes a degree of prior knowledge. Moreover, incomprehensibility is relative: it may range from complete incomprehensibility to partial incomprehensibility, from bewilderment to some degree of understanding.

In systematic theology, *incomprehensibility* is often distinguished from two related concepts, namely *inapprehensibility* and *ineffability*:

- An object is described as *inapprehensible* when it is either unknown or unknowable.[8] In theological terms, God would remain unknown if he does not disclose or reveal himself. To say that God is unknowable suggests that he lies beyond the limits of human knowledge or perception and is therefore inaccessible to any form of understanding or discovery. By contrast, when something or someone—such as God—is said to be *incomprehensible*, a degree of prior knowledge is presupposed. One cannot fail to understand something of which one is entirely unaware. The term *incomprehensible* thus implies a level of

---

4. "Comprehendere," *Latdict*.
5. Klooster, *Incomprehensibility of God*, 28.
6. "Comprehend," *Merriam-Webster*; "Comprehend," *Oxford English Dictionary*.
7. "Incomprehensible," *Encarta Dictionary Tools*.
8. Klooster, *Incomprehensibility of God*, 24–28, 59, 110, 116.

awareness of the object, even if its full nature cannot be grasped. As one theologian puts it, "God remains incomprehensible because he reveals himself without revealing everything there is to know about him."[9] In this light, when God is regarded as the Wholly Other (*der Ganz Andere*), as in the theology of Rudolf Otto and Karl Barth, or as the hidden God (*Deus absconditus*),[10] the discussion centers on the inapprehensibility (unknowability) of God, rather than on the incomprehensibility (unintelligibility) of God. Similarly, biblical imagery that speaks of God[11] dwelling "in thick darkness" (עֲרָפֶל, 1 Kgs 8:12) or hiding himself (סתר hitp, Isa 45:15), refers to situations in which God is unapproachable or inapprehensible. The same applies to the "secret things" (הַנִּסְתָּרֹת) mentioned in Deuteronomy 29:28 (MT). These secret things are God's decisions. They belong to him because they are not revealed. They are inapprehensible.

- Incomprehensibility is also distinct from *ineffability*, which refers to the inability to put something into words.[12] In apophatic theology, God is described through negation—by stating what *cannot* be said about him—based on the assumption that created beings cannot adequately express the essence of God through positive affirmations. The things the apostle Paul witnessed in heaven were ineffable or inexpressible (ἄρρητα, 2 Cor 12:4), meaning that he could not or was not permitted to express what he had experienced, irrespective of whether it was comprehensible to him or not. In an absolute sense, mortals can only speak of God by way of anthropomorphisms.

The Hebrew Bible uses *metaphors* and *specific terms* to describe God's incomprehensibility:

1. *Metaphors*: When God himself, his thoughts, ways, knowledge, and steadfast love are said to be much higher than that of human beings (Isa 55:8–9; Ps 139:6; 1 Kgs 8:27; cf. Ps 103:11), a *spatial metaphor* is used.[13] In comparison to God, humans are too "small"—too limited—

---

9. Sproul, "Divine Incomprehensibility."
10. Klooster, *Incomprehensibility of God*, 107, 111–14.
11. The text refers to the Lord (יהוה). For ease of discussion, this chapter makes no distinction between the divine names, even if different names are used in the respective texts, except where the context calls for a distinction.
12. The Fourth Lateral Council distinguishes God's ineffability as a separate attribute of God, apart from his incomprehensibility (Fourth Lateran Council, *Confession of Faith* (1215), in *Enchiridion Symbolorum* (DS 800)).
13. The spatial metaphor in 1 Kgs 8:27 is used in the *Westminster Larger Catechism*,

to reach or grasp God's thoughts, ways, knowledge, and steadfast love. In Ps 139:17–18, where God's thoughts are described as "difficult,"[14] a *metaphor of complexity* is used, along with a *numerical metaphor*. The sheer intricacy and multitude of God's thoughts are beyond human comprehension—like grains of sand, incalculable and innumerable. In Isa 40:28, a *temporal metaphor* is used. God is portrayed as the everlasting God, the Creator of the ends of the earth. He exists before and beyond all things known to humanity. As such, his understanding is incomprehensible to evanescent humans.

2. The Hebrew term אֵין חֵקֶר (*without searching*) is frequently used to indicate incomprehensibility.[15] In Ps 145:3, this term expresses that *God's greatness* cannot be explored or searched out.[16] Psalm 145 explicitly links God's greatness to his dealings with his people, his works, and deeds (vv. 4–5). While God's actions are perceived and known, they ultimately exceed human understanding. Similar uses of this technical term appear in the books of *Job* and *Isaiah*, where אֵין חֵקֶר is applied to *God's deeds* (Job 5:9; 9:10) and *God's understanding* (e.g., Isa 40:28; cf. Rom 11:33). Likewise, the *number of God's years* (i.e., him being eternal) is beyond understanding (לֹא־חֵקֶר, Job 36:26). Mortals do not understand God because they were not there when God laid the foundation of the earth (Job 38:4). Together, these texts emphasize that God surpasses the comprehension of created beings—not only in His essence, but also in His thoughts and deeds.

3. Various words related to the Hebrew verbal root פלא are used convey the notion that something is *wonderful*—in the sense of being extraordinary, beyond human capacity to duplicate, and difficult to fully comprehend. The related terms נִפְלָאת and נִפְלָאוֹת (nominalized participles *nif* of פלא) are frequently used to describe God's *miraculous acts* in both judgment and redemption. These acts, as manifestations

---

Q&A 7, as proof text for the incomprehensibility of God.

14. The Hebrew word יקר is interpreted as "difficult" (Köhler et al., s.v. "יקר," meaning 1) or "hard to be understood" (Gesenius, *Hebrew and Chaldee Lexicon*, s.v. "יקר," meaning 1).

15. The term is usually used when something is deemed impossible. Six of the nine occurrences in the Hebrew Bible where חֵקֶר is negated, refer to God, or to his attributes and deeds, which are "unsearchable" or "immeasurable." (Tsevat, s.v. "חָקַר ḥāqar חֵקֶר ḥēqer מֶחְקָר meḥqār." Harris, s.v. "חקר," Q.v. Köhler et al., s.v. "חקר"; Klooster, *Incomprehensibility of God*, 43.

16. The metaphor in Ps 145:3 is used in the Westminster Confession of Faith, article 2.1, as proof text for the incomprehensibility of God.

of God's power, are not only unfathomable but also cannot be replicated.¹⁷ There are only two occurrences of these terms in the narratives of the Hebrew Bible,¹⁸ yet they appear extensively throughout the hymnic parts of the Old Testament. God's extraordinary acts in history are described as wonders, miracles, or marvels—not only because of their magnitude, but more significantly because they transcend human understanding and are thus unfathomable. They are "humanly inexplicable and indescribable."¹⁹ In Ps 139:6, the psalmist declares that God's knowledge of the individual is "too wonderful for me." The second half of the verse elaborates: "It is so high that I cannot attain it," highlighting the incomprehensibility of God's knowledge.²⁰ Likewise, when Manoah inquires about God's name, the response is that it is "too wonderful" (Judg 13:18), indicating that it cannot be fathomed.²¹ In Job 5:9, God's incomprehensible (לֹא־חֵקֶר) deeds are juxtaposed with his countless marvels (נִפְלָאוֹת). A marvel is awe-inspiring precisely because it can be perceived but not fully understood. Owing to their incomprehensible nature, such acts are both unfathomable and, in many cases, ineffable.²² Numerous biblical texts refer to God's wonders in the contexts of *awe* and *adoration*.²³

THE NOTION OF DIVINE ATTRIBUTES

Before turning to the theme of God's incomprehensibility in Old Testament narratives, it is important to clarify what is meant by the concept of a *divine attribute*. The Old and New Testaments do not contain a single, generic term that refers to a unified set of divine characteristics—such as

---

17. Köhler et al., s.v. "פלא nif,'" meaning 3. The verb can refer to something that is difficult, beyond one's power or difficult to understand, hence incomprehensible (Brown, et al., s.v. "פֶּלֶא," meaning 1 and 2). In texts like Ps 40:6, 78:4, 86:10, and Job 5:9, 9:10, where נִפְלָאוֹת is used, God's greatness and our limited understanding is evident.

18. Exod 3:20 and 34:10.

19. Conrad, s.v. "פלא pl' III Nouns."

20. The word written in the consonantal Hebrew text (*ketiv*) of Ps 139:6 is the feminine adjective פְּלִאיָה, meaning "wonderful, fantastic, beyond understanding, i.e., pertaining to that which is impossible to understand" (Swanson, s.v. "7100 פְּלִי"). Harris (s.v. "1768b פֶּלְאִי") links this word to God's incomprehensibility. Brown et al. (s.v. "פֶּלְאִי") explains this adjective as "wonderful, incomprehensible."

21. The same adjective is used as in Ps 139:6. The NIV (New International Version) translates this adjective in Judg 13:18 as "beyond understanding."

22. Conrad, s.v. "פלא pl'."

23. For example, in Exod 15:11; Ps 77:12; 88:13; 89:6.

God's eternality, incomprehensibility, invisibility, immutability, infinitude, omnipotence, perfect wisdom, righteousness, and goodness.[24] Nevertheless, some biblical texts present clusters of descriptions, characteristics, or qualities of God,[25] suggesting a generic identifier, label, or concept. In systematic theology and confessions, this general category is typically referred to as "attributes."

No list of attributes is exhaustive or capable of adequately describing God. These attributes are, at best, analogical descriptions—humans attempt to speak meaningfully about the divine using concepts accessible to us as created beings. God is "only one God, who is a simple and spiritual being";[26] thus, his attributes are merely aspects of his being, who, as a person, is indivisible. They represent different perspectives on the one and only God, who ultimately surpasses all his attributes. These attributes exist in perfect harmony and cannot be contradictory, at least not within the framework of monotheistic thought as witnessed in the Old and New Testaments.

As mere aspects or descriptions of God, attributes are often difficult to distinguish clearly. They are interrelated concepts, identified and categorized by the human mind in an attempt to understand and speak meaningfully about the divine.

The harmony and interrelatedness of the divine attributes have significant implications for understanding God's incomprehensibility:

- God's incomprehensibility is *not the only attribute that confirms God's transcendence* (i.e., that God is God). Augustine of Hippo is known for the statement "*Si [enim] comprehendis, non est Deus*" (If you understand [something], it is not God).[27] The implication of this maxim is: if God were comprehensible, he would no longer be God; then we would have mastered God. In the light of the close interconnection of the divine attributes, the same would apply to any of the other attributes:

---

24. *Belgic Confession*, article 2: "He is eternal, incomprehensible, invisible, immutable, infinite, almighty, perfectly wise, just [and] good."

25. For example, in Ps 145, where the following are mentioned along with his incomprehensibility (אֵין חֵקֶר, v. 3): his goodness (טוֹב, v 7, 9), righteousness (צְדָקָה, v 7, 17), compassion (רַחוּם, v 8, 9), grace (חַנּוּן, v 8), the slowness of his anger (אֶרֶךְ אַפַּיִם, v 8), and his steadfast love (חֶסֶד, v 8). Likewise, in Exod 34, a list of characteristics of God is given: his compassion (רַחוּם, v 6), his grace (חַנּוּן, v 6), the slowness of his anger (אֶרֶךְ אַפַּיִם, v 6), his steadfast love (חֶסֶד, v 6, 7), his faithfulness (אֱמֶת, v 6), and his righteousness (described in v 7).

26. *Belgic Confession*, article 2, with reference to Deut 6:4, 1 Cor 8:4, 1 Tim 2:5, and John 4:24.

27. Augustine, "Sermon 117."

if God were temporal, visible, mutable, finite, unjust . . . he would no longer be God.

- *Incomprehensibility is not only about God's being.* When we talk about God's incomprehensibility, it does not only refer to his being. God surpasses our comprehension in his whole being, as well as in his counsels, judgments, thoughts, ways, and works, etcetera. We as creational beings cannot fully comprehend the scope and implications of God himself and of the "things pertaining to God" (cf. Heb 5:1).

- *God's incomprehensibility is proof of human limitations.* As finite creatures, human beings are incapable of containing or fully grasping the infinite God, who exists, moves, and acts on an infinite level or scale. God's being, attributes, and deeds surpass what we are and what we can grasp—not because God is incomprehensible to himself or because his revelation is inadequate[28] but because of the limited capacity of our finite understanding. There is an inherent restriction to the knowledge of God, both quantitively and qualitatively. Despite all human effort, God cannot be fully comprehended (cf. Eccl 3:11–12). Thus, God's incomprehensibility is not a quality that exists independently of humankind, but rather one that reflects the limitations of the human condition. The same principle applies to other divine attributes: to call God "eternal" is to speak in terms shaped by the creational concept of time; to describe him as "infinite" is to use categories derived from the notion of space. Within the framework of monotheism, God is God—and God alone—and therefore exceeds the sum of all his attributes.

TYPES OF INCOMPREHENSIBILITY IN NARRATIVES

Hebrew biblical narratives suggest at least two primary reasons why God is portrayed as incomprehensible. These reasons reflect two distinct types of divine incomprehensibility.

Incomprehensibility of Scale

Firstly, God is incomprehensible due to the *magnitude* of his attributes and deeds. As humans, we possess far less understanding than God. His

---

28. Sproul, "Divine Incomprehensibility." Klooster, *Incomprehensibility of God*, 124, 135.

thoughts are higher, his reach is farther, his existence is eternal, and his power is unmatched. Therefore, God is truly incomparable.

In his prayer of dedication, King Solomon refers to God's incomprehensibility as a result of his magnitude:

> Even heaven and the highest heaven cannot contain you, much less this house that I have built! (1 Kgs 8:27)

References to the magnitude of God's attributes and deeds may suggest that incomprehension arises solely from a quantitative difference between God and humankind; that is, humans simply lack exhaustive understanding and knowledge of God. However, our understanding and knowledge as created beings are *qualitatively different* from God's wisdom due to his transcendence.[29] The various ways in which God surpasses humanity do not fully explain his incomprehensibility. God is incomprehensible simply because he is God, not a human.

The incomprehension of scale is often expressed through metaphors, or by referencing God's unsurpassable deeds in history that evoke a sense of amazement and awe. Frequently, this occurs in contexts where the gods are contrasted with the Lord God (יהוה):

> Who is like you, O Lord, among the gods? Who is like you, majestic in holiness, awesome in splendor, doing wonders? (Exod 15:11).

> I will make all my goodness pass before you . . . but you cannot see my face; for no one shall see me and live . . . while my glory passes by I will put you in a cleft of the rock, and I will cover you with my hand until I have passed by. (Exod 33:19–22).

> What god is there who can do such works and mighty acts? (Deut 3:24).

> For what other great nation has a god so near to it as the Lord our God is whenever we call to him? (Deut 4:7).

> Such knowledge [that God holds] is too wonderful for me; it is so high that I cannot attain it (Ps 139:6).

The incomprehensibility of scale is implied in Exod 33:18–23. When Moses asked to see God's glory, God replied that he would allow him to see his

---

29. The epistemological question of whether God is incomprehensible due to a *quantitative* difference between divine knowledge and the knowledge possible to humans, or whether God's incomprehensibility is due to a *qualitative* distinction between God and humans as temporal and finite beings, is argued at length by Fred Klooster in his dissertation about the views of Dr. Gordon Clark and the ensuing conflict in the Orthodox Presbyterian Church. Klooster, *Incomprehensibility of God*, 16–17, 22–25, 30.

goodness and grace, but not his face. God's glory is not only incomprehensible but also so overwhelming that no one can behold it and live. The text employs the anthropomorphism of God's "face" to represent his direct presence. Additionally, it refers to another anthropomorphism when God states that Moses will only see his "back" as he passes by. This signifies that Moses will experience a *partial* glimpse of God's glory and presence, as only that would be comprehensible and bearable.

Some of the other chapters in this book, such as those by Donatel and Van der Walt, focus on the incomprehensibility of scale.

Incomprehensibility of Incongruency

Secondly, God's attributes often appear contradictory. He acts in one way, yet also in another. He says one thing yet does another. The human mind cannot fully grasp these apparent discrepancies; thus, God is incomprehensible to us.

- One paradox occurs in Exod 34:6–7 (cf. Num 14:18), where God is described as merciful and gracious, slow to anger, and abounding in steadfast love and faithfulness, forgiving iniquity, transgression, and sin. Yet, at the same time, he will by no means clear the guilty and will visit the iniquity of parents upon the third and fourth generation.

Another example is when Solomon declares that God is omnipresent. The highest heavens cannot contain him (1 Kgs 8:27). Yet the context is the consecration of the temple, where it is said God dwells in a specific space among his people (2 Kgs 8:14).

One of God's attributes is his immutability, meaning his constancy and unchangeability. "God is not a human being, that he should lie, or a mortal, that he should change his mind" (Num 23:19; see also 1 Sam 15:29). This attribute closely relates to other divine attributes like righteousness (צְדָקָה), faithfulness (אֱמוּנָה), and loyalty (חֶסֶד), all of which presuppose consistency.[30] Yet, God is "most free,"[31] not bound by anyone or anything. He may overturn his previous pronouncements or acts. If that occurs, it may appear as if he is frivolous, changeable, unrighteous, unfaithful, or disloyal. The rest

---

30. The concept of righteousness, expressed by the צדק word group in Hebrew, serves as a prime example. The general meaning of this word group is "doing what is required according to a standard (Swanson, s.v. "7406 צָדַק" and s.v. "7407 צְדָקָה"). If the standard is set by God who is expected to act accordingly, righteousness indicates consistency.

31. The Westminster Confession of Faith, article 2.1, denotes the divine attribute of God's sovereignty by the words "most free."

of this chapter will focus on this incongruency found throughout the grand narrative of the Hebrew Bible.

DIVINE REVERSALS

In several narratives, the reader encounters a portrayal of God reversing what he had previously said or done. In some of these accounts, the *nif* or *hitp* forms of the verb נחם[32] are used, though in many cases the reversal is evident from the narrative context without the explicit use of this verb.

There are two lines of thought regarding these divine reversals:

- When the apparent reversals are interpreted, they align with attributes such as God's immutability. From God's perspective, he does not reverse prior pronouncements or actions, but he may change his attitude.[33] It is only from a human perspective that God appears to change his actions. The verb נחם can be translated emotively, for example, as *to regret, to repent, to be grieved, to console oneself*, or *to avenge oneself*.[34] This raises a related question: is God subject to human-like emotions, or should he, in accordance with other divine attributes, be considered unemotional (impassible)? The solution to this question invokes the notion of anthropopathism (the attribution of human feelings to God). When God relents, he does not truly regret or console himself; rather, human-like emotions are ascribed to him.

- Another line of thought explored in this chapter is that God can indeed reverse prior pronouncements or actions. He does not merely change his attitude; he begins to act differently.[35] In light of God's other attributes, this notion seems incongruent and is thus incomprehensible to the human mind. Aside from events indicating divine reversals where no Hebrew word or phrase signifies the change, the verb נחם does indicate reversals of intent or actions in certain contexts and is typically translated as *relent, reconsider, or change one's mind*.

---

32. Parunak discusses this verb extensively as does Jeremias. See Parunak, "Semantic Survey of nḥm," and Jeremias, *Die Reue Gottes*.

33. Steinman, *1 Samuel*, 285: "God 'relents' of the punishment as his disposition toward people changes from anger . . . to grace."

34. Swanson, s.v. "5714 נָחַם," meaning 1, 3 and 4; Köhler et al., s.v. "נחם"; Gesenius s.v. "נָחַם"; Brown et al., s.v. "נחם," suggest only emotive meanings such as regret, console oneself, be sorry, revenge, be grieved, and allow oneself to be comforted.

35. Wenham, *Genesis 1–15*, 144.

In the narrative texts discussed below, God reverses his intentions, actions, or pronouncements. In some of these texts, the verb נחם is used, while in others, the reversals are evident from the context without this specific verb.

Reversal of Doom

There are numerous examples in the Hebrew Bible where God relents from impending doom that he has both decided upon and explicitly announced. When God shows mercy and relents, his kindness supersedes his immutability and justice. This creates an apparent incongruence between divine attributes that can be difficult for the human mind to reconcile. According to human logic, this is not only incomprehensible but also seems unfair.

In the Hebrew Bible, the verb נחם is sometimes used in contexts where God refrains from doom, e.g., in the Latter Prophets.[36] The verb נחם (*nif*) is used three times in Israel's grand narrative where God withheld judgment:

1. The first instance occurs after the Israelites fashioned a golden calf at Mount Sinai (Exod 32:4, 7–8). In response, God wanted to destroy them and raise a new nation from Moses (Exod 32:10). However, after Moses interceded, appealing to God's covenantal promises and reputation among the nations, God *relented* (נחם, *nif*) from the disaster he had threatened (Exod 32:14). God, in this sense, "changed his mind."[37]

2. A second instance appears during the period of the judges. The Israelites repeatedly turned away from God to worship other deities. Nevertheless, when they groaned under the oppression of their enemies, God would raise up judges to deliver them. This was because he was "moved to pity" (נחם *nif*) (Judg 2:18). In effect, God "relented" or "repented" because of their groanings.[38] He reversed their well-deserved plight.

3. After David had commissioned a census, the prophet Gad announced God's judgment. However, God relented (נחם *nif*) concerning the evil, specifically the pestilence he had sent upon Israel. By ordering the angel of the LORD not to destroy Jerusalem, he prevented the full execution of his judgment (2 Sam 24:16).

36. Jer 15:6; 18:8, 26:3, 13, 19; 42:10; Joel 2:13–14; Amos 7:3, 6; Jonah 3:9–10; 4:2.

37. Translation of נחם *nif* in the New Revised Standard Version (NRSV), Today's English Version (TEV), and the New Jerusalem Bible (NJB).

38. Respective translations of נחם *nif* in the New Jerusalem Bible (NJB) and King James Version (KJV).

There are other instances of doom being reversed in the Hebrew narratives where the verb נחם is not used, but where God clearly *"changed his mind"*:

- In the garden, God forbade the man (Adam) to eat from the tree of the knowledge of good and evil, with the emphatic warning: "In the day that you eat of it you shall die" (Gen 2:17). However, after the man and his wife ate from the forbidden tree (Gen 3:6), God relented, and they did not die immediately.

- God bore with his people in the wilderness even after they had repeatedly disobeyed (Num 14:22; see also Exod 32). He kept his promises, but now, in the wilderness of Paran, the Israelites refused to enter the promised land and decided to return to Egypt. As at Mount Sinai, God considered destroying his people and making Moses the progenitor of a great nation (Num 14:11–12). Once again, Moses pleaded for his people (Num 14:13–19), and once again, God relented (Num 14:19).

- God sent the prophet Nathan to King David after he committed adultery and murder. Unwittingly, David passed his own judgment: "As the Lord lives, the man who has done this deserves to die" (2 Sam 12:5). However, God relented after David's repentance and did not let him die for his wrongdoings (2 Sam 12:13).

- The theme of a *remnant* that survives a catastrophe reflects God's ability to turn his inevitable judgment around.[39] God became angry with Solomon when he followed other gods. God declared that he would tear his kingdom away from him and give it to one of his subordinates. However, for the sake of David and Jerusalem, which God had chosen, he maintained the Davidic dynasty through one of the tribes of Israel (1 Kgs 11:4–13). At the end of the eighth century, the prophet Isaiah announced that God would destroy the Judean cities (e.g., Is 6:11–33). This destruction occurred when the Assyrians captured all the fortified cities of Judah, except Jerusalem, during the reign of King Hezekiah (2 Kgs 18:13). In a sense, God relented when he delivered

---

39. The term "שְׁאֵרִית" (remnant) is used for survivors of a catastrophe, e.g., Joseph's brothers surviving a famine (Gen 45:7); Israelites who would survive the Assyrian onslaught (Amos 5:15); Judeans who were spared the Assyrian onslaught (2 Kgs 19:4, 30–31); Judeans who were left behind after the destruction of Jerusalem (Jer 40–44); and the Judeans who returned from exile (Ezra 9:8, 13; 15; Neh 1:2). The term is specifically used as a technical term for the faithful remnant of Israel and Judah, e.g., in Isa 10:20–22; 11:11, 16; 28:5; 37:31–32; Jer 31:7; Mic 2:12; 4:7; 5:7–8; 7:18; Zeph 2:7; 3:13; Hag 2:2; Zech 8:11–12. Cf. Köhler et al., s.v. "שְׁאֵרִית"; Harris, s.v. "2307b שְׁאֵרִית." The collective noun "פְּלֵיטָה" (*escapees, survivors*) is used as an alternative term for the remnant (Isa 4:2; 10:20, 37:31–32; Ezra 8:8, 13–15; Neh 1:2). Cf. Köhler et al., s.v. "פְּלֵיטָה"; Harris, s.v. "1774d פְּלֵיטָה."

Jerusalem (Isa 37:35–38; 2 Kgs 19:35–37), thus fulfilling His promise of a remnant (שְׁאֵרִית/שְׁאָר) of survivors (פְּלֵיטָה) (Isa 37:31–32; 2 Kgs 19:30–31). More than a hundred years later, Jeremiah announced that God would hand over Judah to the king of Babylon, who would carry them away to Babylon (Jer 20:4; 43:3). Yet, a remnant would return after the exile.

The reversals of doom in the narratives are characterized by the following:

a. The reversal of doom is *solely based on God's mercy*. Psalm 106 provides an overview of Israel's grand narrative, particularly their time in the wilderness, concluding that God reversed his anger and relented (נחם *nif*), demonstrating compassion *according to the abundance of his steadfast love* (Ps 106:45). God shows mercy even without human repentance, unconditionally refraining from total destruction. Notable exceptions include Moses pleading on behalf of the people (Exod 32) and David acknowledging his sin (2 Sam 12).

b. *God does not regret what he has done, but rather what he has decided.* He rescinds his decisions. This suggests that God's resolve may be conditional. "No word is God's final word. Judgment, far from being absolute, is conditional. A change in man's conduct brings about a change in God's judgment."[40] God allows for leniency or mitigation of sentences. The conditionality of judgment makes reversals of doom somewhat more comprehensible to readers of the biblical narratives.

c. In some instances, these reversals occur in the *context of supplications* by the human recipients of God's judgments. They cry out for mercy, and God leaves the door open for prayer and intercession. "He allows himself to be persuaded."[41]

d. When God decides to set aside doom or destruction, *his wrath is not entirely removed*. The perpetrators, whether individually or collectively, still bear the dire consequences of their actions. In a sense, he still fulfils what he has declared. When God spared the man and his wife in the garden, paradise was still lost for humankind, resulting in suffering and eventual death (Gen 3:16–19, 23–24; 5:5). At Sinai, the incident with the golden calf had severe repercussions: about three thousand Israelites died by the sword (Exod 32:28), and God struck them with a plague (Exod 32:35). Although God forgave his people, the generation

---

40. Harris, s.v. "1344 נָחַם."
41. Ryken, *Exodus*, 987.

that rebelled at Paran would die in the wilderness (Num 14:20–24, 28–30a, 32–35). Similarly, though God forgave David, there would still be strife in his household, and four of his sons would die young (2 Sam 12:10, 14; 13:28–29; 18:14; 1 Kgs 2:25).

e. At the same time, there is *continuity of God's favor*. God gives second chances and maintains his original plan through a faithful offspring or remnant. He granted Adam and Eve a new lease on life with an implied promise of victory over the serpent (Gen 3:15). He also provided clothing (Gen 3:20) and a means of living outside the garden (Gen 3:17–19, 23; 4:2–4). Additionally, he gave them an offspring (Gen 3:15–16, 20; Gen 4:1–2; 25–26). After the events at Sinai, where God relented from the disaster he had spoken of (Exod 32:14), he reiterated his promises of a homeland and that he would send an angel before them to drive out the local population (Exod 33:1–2; see 23:23). He relented based on his covenant promises. God promised even more at the request of Moses: his presence would accompany them (Exod 33:12–14). At Paran, God declared that Caleb and Joshua, along with the next generation—those under twenty years old—would enter the land (Num 14:30b–31). God promised, against all odds, that Bathsheba, involved in the scandal with David, would become the matriarch of the Davidic dynasty. Among David's harem, she would receive God's special favor (2 Sam 12:24–25; 2 Kgs 1:13).

God changing his mind for the better remains an enigma. On the one hand, there is some logic to these reversals. When God relents from what he has intended or announced, there can still be a form of reprisal, and it can be argued that his intentions or announcements were conditional, even if the text does not state this explicitly. On the other hand, God's change of mind retains a significant measure of incomprehensibility. Mercy, even when it involves only the mitigation of punishment, is not strictly fair. God's mercy does not merely mean that full punishment is set aside; often, he reinvigorates his original plan by providing relief and hope. This amounts to mercy plus renewed favor, which, from a strict logical perspective, is incomprehensible in light of God's transcendence, holiness, and righteousness. However, the Hebrew narratives frame these reversals of doom within the context of God fulfilling his covenant promises. According to that logic, it makes sense that God provides grace amid or despite judgment.[42]

---

42. Beakley, *God's nhḥm*, 203. As an advocate of this view, Beakley prefers to translate the verb נחם with "comfort himself" when God is the subject. God comforts himself in providing judgment, and God at the same time comforts himself in providing grace based on his covenant promises.

Reversal of Favor

There are two instances in the narratives where God reverses a positive situation due to unacceptable human behavior, and where the verb נחם (*nif*) is used in the sense that God "regretted" his prior actions.

1. God created humankind and even granted them a new lease on life after their transgression, as narrated in Gen 3-4. One might expect that God would indefinitely sustain life. Yet, the flood narrative states twice that God "regretted" (נחם *nif*) having made humankind (Gen 6:6-7). In Gen 6:6, the *nif* form of נחם is juxtaposed with עצב (to feel pain), suggesting an emotion. However, the verb נחם (*nif*) does not merely express an emotion; the context clearly indicates a reversal of God's favor and long-suffering toward humankind.

2. God sent Samuel to anoint Saul as leader over Israel (1 Sam 9:15-16; 10:1). At Mizpah, after being designated king by lot, Saul was formally instated (1 Sam 10:20-21; 24). Subsequently, the biblical text depicts him as unfit to be a king after God's own heart (1 Sam 13:7-14; 14:24-30, 40-45; 15:1-3, 9). Eventually, God told Samuel, "I regret (נחם *nif*) that I made Saul king" (1 Sam 15:11, 35). As in Gen 6:6, the verb נחם (*nif*) signifies more than emotions; the context reveals God announcing that he would terminate Saul's kingship and dynasty.

These reversals of favor differ from the reversals of doom:

a. God does not regret what he has decided, but rather what he has *done*, making it even more incomprehensible than reversals of doom. The regret is expressed in *direct speech*, underscoring the importance: God himself asserts that he changes his plan. It is incomprehensible that the Almighty God regrets his own handiwork and chooses to destroy it as if it were incomplete.

b. There is *no mitigation* when God transforms favor into destruction. He decided to destroy humankind and animals because of the corrupt behavior of humankind (Gen 6:5; 11-14), which he executed by sending a total deluge, blotting out every living thing on the face of the earth (Gen 6:17; 7:10-12, 19-24). Samuel told Saul that God had decided to reverse the favor he had bestowed upon him because Saul turned away from God and failed to carry out his instructions (1 Sam 13:41; 15:17, 27-28). The same passage where God states that he regretted (נחם *nif*) making Saul king also declares that God will *not* recant or change his mind (נחם *nif*), for he is not a mortal who should change his mind (נחם *nif*) (1 Sam 15:29). This means that God relenting his favor is not a trivial decision. His judgment is final and extensive. Not only would King Saul and three of his sons be killed in battle (1 Sam 31:2–4), but Saul's entire royal lineage would be erased (2 Sam 4:1–7; 6:20–23; 9:1–13; 16:1–4; 19:24–30; 21:3–9).

c. As a result of destruction, there is *discontinuity*. In Genesis, the Flood is described as the destruction of the earth (Gen 6:13). In an act of recreation,[43] God reestablished his creational plan through a single person and his family. By selecting only two or a small number of each animal, he indicated that he would start anew. After the flood, God established a new world in place of the old, providing instructions that echo those given at creation (Gen 9:1, 3, 7). Following the "false start" of the monarchy with Saul as king, God effectively began anew with David, the most unlikely choice (1 Sam 16:10–13), who came from a different place, family, and tribe than Saul. This also constitutes an "act of recreation."

CONCLUSION

God's incomprehensibility emerges in the narrative texts of the Hebrew Bible, where God performs *acts of salvation* (wonders) that transcend human understanding. These acts are incomprehensible and lead to wonder and praise.

His incomprehensibility is also evident in texts where he relents on his *prior decisions or announcements of doom*. He mitigates doom and even extends his favor to those who deserve punishment.

There are two instances in the narratives that are particularly perplexing, where God is said to *regret his own actions*. In both instances, God reverses his handiwork and replaces it with something new. Not only are human emotions attributed to God when it is said that he regrets, but God's regret or relenting also appears to contradict the notion of his immutability, omnipotence, and eternal wisdom. This is indeed incomprehensible.

Should the Bible reader attempt to resolve the incomprehensibility of God, his greatness, wisdom, and deeds? Instead of offering various explanations, we must accept that God remains incomprehensible to humankind simply because he is God and God alone.

---

43. Krüger, "Life in the Pentateuch (1)," 27–32.

BIBLIOGRAPHY

Augustine. "Sermon 117." In *Patrologia Latina*, vol. 38, edited by Jacques-Paul Migne, 661–71. Paris: Imprimerie Catholique, 1841–49.

Bavinck, Herman. *Gereformeerde Dogmatiek*, vol 2. Kampen: Kok, 1928.

Beakley, David L. "God's nḥm ('comfort') as the Unfolding of God's Promise in Four Old Testament Historical Passages." PhD diss., Northwest University, 2013.

Belgic Confession. In *Our Faith: Ecumenical Creeds, Reformed Confessions, and Other Resources*, 25–34. Grand Rapids: Faith Alive Christian Resources, 2013.

Brown, Francis, et al. *The Enhanced Brown-Driver-Briggs Hebrew and English Lexicon*, edited by James Strong. Oak Harbor, WA: Logos, 2000.

"Comprehend." *Merriam-Webster Dictionary*. https://www.merriam-webster.com/dictionary/comprehend.

"Comprehend." *Oxford English Dictionary*. https://www.oed.com/dictionary/comprehend_v?tab=factsheet#8602876.

"Comprehendere." *Latin Dictionary and Grammar Resource*. 1982. https://latin-dictionary.net/definition/11805/comprehendo-comprehendere-comprehendi-comprehensus.

Conrad, J. "פלא pl' III Nouns." In *Theological Dictionary of the Old Testament*, vol. 11, edited by G. Johannes Botterweck and Helmer Ringgren, 540–43. Translated by David E. Green. Grand Rapids: Eerdmans, 2001.

Fourth Lateran Council. "Confession of Faith (1215)." In *Enchiridion Symbolorum: A Compendium of Creeds, Definitions, and Declarations of the Catholic Church*, edited by Heinrich Denzinger and revised by Peter Hünermann, no. 800. San Francisco: Ignatius, 2012.

Gesenius, Wilhelm. *Gesenius' Hebrew and Chaldee Lexicon to the Old Testament Scriptures*. Translated by Samuel P. Tregelles. London: Bagster, 1979.

Harris, R. Laird, ed. *Theological Wordbook of The Old Testament* (TWOT). Chicago: Moody, 1980.

"Incomprehensible." *Encarta Dictionary Tools*. CD-ROM. Redmond, WA: Microsoft, 2006.

Jeremias, Jörg. *Die Reue Gottes: Aspekte Alttestamentlicher Gottesvorstellung*. 2nd ed. Neukirchen-Vluyn: Neukirchener Verlag, 1997.

Klooster, Fred H. *The Incomprehensibility of God in the Orthodox Presbyterian Conflict*. Franeker: Wever, 1951.

Köhler, Ludwig, et al., eds. *The Hebrew and Aramaic Lexicon of the Old Testament* (HALOT). Translated and edited by Mervin E. J. Richardson. Leiden: Brill, 2024.

Krüger, P. Paul, "Life in the Pentateuch (1): Genesis 1–11: Life Created and Sustained." In *Biblical Theology of Life in the Old Testament*, edited by Albert J. Coetsee and Francois P. Viljoen, 11–34. Cape Town: AOSIS, 2021.

Parunak, Howard V. "A Semantic Survey of NHM." *Biblica* 56 (1975) 512–32.

Ryken, Philip G. *Exodus: Saved for God's Glory*. Wheaton, IL: Crossway, 2005.

Sproul, Robert C. "Divine Incomprehensibility." *Ligonier Ministries*, July 25, 2014.

Steinmann, Andrew E. *1 Samuel*. Concordia Commentary. St. Louis: Concordia, 2016.

Swanson, James A., ed. *Dictionary of Biblical Languages with Semantic Domains: Hebrew Old Testament* (DBLH). Oak Harbor, WA: Logos, 2001.

Tsevat, Matitiahu, "חָקַר ḥāqar חֵקֶר ḥēqer מֶחְקָר meḥqār." In *Theological Dictionary of the Old Testament*, vol. 5, edited by G. Johannes Botterweck and Helmer Ringgren, 148–50. Translated by David E. Green. Grand Rapids: Eerdmans, 1986.

Wenham, Gordon J. *Genesis 1–15*. Word Biblical Commentary, vol. 1. Dallas: Word Books, 1987.

Westminster Assembly. "The Westminster Confession of Faith." In *The Westminster Standard*. https://thewestminsterstandard.org/the-westminster-confession/.

———. "The Westminster Larger Catechism: Text and Scripture Proofs." In *The Westminster Standard*. https://thewestminsterstandard.org/the-westminster-confession/.

Chapter 2

Divine Incomprehensibility Fostering Human Responsibility: The Structure and Rhetorical Aim of Deuteronomy 10:12–22

—Albert J. Coetsee

>Unit for Reformational Theology and the Development of the South African Society, Faculty of Theology, North-West University, Potchefstroom, South Africa

ABSTRACT

Due to a lack of scholarly consensus concerning the structure of Deut 10:12–22, the current chapter investigated the structure and rhetorical aim of the passage anew. This was done by providing an overview of previous analyses of the structure of the passage and examining Deut 10:12–22 on a verse-by-verse basis in order to identify aspects of the passage that influence and contribute to its structure. Based on this, a new proposal for the structure of the passage was supplied, followed by reflection on its rhetorical aim. The chapter found that the passage contains exhortations that are supported by motivations that focus on divine transcendence and immanence, and that the passage has a deliberate and consistent alternation between human responsibility and divine incomprehensibility, highlighting the latter in order to foster the former.

INTRODUCTION

Deuteronomy 10:12–22 is arguably one of the most important passages within the basic stipulations of the book of Deuteronomy (Deut 6:1–11:32).

The passage has been described as "one of the loveliest, most powerful, most freighted summations of covenant theology offered in the book of Deuteronomy,"[1] and a passage that "purposely tries to 'boil down' the theological and ethical content of the book into memorable phraseology."[2]

Yet, for all its importance and beauty, the structure of the passage is not entirely clear. This is mostly due to the sermonic nature of the passage, which leads to a variety of ways in which the structure can be viewed (see the discussion that follows). This dissensus results in the interesting phenomenon: On the one hand, virtually all scholars agree what Deut 10:12–22 is a very important passage within the book of Deuteronomy; on the other hand, few scholars agree about its structure.

The purpose of the current chapter is to investigate the structure and rhetorical aim of Deut 10:12–22 anew. The chapter starts by providing an overview of previous analyses of the structure of the passage, reflecting on matters that should be considered in any structural analysis of Deut 10:12–22. Next, the chapter provides an overview of the content and form of Deut 10:12–22 on a verse-by-verse basis in order to identify aspects of the passage that influence and contribute to its structure. The chapter limits itself to a synchronic investigation,[3] focusing on the final form of the passage in the critical text of the BHQ.[4] Based on its findings, the chapter provides a new suggestion of the structure of Deut 10:12–22 and concludes by reflecting on the rhetorical aim of the passage.

PREVIOUS ANALYSES OF THE STRUCTURE OF DEUTERONOMY 10:12–22

Broadly speaking, most scholars analyze the structure of Deut 10:12–22 according to its content and form. While there is no watertight distinction between analyzing the structure of a passage according to its content or

---

1. Brueggemann, *Deuteronomy*, 128.

2. Wright, *Deuteronomy*, 144.

3. Talstra, "Deuteronomy 9 and 10," 189–90, fittingly captures the gist of a synchronic, rhetorical analysis as an analysis based on "*admiration*," attempting "to explain *all* the details of the text as *intentionally* constructed by an artistic writer . . . to persuade the reader of the theological insights presented with the text" (emphasis original).

4. Where relevant for the argumentation of the current chapter, certain diachronic matters are discussed. For a diachronic analysis of the passage, see Otto, *Deuteronomium*, 1025–33. For discussion of text-critical issues in Deut 10:12–22, see Arnold, *Deuteronomy*, 552–553; Christensen, *Deuteronomy*, 200; McCarthy, *Deuteronomy*, 80*; and Weinfeld, *Deuteronomy*, 431. For the critical text of Deut 10:12–22 in the LXX, see Wevers, *Deuteronomium*, 159–62.

form, virtually all scholars tend to emphasize the one more than the other. Accordingly, in what follows, an overview is provided of previous analyses of the structure of Deut 10:12–22 using "content" and "form" as the major categories. This overview is preceded by a discussion of the place of the passage within the literary context of the book of Deuteronomy. Based on these findings, the section ends by reflecting on matters that should be considered in any structural analysis of Deut 10:12–22.

Before continuing, however, a caveat is in order. Various commentators provide an overview of the structure of a passage in a memorable way and consequently do not provide a detailed analysis of the various intricacies of the structure of a passage. This, per definition, is the very nature of a structural analysis: to provide the bigger contours of a passage according to patterns. This needs to be kept in mind in order to be fair to the scholars whose structural analyses are discussed below.

Deuteronomy 10:12–22 Within the Structure of Deuteronomy

Deuteronomy 10:12–22 forms part of Moses's second speech in the book of Deuteronomy (Deut 4:44—28:68). Zooming in on the second speech, the passage is found within the so-called "basic stipulations" of the book (Deut 6:1—11:32) which emphasize the inner disposition that should characterize the people in their covenant relationship with YHWH. In sum, they are to fear and love YHWH, and they are not to disobey him or forget him amid prosperity. Deuteronomy 10:12–22 links on to the overall gist of the basic stipulations by summarizing what YHWH expects of his people: they should fear him, walk in his ways, love him, serve him, keep his commandments, hold fast to him and swear by his name (Deut 10:12–13, 20).

Deuteronomy 10:12–22 links on to the passages that immediately precede and succeed it. On the one hand, Deut 9:1—10:11 contains an interpreted account of Israel's stubbornness and rebellion at Horeb amid the golden calf incident, providing an example the addressees are not to follow. Deuteronomy 11:1–32, on the other hand, echoes Deut 10:12–22 in its call to love YHWH, to serve him and to keep his commandments in the promised land, intertwined with an overview of blessings which would follow if the people were obedient, and curses should they be disobedient and commit idolatry (cf. Deut 11:13–17, 26–32). Because of the close connection between themes in Deut 9:1—10:11, 10:12—22 and 11:1—32, scholars view either Deut 9:1—10:22[5] or Deut 10:12—11:32[6] as a unit.

The Structure of Deuteronomy 10:12-22 Based on Content

The structural analyses of Arnold and Merrill can be viewed as analyses of the structure of Deut 10:12-22 based on its content.

Arnold views Deut 10:12-22 as consisting of three parts:[7]

Deut 10:12-13   A question and its answer (theological crux)

Deut 10:14-16   Justification 1: Who Israel is (the Israel of God)

Deut 10:17-22   Justification 2: Who YHWH is (the God of Israel)

While this analysis fittingly captures the essence of Deut 10:12-13, the headings for Deut 10:14-16 and Deut 10:17-22 can be a bit misleading. Deuteronomy 10:14, for example, clearly expresses who YHWH is, while Deut 10:19 stresses who Israel were and consequently how they should conduct themselves at present.

Merrill too bases his view of the structure of in Deut 10:12-22 on the content of the passage. He sees an "enveloping pattern" of injunctions to obey God as embracing the corollary command to exhibit the proper care for other people:[8]

Deut 10:12-13   Obey God

Deut 10:14-19   Care for other people

Deut 10:20-22   Obey God

Like the analysis of Arnold, Merrill is correct to view Deut 10:12-13 as a command to obey God. The same is true for Deut 10:20. But to view Deut 10:21-22 as a command to obey God is too simplistic. These verses rather emphasize who God is and what he has done. In addition, while Deut 10:19 is an explicit exhortation to love the sojourner, it is difficult to apply the heading "care for other people" to Deut 10:14-18.

The analyses of these scholars highlight the importance of fitting headings for the different parts of a structural analysis based on the content of

---

5. E.g., Tigay, *Deuteronomy*, 96-109. Based on the vocative "O Israel" (יִשְׂרָאֵל) found in Deut 9:1 and 10:12, Talstra views Deut 10:12-22 as the conclusion of Deut 9:1-10:22. See Talstra, "Deuteronomy 9 and 10," 195, 200.

6. E.g., Otto, *Deuteronomium*, 1003-72; Arnold, *Deuteronomy*, 553.

7. Arnold, *Deuteronomy*, 554, 558, 562.

8. Merrill, *Deuteronomy*, 201.

a passage. In addition, they suggest that more than the content should be considered when reflecting on the structure of a passage; the form of the passage plays a crucial role.

The Structure of Deuteronomy 10:12–22 Based on Form

A number of scholars base their analyses of the structure of Deut 10:12–22 on the form of the passage. This includes views of the structure of the passage based on chiasms, structural parallels and what can be called "sermonic rhythms."

Both Christensen and Meade can be viewed as scholars who view the structure of Deuteronomy 10:12–22 according to chiastic patterns. Christensen calls the passage "a simple chiasm," which he depicts as follows:[9]

> A   The "great commandment"—fear YHWH your God
> (Deut 10:12–13)
>
> B   YHWH owns the whole universe, but he has chosen you
> (Deut 10:14–16)
>
> B' YHWH is "God of gods," and he loves the sojourner
> (Deut 10:17–19)
>
> A' Fear YHWH, for he is your God
> (Deut 10:20–22)

This chiastic structure has various aspects of commendation. There are, however, other ways in which the paragraphs that make up the overall structure can be viewed (e.g., Deut 10:12–13, 14–15, 16–18, 19, 20–22; discussion follows), and a more detailed analysis would enable a reader to notice and follow more of the arguments found in the passage.

In the same vein, Meade views the literary structure of Deut 10:12–22 in a semi-chiastic fashion, consisting of three exhortations of loyal devotion each followed by praises to YHWH:[10]

> A¹ Exhortation to loyal devotion: fear, walk, love, serve, keep
> (Deut 10:12–13)
>
> B¹ Yahweh is praised: sovereign Creator and Redeemer
> (Deut 10:14–15)
>
> A² Exhortation to loyal devotion: circumcise and do not stiffen
> (Deut 10:16)

---

9. Christensen, *Deuteronomy*, 202.
10. Meade, "Circumcision of the Heart," 72.

B² Yahweh is praised: supreme God and faithful to weak
(Deut 10:17–18)

A³ Exhortation to loyal devotion: love, fear, serve, cling, swear
(Deut 10:19–20)

B³ Yahweh is praised: faithful God of the patriarchs and exodus
(Deut 10:21–22)

Although this analysis is very similar to views of the structure of the passage based on sermonic rhythms (discussion follows), the semi-chiastic nature of Meade's view of the structure is confirmed by his argument that A² forms the "center" of the passage.[11] In my view, while Deut 10:16 unquestionably contains a crucial exhortation within the passage, the parallel exhortations found in Deut 10:12–13 and 20 are emphasized by means of repetition and placement (at the beginning and near the end of the passage), and should consequently be highlighted.

Wright, Block and Otto can all be viewed as scholars who view the structure of Deut 10:12–22 based on structural parallels. Wright interprets Deut 10:14–19 as a "carefully structured . . . pair of matching triplets,"[12] which he identifies as follows:

Opening: A hymn-like exaltation of Yahweh with a resounding superlative (Deut 10:14)

Description of something unexpected about God's action or character (Deut 10:15)

Conclusion: A command for Israel to respond appropriately (Deut 10:16)

Opening: A hymn-like exaltation of Yahweh with resounding superlatives (Deut 10:17)

Description of something unexpected about God's action or character (Deut 10:18)

Conclusion: A command for Israel to respond appropriately (Deut 10:19)

Block views Deut 10:12—11:1 (note the inclusion of Deut 11:1) as addressing "a single issue from three different but complementary angles,"[13] of

---

11. Meade, "Circumcision of the Heart," 72. Lemke, "Circumcision of the Heart," 301–2, is of the opinion that Deut 10:16 is a secondary insertion in the passage. Meade, "Circumcision of the Heart," 73–74, rightly challenges and disproves this.

12. Wright, *Deuteronomy*, 145–46.

13. Block, *Deuteronomy*, 269.

which "the result is a glorious theology of covenant relationship built on three pillars of cosmic theology and grounded on three marvelous acts of grace."[14] This can be depicted as follows:

Table 1: Block's view of Deuteronomy 10:12—11:1

Issue		Deut 10:12a		
Requirement Deut 10:12b–13		I (Deut 10:12b–15)	II (Deut 10:16–19)	III (Deut 10:20–22)
		Deut 10:16	Deut 10:20	
Basis of the requirement	Doxology	Deut 10:14	Deut 10:17	Deut 10:21
	Application	Deut 10:15	Deut 10:18–19	Deut 10:22
Conclusion		Deut 11:1		

Otto too sees a number of parallels between the various parts of Deut 10:12–22. While he identifies similar patterns throughout Deut 10:12—11:32, for the sake of the current chapter only a visual presentation of the structure of Deut 10:12–11:1 is presented here:[15]

    Series of commandments   Deut 10:12–13
      A: Statement of sovereignty   Deut 10:14
         B: YHWH's exemplary actions   Deut 10:15
            C: Call to Moses's addressees to act accordingly   Deut 10:16
      A: Statement of sovereignty   Deut 10:17
         B: YHWH's exemplary actions   Deut 10:17–18
            C: Call to Moses's addressees to act accordingly   Deut 10:19
    Series of commandments   Deut 10:20, 11:1
      A: Statement of sovereignty   Deut 10:21–22

Various aspects of these structural analyses of Deut 10:12–22 according to structural parallels are commendable and convincing. There seems to be a level of consensus that some verses go together, contributing to its "quasi-poetic style" which "would have facilitated memorization."[16] For example, all three scholars view Deut 10:14 and 10:17 as parallel, and all of them view Deut 10:15 as having a parallel with parts of Deut 10:17–19 (Wright: Deut 10:15||10:18; Block: Deut 10:15||10:18–19; Otto: Deut 10:15||10:17–18).

---

14. Block, *Deuteronomy*, 270.
15. Otto, *Deuteronomium*, 1021, 1023.
16. Tigay, *Deuteronomy*, 107.

The previous example, however, also indicates that there is difference of opinion about exactly which verses go together. The greatest difference is that Wright and Otto view Deut 10:12–22 as consisting of two pairs of material, while Block views it as consisting of three. This explains why Wright and Otto view Deut 10:16 and 10:19 as parallel, but Block doesn't. The second greatest difference is the inclusion or exclusion of Deut 11:1.

Third and finally, Brueggemann and Lundbom base their analyses of the structural form of Deut 10:12–22 on what can be called "sermonic rhythms." Brueggemann views the passage as "a series of imperatives supported by a corresponding series of quite expansive motivations,"[17] which results in a "rhythm of *imperative* and *motivation*" (emphasis his).[18] Based on his commentary of the passage, Brueggemann's view of the structure of the passage can be depicted as follows:[19]

Imperative	Deut 10:12–13
Motivation	Deut 10:14–15
Imperative	Deut 10:16
Motivation	Deut 10:17–18
Imperative	Deut 10:19a
Motivation	Deut 10:19b
Imperative	Deut 10:20
Motivation	Deut 10:21–22

Lundbom's view of the structure of the passage is virtually identical. He does, however, highlight the balance between the opening (Deut 10:12–13) and closing command (Deut 10:20):[20]

Command	Deut 10:12–13
Reason	Deut 10:14–15
Command	Deut 10:16
Reason	Deut 10:17–18
Command	Deut 10:19a
Reason	Deut 10:19b
Command	Deut 10:20
Reason	Deut 10:21–22

The greatest benefit of viewing the structure according to "sermonic rhythms" is that it is the most natural way to read the text. The passage indeed contains an ebb and flow of exhortations and motivations, all of which

17. Brueggemann, *Deuteronomy*, 129.
18. Brueggemann, *Deuteronomy*, 133.
19. Brueggemann, *Deuteronomy*, 129–33.
20. Lundbom, *Deuteronomy*, 388–89.

contribute to the sermonic nature of the passage. The drawback, however, is that it does not highlight the deliberate parallels between some verses that are visibly discernible.

Matters that Should Be Considered in a Structural Analysis of Deuteronomy 10:12–22

Based on the overview of previous analyses of the structure of the passage, it is clear that the following should be considered in any structural analysis of Deut 10:12–22:

- Deuteronomy 10:12–22 is part of the basic stipulations of the book of Deuteronomy and link on to the passages that immediately precede and succeed it, namely Deut 9:1–10:11 and 11:1–32.
- Both the content and the form of the passage should be considered when reflecting on a structural analysis of Deut 10:12–22.
- Deuteronomy 10:12–22 seems to contain a series of commands, each followed by a motivation.
- Deuteronomy 10:12–13 seems to form the heart of the passage by providing the main exhortation by means of a question and an answer.
- There are several parallels between the verses that make up Deut 10:12–22: Deut 10:12–13 forms a parallel with 10:20, 10:14 with 10:17, and 10:15 with parts of 10:17–19.
- Based on these parallels, it is possible that Deut 10:12–22 is made up of two or three pairs of material that mirror each other in a way.
- The question of whether Deut 11:1 forms part of Deut 10:12–22 needs to be answered in a structural analysis of the passage.
- When providing a visual overview of the structure of Deut 10:12–22, headings that fittingly capture the heart of the content under discussion should be provided.

A VERSE-BY-VERSE OVERVIEW OF THE CONTENT AND FORM OF DEUTERONOMY 10:12-22

The current section of the chapter provides an overview of the content and form of Deut 10:12–22 on a verse-by-verse basis (where relevant verses are grouped together) in order to identify aspects of the passage that influence and contribute to its structure. Since this section provides the building blocks for the new structural analysis that follows, it forms the bulk of the chapter. The verse-by-verse discussion is preceded by reflection on the demarcation of the passage, as it has a bearing on the parameters of the investigation.

Demarcation of the Passage

To view Deut 10:12 as the start of the passage is strongly suggested by to two factors. First, the occurrence of the *petuhah* (פ) marker in the Hebrew text at the end of Deut 10:11 indicates that a new section of the text begins at Deut 10:12. Secondly, the use of the conjunction-adverb combination "and now" (וְעַתָּה) followed by the vocative "O Israel" (יִשְׂרָאֵל) in Deut 10:12 indicates a transition in the text.[21] In Deut 4:1, the only other place in the book where the similar phrase "and now, Israel" is found, it signals the start of a new passage.[22] The way in which Deut 10:12 starts indicates that the passage can be viewed as a logical "conclusion" of the previous pericope. Theologically, in light of YHWH's unwillingness to destroy Israel after their rebellion with the golden calf (Deut 9:1–10:11), Israel is called to conduct themselves in a certain way (Deut 10:12–11:32).

To determine the end of the passage is trickier. There are no *petuhah* (פ) or *setumah* (ס) markers at the end of Deut 10:22 or any of the surrounding verses. That Deut 10:22 should be viewed as part of Deut 10:12–22, is not contested. The question is whether Deut 11:1 should be included in the pericope. A number of prominent scholars view the exhortations in Deut 11:1 to "love" (אָהֵב) YHWH and to "keep" (שָׁמַר) his commandments as forming an *inclusio* with the opening exhortations in Deut 10:12–13 ("love" in Deut 10:12; "keep" in Deut 10:13).[23] While this *inclusio* can indicate the start and end of the passage, it has already been indicated that Deut 10:12–22 thematically links on to the passages that precede and succeed it. This is confirmed by the fact that apart from Deut 11:1, some of the exhortations in Deut 10:12–13 are also repeated in Deut 11:13 and 11:22 (namely, to "love" YHWH [Deut 11:13, 22], to "serve" him [Deut 11:13] and to "walk"

---

21. Interestingly, Craigie, *Deuteronomy*, 201–4, views Deut 10:11 as the start of the passage.

22. Various scholars have noted the resemblance between Deut 4:1–40 and Deut 10:12–22. Based on these similarities, some view Deut 10:12–22 as being a later edition to the book of Deuteronomy.

23. Block, *Deuteronomy*, 275; Otto, *Deuteronomium*, 1019–23; Weinfeld, *Deuteronomy*, 441.

in his ways [Deut 11:22]). Consequently, Deut 11:1 can be viewed as the start of a new passage, albeit intricately linked to the preceding pericope. In addition, the use of the conjunction-adverb combination "and now" (וְעַתָּה) in Deut 10:12 and 10:22 forms an *inclusio*, bracketing Deut 10:12–22 as a unit.[24] Accordingly, most commentators view Deut 10:22 as the end of the passage,[25] and Deut 11:1 as the start of the new.[26]

Deuteronomy 10:12–13

Deuteronomy 10:12–13 is the main exhortation of the passage. The conjunction-adverb and vocative combination "and now, O Israel" in Deut 10:12 is followed by a rhetorical question, asking Israel what YHWH "requires" (שָׁאַל) of them. While the verb refers to the action of "ask" in a number of contexts, the context of Deut 10:12 indicates that here the verb has the nuance of an insistent request or demand rather than an invitation. The rhetorical nature of the question is confirmed by the fact that the remainder of Deut 10:12–13 provides the answer to the question.

What YHWH requires of Israel is introduced by the two conjunctions כִּי אִם in combination. The construction is used to express an antithesis presupposing a negative answer,[27] and is best translated as "except" (cf. "only" in the NRSV; "but" in the ESV). The detail of what is expected of Israel is spelled out by means of five *Qal* infinitives, each reiterating previous and subsequent Deuteronomic exhortations: Israel should (1) "fear" YHWH (יָרֵא; cf. Deut 5:29; 6:2, 13, 24; 10:20; 13:4; 31:12–13), (2) "walk" in his ways (הָלַךְ; cf. Deut 5:33; 8:6; 11:22; 19:9; 26:17; 28:9; 30:16), (3) "love" him (אָהַב; cf. Deut 6:5; 11:1, 13, 22; 19:9; 30:16), (4) "serve" him (עָבַד; cf. Deut 10:20; 11:13; 13:4) and (5) "keep" his commandments (שָׁמַר; cf. Deut 4:40; 5:29; 6:2; 8:6; 11:1, 8; 13:4; 19:9; 26:17; 28:9; 30:16). The second and fourth infinitives emphasize the comprehensive nature of these exhortations by stating that Israel should walk "in all his ways" (בְּכָל־דְּרָכָיו) and serve him "with all your heart and with all your soul" (וּבְכָל־נַפְשֶׁךָ בְּכָל־לְבָבְךָ) (cf. Deut 4:29; 6:5; 11:13; 13:4; 26:16; 30:2, 6, 10). The exhortation to "love" YHWH and to serve him "with all your heart and with all your soul" echoes the Shema

---

24. Lundbom, *Deuteronomy*, 389, 397; McConville, *Deuteronomy*, 198, 201.

25. E.g., Arnold, *Deuteronomy*, 568–69; Brueggemann, *Deuteronomy*, 132–33; Harstad, *Deuteronomy*, 359; Lundbom, *Deuteronomy*, 397; McConville, *Deuteronomy*, 201; Wright, *Deuteronomy*, 151.

26. Tigay, *Deuteronomy*, 109–110, takes a middle position by viewing Deut 11:1 as "transitional," serving as both the end of the present unit and the introduction to the next.

27. Harstad, *Deuteronomy*, 343.

in Deut 6:5, which is repeated in Deut 11:18–20. Pursuing all these matters will result in the well-being of Israel, which is elsewhere in Deut depicted as "life," that is, quality of life.[28]

Overall, the introductory rhetorical question and answer of Deut 10:12–13 provides a core summary of what YHWH requires of the people with whom he has covenanted himself. He requires "total and exclusive"[29] or "complete commitment . . . without reserve."[30]

Deuteronomy 10:14

The first word in Deut 10:14 is the interjection הֵן, which is usually employed for emphasis.[31] A literal translation of the particle is "lo" or "behold," but in the current context, where it is used in conjunction with the adverb רַק in Deut 10:15 in order to form a contrast, it is best translated as "although."[32]

Deuteronomy 10:14 consists of a nominal sentence which implies the use of the verb הָיָה ("to be"). The verse states that "(the) heaven" (הַשָּׁמַיִם) and "the heaven of heavens" (וּשְׁמֵי הַשָּׁמַיִם) "is" YHWH's, that is, belongs to him. The distinction seems to refer to the literal sky above versus whatever is beyond that, namely "the heavens" in a cosmological scheme.[33] The superlative "heaven of heavens" indicates that in addition to the visible heaven, the "highest" or the "greatest" heaven belong to YHWH as well.

On closer investigation, Deut 10:14 contains a merism with elaboration that expands and narrows down on YHWH's ownership and sovereignty:

	Merism	Elaboration	Expansion/Narrowing down
To YHWH belongs	[a] heaven	[a'] and the heaven of heavens	Expansion: space
	[b] earth	[b'] with all that is in it	Narrowing down: content

The overarching effect of the merism is to emphasize that YHWH is owner of everything and sovereign over everyone (cf. Ps 24:1; 1 Kgs 8:27). In addition, the merism also paves the way for Deut 10:15 by suggesting that

---

28. Coetsee, "YHWH and Israel," 106–14.
29. Wright, *Deuteronomy*, 144.
30. Brueggemann, *Deuteronomy*, 129.
31. Weinfeld, *Deuteronomy*, 436.
32. McConville, *Deuteronomy*, 200.
33. Craigie, *Deuteronomy*, 204–5.

although even the highest heaven belong to YHWH, he has an interest in the earth and all it contains.

Deuteronomy 10:15

Deuteronomy 10:15 starts with the adverbial particle רַק, which is usually translated as "only." This adverbial particle has many similarities with emphatic adverbs, and can either have a restrictive or asseverative force.[34] Within the current context, it has a restrictive force by building on the verse that precedes it.[35] Some Bible translations opt to translate the particle in this context as "yet" (e.g., NRSV; NIV; ESV), although some keep the translation of "only" (e.g., KJV; NKJV).

Deuteronomy 10:15 makes the striking assertion: although everything belongs to YHWH, and although he is sovereign over everyone (Deut 10:14), he "attached" (חָשַׁק) himself to Israel to "love" (אָהֵב) them, and he "chose" (בָּחַר) them. Out of all the peoples he loved and chose only them. The cosmic claim of Deut 10:14 is consequently contrasted to YHWH's particular choice of Israel in Deut 10:14.[36] Deuteronomy 10:15 also emphasizes the enduring nature of YHWH's love and choice of Israel: he attached himself "on your fathers" (בַּאֲבֹתֶיךָ) to love them, he chose "their offspring after them" (בְּזַרְעָם אַחֲרֵיהֶם בָּכֶם),[37] and this is still the case "this day" (כַּיּוֹם הַזֶּה). From generation to generation YHWH's choice of loving and choosing Israel as his people remains.

With these words, the addressees are placed before the mystery of God's love for Israel, and his choice of them as his people. Both are recurring concepts in the book of Deuteronomy (cf. Deut 4:37; 32:8–9). The locus classicus is Deut 7:6–8, which has numerous overlaps with Deut 10:15, and states that YHWH chose Israel out of all the peoples on the face of the earth

---

34. Harman, "Particles," 1031.

35. Lundbom, *Deuteronomy*, 391. Christensen, *Deuteronomy*, 200, indicates that the Dead Sea Scrolls read כן על instead of רק.

36. Brueggemann, *Deuteronomy*, 129.

37. There is a notable number change in Deut 10:15b up to Deut 10:19 (the so-called *Numeruswechsel*). In Deut 10:12–15a and Deut 10:20–22, the passage employs the second person singular to refer to Israel; in Deut 10:15b–19, the second person plural is employed. Some have viewed the number change as an indication of different sources that are now intertwined. Otto, *Deuteronomium*, 1012, correctly argues that the number change in Deut 10:15b–19 has the hermeneutic function of focusing the attention of the addressees of Moses and distinguishing them from the previous generation. In my view, the change of number indicates that unlike their rebellious forefathers, they are called to circumcise their hearts (Deut 10:16), and they receive the assurance that the "Lord your God" is still their God (Deut 10:17).

to be a people for his treasured possession; he did this because he loves them and keeps the oath he made to their fathers (cf. Exod 19:5–6; Neh 9:6–7). No specific reason for YHWH's choice apart from this is given. In other words, he did this because he wanted to.

Deuteronomy 10:15 consequently stresses two interrelated theological facts:

- On the one hand, the verse emphasizes the absolute freedom and incomprehensibility of YHWH. Since everything belongs to him and he is sovereign to everyone, he can love and choose whomever he wants. In his freedom he decided to love and choose Israel.[38] Why he did this, considering the small size of Israel (Deut 7:7), is beyond human understanding.

- On the other hand, the verse also emphasizes the special nature of Israel. Although YHWH's choice of them is unfathomable, he has loved them, and he has chosen them. They are therefore his treasured possession among all the peoples. This special privilege comes with a great responsibility. As the main exhortation of the passage indicates, they should live completely committed to him (Deut 10:12–13).

Deuteronomy 10:16

Israel's response to YHWH singling them out in his love and election (Deut 10:15) is spelled out in the very next verse, Deut 10:16. Unlike the previous and subsequent verses that begin with an interjection (הֵן; Deut 10:14), adverb (רַק; Deut 10:15) and conjunction (כִּי; Deut 10:17), Deut 10:16 begins with a *waw* consecutive. Several scholars and Bible translations interpret the *waw* adverbially as an indication of reason (e.g., "therefore" in the ESV, NIV, (N)KJV, or "then" in the NRSV). Because YHWH loves and chose Israel, they should respond as instructed in Deut 10:16.

Israel is instructed to "circumcise the foreskin of your heart" (וּמַלְתֶּם אֵת עָרְלַת לְבַבְכֶם).[39] The metaphor recalls the covenant sign God instructed Abram and his descendants to keep (Gen 17:9–14). Here, however, the object that is to be circumcised is the heart. What is meant by the metaphor is explained by the metaphor in the parallel clause of Deut 10:16: to circumcise their foreskin of the heart is to not "harden" or "stiffen" (a *Hiph'il* form

---

38. Driver, *Deuteronomy*, 125.

39. Craigie, *Deuteronomy*, 205, followed by Christensen, *Deuteronomy*, 200, accepts the plural reading "foreskins" based on evidence from the Dead Sea Scrolls. See Baillet, *Les 'Petites Grottes'*, 158–61.

of קָשָׁה) the neck. The solemnity of the exhortation is strengthened by the inverted word order; literally the Hebrew clause reads "your neck do not harden any longer." To harden or stiffen the neck is a common biblical metaphor for being stubborn or obstinate (e.g., Jer 7:26; 17:23; 19:15; Prov 29:1; 2 Chr 30:8; 36:13; Neh 9:16–17, 29). This is exactly what Israel is accused of in the previous passage: their rebellion against God with the molten image indicated that they are "a people hard of neck" (עַם־קְשֵׁה־עֹרֶף), that is, "a stubborn people" (Deut 9:6, 13). During his intercession Moses explicitly asks God "not to remember the stubbornness of this people" (אֶל־קְשִׁי הָעָם הַזֶּה; Deut 9:27; cf. Exod 32:9; 33:3; 34:9).[40]

From the wider context the phrase "to circumcise the heart" refers to removing any stubbornness from the human heart. By doing this, the people would be different from the previous generation depicted in Deut 9:1–10:11. When heart-circumcision is done, everything that blocks their hearts and make them resist YHWH's commandments will be removed;[41] the people will willingly submit themselves to him; they will embody the main exhortation of Deut 10:12–13. That this is the meaning of heart-circumcision, is also implied from other passages in the Old Testament where the metaphor occurs (Deut 30:6; Lev 26:41; Jer 9:25; Ezek 44:7).[42] It refers to "the renewal and spiritual nature of the divine-human relationship."[43] While Deut 10:12–22 nowhere downplays the importance of the physical circumcision, it does emphasize the importance of the inward attitude that should characterize the lives the people. This in turn links on to the overarching aim of the basic stipulations, which emphasize the inner disposition that should characterize Israel.

Deuteronomy 10:17–18

Deuteronomy 10:17 starts with the conjunction כִּי, signaling a logical connection with the preceding Deut 10:16, and more specifically, indicating that Deut 10:17 provides the reason why Deut 10:16's exhortation should be obeyed.

Zooming in on the content of Deut 10:17–18, it becomes clear that these verses provide a lyrical description of who YHWH is and what he

---

40. Moses's fear that the people will remain rebellious and stubborn—especially after his death—is highlighted in Deut 31:27.

41. Tigay, *Deuteronomy*, 107–8.

42. For discussion of the biblical metaphor, see Lemke, "Circumcision of the Heart," 299–319, and Meade, "Circumcision of the Heart," 59–85.

43. Lemke, "Circumcision of the Heart," 317.

does.⁴⁴ Deuteronomy 10:17a contains a threefold description of YHWH's being, while Deut 10:17b–18 contains a fourfold description of YHWH's actions. The logic of the opening conjunction now becomes clear: Israel should circumcise their hearts (Deut 10:16) because of YHWH's being and actions (Deut 10:17–18).

The threefold description of YHWH's being starts with two striking superlatives: he is described as "God of gods" (אֱלֹהֵי הָאֱלֹהִים) and "Lord of lords" (וַאֲדֹנֵי הָאֲדֹנִים). As with other superlatives in Hebrew, the phrasing emphasizes that YHWH is the "greatest" or "highest" God and Lord.⁴⁵ At first sight, the verse might be interpreted to acknowledge the existence of other gods, with YHWH at the top of the pantheon. While some interpret the verse in this sense,⁴⁶ other parts of Deuteronomy (esp. Deut 3:24; 4:35, 39) affirm that YHWH is the only God, and consequently, Deut 10:17 should be understood as an expression of YHWH's uniqueness, incomparability and sovereignty (cf. Ps 136:2–3; Dan 2:47).⁴⁷ Otto strikingly states, "In the superlative statements, other gods are no longer given any existence. Rather, they have become language games for denoting YHWH's uniqueness" (translation mine).⁴⁸ Third and finally, YHWH is described as "the great, mighty and frightening God" (הָאֵל הַגָּדֹל הַגִּבֹּר וְהַנּוֹרָא), which are common expressions for God's dealings in the exodus.⁴⁹

The fourfold description of YHWH's actions starts with three references to his judicial character, of which the first two are put in the negative. First, he "does not lift up faces" (לֹא־יִשָּׂא פָנִים), which is a metaphor for unfairly regarding faces during judicial procedures and so doing influencing the verdict. The metaphor is often translated as "being partial" (e.g., ESV, NRSV). Secondly, YHWH "does not take a present" (וְלֹא יִקַּח שֹׁחַד), that is, a bribe, given to influence the outcome of a case (cf. Exod 23:8; Deut 27:25). Thirdly, he "does justice" (עֹשֶׂה מִשְׁפַּט) for the orphan and widow, namely those without a male head of a family who usually dealt with judicial matters, and who were consequently at risk of victimization. And fourthly, YHWH "loves the sojourner" (אֹהֵב גֵּר), and gives him food and clothing (cf. Deut 8:3–4).⁵⁰

44. Lundbom, *Deuteronomy*, 391.
45. Arnold, *Deuteronomy*, 563.
46. E.g., Brueggemann, *Deuteronomy*, 130.
47. Lundbom, *Deuteronomy*, 392; McConville, *Deuteronomy*, 200.
48. Otto, *Deuteronomium*, 1037.
49. Coetsee, "YHWH's 'Greatness,'" 114–40.
50. Syntactically, "giving food and clothing" is subordinate to YHWH "loving the sojourner." The latter is a *Qal* participle, which links it to the *Qal* participle "does [justice]" (עֹשֶׂה), while the former is a *Qal* infinitive construct.

Two matters should be noted from Deut 10:17b–18's description of YHWH's actions:

- The first three descriptions of what YHWH does are stated elsewhere in Deuteronomy as actions that are required from Israel's judges. Among others, they were to judge fairly between people (Deut 1:16), they were not to be partial in judgment (Deut 1:17; 16:19), and they were not to accept bribes (Deut 16:19).[51] As supreme Lord and judge, YHWH does not do these things; Israel's judges were to imitate his character.

- YHWH's actions in Deut 10:18 are specifically directed toward *personae miserae*, namely those who are on the margins of society, and who could easily have been exploited, namely the orphans, widows and sojourners. Strikingly, YHWH is said to "love" (אָהֵב) the sojourner—the same verb that is employed in Deut 10:15 to express YHWH's love for Israel as his special people.[52]

A striking flow within these verses becomes clear: the description of YHWH's being focuses on his transcendence: he is God of gods, Lord of lords, a great God, mighty and terrible. The description of his actions, however, focuses on his immanence, especially his care for those on the margins of society.[53]

Deuteronomy 10:19

Structurally, Deut 10:19 seems like an interlude or digression of sorts. This is also noted by some scholars.[54] But the flow from verse 18 to verse 19 is logical and fitting. The verse opens with a *waw* consecutive, which is interpreted by various Bible translations and scholars as an indication of reason (e.g., "therefore" in the ESV and KJV). Directly following the announcement that YHWH loves the sojourner, Deut 10:19 explicitly exhorts the addressees to do the same: "therefore love the sojourner" (וַאֲהַבְתֶּם אֶת־הַגֵּר). They should imitate their God.[55]

In the Old Testament, a "sojourner" was usually someone who left his or her homeland and relatives due to famine or warfare and sought

---

51. Cf. Coetsee, "By Everyone and for Everyone," 1–11.
52. Wright, *Deuteronomy*, 149.
53. Harstad, *Deuteronomy*, 356.
54. Arnold, *Deuteronomy*, 566; Tigay, *Deuteronomy*, 108.
55. Cf. Harstad, *Deuteronomy*, 356; Merrill, *Deuteronomy*, 201.

protection in another community. They were often poor and in need of protection.[56] As an outsider, the sojourner had no inherited rights and lacked the protection and privileges of the native. The Torah, however, contains explicit legislation of how the people of Israel were to treat sojourners. They enjoyed a number of conceded rights. The Torah explicitly stipulate how the Israelites were expected to conduct themselves toward the sojourner.[57] Deuteronomy 10:19 is one of these laws.

What is striking of the exhortation in Deut 10:19 is that YHWH exhorts Israel to love someone apart from himself.[58] This is significant considering Deut 10:12's indication that part of the heart of Israel's covenant fidelity is to love YHWH, and per implication, only him.

Deuteronomy 10:19b provides motivation for why the people were to love the sojourner: "for" (כִּי) they were sojourners in the land of Egypt. This is also the motivation provided in other similar stipulations in the Torah (Exod 22:20; 23:9; Lev 19:33–34; Deut 24:17–18, 21–22; cf. Deut 23:9). Once again exodus motifs are apparent in the verse.

Deuteronomy 10:20

Deuteronomy 10:20 echoes Deut 10:12–13. Similar to Deut 10:12–13, Deut 10:20 explicitly refers to "the Lord your God" (יְהוָה אֱלֹהֶיךָ), placed first in the sentence for emphasis, and it repeats the exhortations that Israel should "fear" (יָרֵא) and "serve" (עָבַד) YHWH. There are, however, also differences. Deuteronomy 10:12–13 is in the form of a rhetorical question followed by an answer, while Deut 10:20 contains direct exhortations (by means of three *Qal* and one *Niph'al* imperfects). In addition, Deut 10:20 contains two exhortations that are not found in Deut 10:12–13, namely that the people should "hold fast" (דָּבַק) to YHWH and "swear" (שָׁבַע) by his name (cf. Deut 6:13; Josh 23:7–8). The first verb expresses an intimate relationship, and the second loyalty.

As with Deut 10:12–13, the overarching meaning of Deut 10:20 is total commitment and obedience to YHWH. The content of Deut 10:12–13 is repeated here for emphasis.[59] In light of the similarities between the two, Deut 10:12–13 and 10:20 are the main exhortations of the passage, and can be viewed as the two pillars on which the rest of the passage rests.

---

56. Coetsee, "Love Thy Sojourner," 18–21.
57. Coetsee, "Love Thy Sojourner," 25–37.
58. Arnold, *Deuteronomy*, 567.
59. Craigie, *Deuteronomy*, 207.

Deuteronomy 10:21

Following the exhortations of Deut 10:20, Deut 10:21 shifts back to explaining who YHWH is (cf. Deut 10:14–15, 17–18). The verse begins with the emphatic personal pronoun "he" (הוּא), which is repeated two words on (וְהוּא), indicating that the nominal sentences that follow are "identification clauses,"[60] and relate to "the Lord your God" (יְהוָה אֱלֹהֶיךָ) mentioned in verse 20.

Verse 21 explains that YHWH is two things:

- "He is your praise" (הוּא תְהִלָּתֶךָ): The noun תְּהִלָּה is usually used to refer to "praise" or "a song of praise,"[61] but it can also be used to express "renown."[62] The phrase has been interpreted in primarily two ways: (1) YHWH is the object of Israel's praise, namely the one who should be praised because of his gracious and awesome acts in the exodus;[63] or (2) YHWH is the reason Israel will receive praise, implying that YHWH's acts for his people will result in other nations praising Israel and their God (cf. Deut 33:29).[64] While the clause may be intentionally ambiguous,[65] the first explanation fits the context the best.

- "And he is your God" (וְהוּא אֱלֹהֶיךָ): The personal nature of the description of YHWH as "your God" links on to the fuller description of "the Lord your God" found throughout the passage (Deut 10:12[3x], 14, 17, 20, 22). The rest of the description describes YHWH in terms frequently used in Deuteronomy for his role in the exodus events: YHWH is the one who has done "for you" (אִתְּךָ) "these great and terrifying things that your eyes have seen" (אֶת־הַגְּדֹלֹת וְאֶת־הַנּוֹרָאֹת הָאֵלֶּה אֲשֶׁר רָאוּ עֵינֶיךָ; cf. Deut 10:17 for "great" [גָּדוֹל], and Deut 10:12, 17, 20 for "terrifying" [from יָרֵא]).

Deuteronomy 10:22

The passage ends with a summary statement of redemption history up to the present day in the narrative context. Linking on to Gen 46:26–27 and

---

60. Arnold, *Deuteronomy*, 568.
61. Brown et al., *Hebrew and English Lexicon*, §239.2.
62. Allen, "הָלַל (hālal II)," 1035–36.
63. Harstad, *Deuteronomy*, 358.
64. Craigie, *Deuteronomy*, 207.
65. Block, *Deuteronomy*, 274.

Exod 1:5, Moses reminds the addressees that their forefathers who went down to Egypt were seventy in total. Now, however, in fulfilment of the promises YHWH made to Abraham and Isaac (Gen 15:5; 22:17; 26:4), they are as numerous as the stars of heaven (cf. Deut 1:10; 28:62).[66] The focus in the verse is on the one that is responsible for this expansive growth among the Israelites: "the LORD your God" (יְהוָה אֱלֹהֶיךָ). Within the larger narrative of Deuteronomy, the growth of Israel (cf. Gen 12:3) recalls the other major promise that is yet to be but soon will be fulfilled: the provision of land through the conquest (cf. Gen 17:8).[67] Consequently, Deut 10:22 provides proof of divine providence and implicitly looks forward to more of the same.

A NEW SUGGESTION OF THE STRUCTURE OF DEUTERONOMY 10:12-22

Based on the overview of the content and form of Deut 10:12-22 on a verse-by-verse basis, the current section of the chapter provides a new suggestion for how the structure of the passage can be viewed. This is done by providing a visual overview of the perceived structure of the passage (Figure 1), and an explanation of the proposed structure.

Figure 1: A visual overview of the structure of Deuteronomy 10:12-22

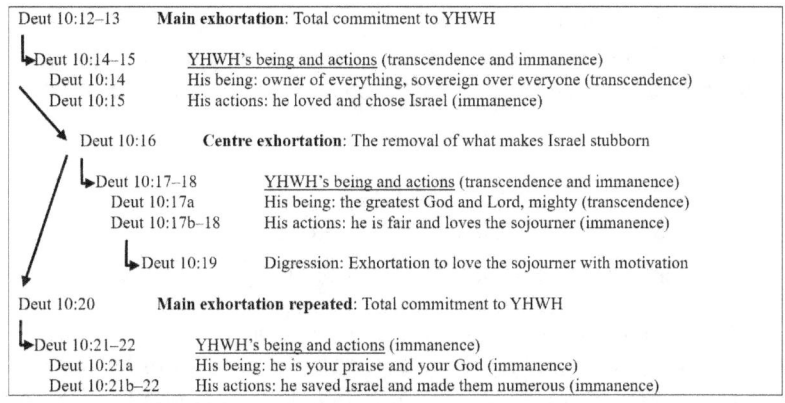

Deuteronomy 10:12-22 is made up of three movements, namely Deut 10:12-15, 10:16-19 and 10:20-22. Each movement consists of an

---

66. Block, *Deuteronomy*, 275, correctly indicates that the statement is hyperbolic, given that Num 1-2 and 26 demonstrate that the people could still be counted.

67. Craigie, *Deuteronomy*, 207.

exhortation (Deut 10:12–13, 16, 20) followed by motivation (Deut 10:14–15, 17–18, 21–22).

The two main exhortations of the passage are Deut 10:12–13 and Deut 10:20. These exhortations are very similar in terms of content, and they can be viewed as the two pillars of the passage. Deuteronomy 10:16 is the center exhortation of the passage. Structurally, Deut 10:12–13 builds up to Deut 10:16, while Deut 10:17–22 flows from Deut 10:16. This is suggested by the use of the *waw* consecutive in Deut 10:16, which, within its context, indicates reason ("therefore"), and the use of the conjunction כִּי ("for") at the start of Deut 10:17. The center exhortation of Deut 10:16 is therefore emphasized. The repetition found in Deut 10:12–13 and 20, however, does not only emphasize the content of these verses, but indicates that these verses should be viewed as the main exhortations of the passage. To put it differently, Deut 10:12–13 and 20 exhort the addressees to total commitment toward YHWH; based on their rebellion revisited in Deut 9:1–10:11, Deut 10:16 indicates how Israel can follow the exhortations contained in Deut 10:12–13 and 20.

Deuteronomy 10:19 also contains an exhortation (Deut 10:19a) followed by motivation (Deut 10:19b). This verse, however, is a digression, albeit a fitting digression. Based on the explanation that YHWH executes justice for the fatherless and widow and loves the sojourner (Deut 10:18), Deut 10:19 then digress from the overall symmetry of the passage by instructing Israel to love the sojourner. This does not suggest that Deut 10:19 is a later addition. That Deut 10:19 is an integral part of the passage, is suggested by the chiasm formed by the fourfold use of the verb "love" (אָהֵב):

> A Israel should love YHWH (Deut 10:12)
>
> B YHWH loves Israel (Deut 10:15)
>
> B' YHWH loves the sojourner (Deut 10:18)
>
> A' Israel should love the sojourner (Deut 10:19)

The three exhortations in Deut 10:12–22 are supported by three motivations: Deut 10:12–13 is motivated by 10:14–15, Deut 10:16 by 10:17–18 and Deut 10:20 by 10:21–22. Each motivation describes who YHWH is and what he does, and strikingly, in the same order. YHWH's being is described in Deut 10:14, 17a and 21a. Of these three descriptions of his being, the first two contain superlatives (Deut 10:14, 17a) and the first and third nominal sentences (Deut 10:14, 21a). YHWH's actions are described in Deut 10:15, 17b–18 and 21b–22.

Upon closer inspection, it becomes clear that the three motivations provided in the passage emphasize YHWH's transcendence and immanence.

The first two motivations describe YHWH's being to emphasize his transcendence (Deut 10:14, 17a), and is immediately followed by descriptions of his actions in order to emphasize his immanence (Deut 10:15, 17b–18). The majestic statements of his transcendence lead to striking statements of his immanence. The third motivation, however, while also describing YHWH's being and actions, solely focuses on his immanence (Deut 10:21–22). This suggests a development within the passage: it ends by focusing on the immanence of this transcendent God.

CONCLUSION: THE RHETORICAL FUNCTION OF DEUTERONOMY 10:12-22

Being part of the basic stipulations, Deut 10:12–22 indicates to the addressees what their inner disposition should be. This is necessary, since Deut 9:1–10:11, which reflects on the people's rebellion during the golden calf incident, explicitly refer to them as "stubborn" (Deut 9:6, 13). YHWH, however, upon Moses's intercession, was unwilling to destroy his people (Deut 10:10). Deuteronomy 10:12–22 then indicates how the addressees should respond to YHWH's gracious acts toward them.

The main aim of the passage is to exhort the people to wholehearted commitment toward YHWH. This is clear from the main exhortations of the passage (Deut 10:12–13, 20), as well as the center exhortation that instructs them to circumcise the foreskin of their heart (Deut 10:16), namely remove whatever makes them stubborn and inhibits them from wholehearted commitment toward YHWH.

As indicated in the previous section, each of the exhortations in the passage is supported by a motivation that focuses on divine transcendence and immanence:

- Israel should be completely committed to YHWH (Deut 10:12–13), because, although he is the owner of everything and sovereign over everyone, he has loved them and chose them as his people (Deut 10:14–15).
- Israel should circumcise their hearts to be completely committed to YHWH (Deut 10:16), because he is the greatest God and Lord, and his character is fair and worthy of imitation (Deut 10:17–18).
- Israel should be completely committed to YHWH (Deut 10:20), because he is their praise and God, and he has fulfilled his promise of their expansion (Deut 10:21–22).

These motivations emphasize who YHWH is (Deut 10:14, 17a, 21) and what he does (Deut 10:15, 17b–18, 22). Throughout the passage, seven times in total, he is referred to as "the Lord your God" (Deut 10:12^{3x}, 14, 17, 20, 22). He is the God who covenanted himself to his people. At its core, Deut 10:12–22 stresses YHWH's being and actions.[68] By doing so, the passage indirectly emphasizes the special status of Israel (Deut 10:15, 21b–22); they alone are YHWH's people.

The exodus events are also referred to throughout the passage (Deut 10:15, 17a, 19b, 21b, 22). YHWH's past dealings with and for Israel are emphasized to change their conduct in the present, and in view of the future. His providence in Israel's expansion (Deut 10:22) indicates that he stays true to his promises and implies that the next great promise that is on the horizon of the people, namely the provision of land by means of the conquest, will be fulfilled as well.

Strikingly, the references to divine transcendence and immanence in the motivations all relate in some way to divine incomprehensibility:

- YHWH's love for and choice of Israel as his people (Deut 10:14–15) is unfathomable and beyond human understanding, emphasizing his absolute freedom as God.
- YHWH's care for the marginalized of society (Deut 10:17–18), the so-called "little people,"[69] is astonishing, given the fact that he is "God of gods and Lord of lords."
- YHWH's providential care for Israel in their redemption from Egypt and their expansion prior to and after the exodus (Deut 10:21–22)—even despite their open rebellion against him (cf. Deut 9:1–10:11)—is astounding.

Deuteronomy 10:12–22 consequently emphasizes that YHWH's being and actions are ultimately unfathomable. He alone is God, and in accordance with his being and character, he does as he likes. And what he has done and promises to do, is and will be to the greatest benefit of Israel.

In consequence, the passage has a deliberate and consistent alternation between human responsibility (Deut 10:12–13, 16, 20) and divine incomprehensibility (Deut 10:14–15, 17–18, 21–22), highlighting the latter to foster the former.

---

68. Brueggemann, *Deuteronomy*, 128.
69. Block, *Deuteronomy*, 273.

BIBLIOGRAPHY

Allen, Leslie C. " הָלַל (hālal II)." In *New International Dictionary of Old Testament Theology and Exegesis*, vol. 2, edited by Willem A. VanGemeren, 1035-38. Grand Rapids: Zondervan, 1997.

Arnold, Bill T. *The Book of Deuteronomy: Chapters 1-11*. New International Commentary on the Old Testament. Grand Rapids: Eerdmans, 2022.

Baillet, Maurice, et al. "Les 'Petites Grottes' de Qumrân: Exploration de la Falaise Les grottes 2Q, 3Q, 5Q, 6Q, 7Q à 10Q, Le Rouleau de Cuivre." In *Discoveries in the Judaean Desert*, vol. 2. Oxford: Clarendon, 1962.

Block, Daniel I. *Deuteronomy*. NIV Application Commentary. Grand Rapids: Zondervan, 2012.

Brown, Francis, et al. *Enhanced Brown-Driver-Briggs Hebrew and English Lexicon*. Oxford: Clarendon, 1977.

Brueggemann, Walter. *Deuteronomy*. Abingdon Old Testament Commentaries. Nashville: Abingdon, 2001.

Christensen, Duane L. *Deuteronomy 1:1-21:9*. Word Biblical Commentary. Nashville, Tennessee: Thomas Nelson, 2001.

Coetsee, Albert J. "By Everyone and for Everyone: The Principles Underlying 'Justice' in Deuteronomy 16:18-20." *In Luce Verbi* 55.3 (2021) 1-11.

———. "'Love Thy Sojourner (by Integrating Them)': Ethical Perspectives from the Pentateuch." In *Life in Transit: Theological and Ethical Contributions on Migration*, edited by Manitza Kotzé and Riaan Rheeder, 15-45. Reformed Theology in Africa Series, 2. Cape Town: AOSIS, 2020.

———. "YHWH and Israel in Terms of the Concept of Life in Deuteronomy." *Old Testament Essays* 32.1 (2019) 101-26.

———. "YHWH's 'Greatness,' 'Mighty Hand,' 'Deeds' and 'Mighty Acts' in Deuteronomy 3:24." *Old Testament Essays* 34.1 (2021) 114-40.

Craigie, Peter C. *The Book of Deuteronomy*. New International Commentary on the Old Testament. Grand Rapids: Eerdmans, 1976.

Driver, Samuel R. *A Critical and Exegetical Commentary on Deuteronomy*. International Critical Commentary. Edinburgh: T&T Clark, 1902.

Harman, Allan. "Particles." In *New International Dictionary of Old Testament Theology and Exegesis*, vol. 4, edited by Willem A. VanGemeren, 1028-42. Grand Rapids: Zondervan, 1997.

Harstad, Adolph L. *Deuteronomy*. Concordia Commentary. Saint Louis: Concordia, 2022.

Lemke, Werner E. "Circumcision of the Heart. The Journey of a Biblical Metaphor." In *A God so Near: Essays on Old Testament Theology in Honor of Patrick D. Miller*, edited by Brent A. Strawn and Nancy R. Bowen, 299-319. Winona Lake, IN: Eisenbrauns, 2003.

Lundbom, Jack R. *Deuteronomy: A Commentary*. Grand Rapids: Eerdmans, 2013.

McCarthy, Carmel. *Deuteronomy: Biblia Hebraica Quinta*. Stuttgart: Deutsche Bibelgesellschaft, 2007.

McConville, J. Gordon. *Deuteronomy*. Apollos Old Testament Commentary. Leicester: Apollos, 2002.

Meade, John D. "Circumcision of the Heart in Leviticus and Deuteronomy: Divine Means for Resolving Curse and Bringing Blessing." *Southern Baptist Journal of Theology* 18.3 (2014) 59–85.

Merrill, Eugene H. *Deuteronomy*. New American Commentary. Nashville: Broadman & Holman, 1994.

Otto, Eckart. *Deuteronomium 4,44–11,32*. Herders Theologischer Kommentar zum Alten Testament. Freiburg im Breisgau: Herder. 2012.

Talstra, Eep. "Deuteronomy 9 and 10: Synchronic and Diachronic Observations." In *Synchronic or Diachronic? A Debate on Method in Old Testament Exegesis*, edited by Johannes C. de Moor, 187–210. Leiden: Brill, 1995.

Tigay, Jeffrey H. *The JPS Torah Commentary: Deuteronomy*. Philadelphia, Pennsylvania: Jewish Publication Society, 1996.

Weinfeld, Moshe. *Deuteronomy 1–11*. Anchor Bible. New York: Doubleday, 1991.

Wevers, John W., ed. *Deuteronomium*. Vol. 3.2, *Septuaginta: Vetus Testamentum Graecum Auctoritate Academiae Scientiarum Gottingensis Editum*. 2nd ed. Göttingen: Vandenhoeck & Ruprecht, 2006.

Wright, Christopher J. H. *Deuteronomy*. New International Biblical Commentary. Peabody, Massachusetts: Hendrickson, 1996.

Chapter 3

Ways the Lord Makes Himself Known in the Book of Job

—Robin Gallaher Branch

Department Religion & Philosophy, Christian Brothers University, Memphis, Tennessee, USA, and Unit for Reformational Theology and the Development of the South African Society, Faculty of Theology, North-West University, Potchefstroom, South Africa

ABSTRACT

This chapter takes issue with a common view that God is inscrutable and difficult to understand. Employing literary tools and a canonical methodology, this chapter argues that God can and wants to be known. He seeks to be understood and jealously values a proper understanding of his character. However, the limits of understanding and knowing him rest not only on his self-revelation but also on our capacity as human beings to understand.

Using the book of Job and Job himself as examples, this chapter examines how God makes himself known. Consider these aspects, namely that God

- Ably administrates (Job 1–2)
- Gambles (1–2)
- Listens (3–37)
- Shows up with theatrics (38:1; 40:6)

- Extends good manners
- Corrects Job's faulty knowledge and theology (38–41)
- Teaches (38–41)
- Excels as a tour guide (38–41)
- Seeks restoration of fellowship (38–42:10)
- Promotes Job and assigns a new duty (42:7–10)
- Honors Job posthumously

INTRODUCTION

The Lord honors Job with probably more "facetime" (to use a modern expression) than any other Hebrew Bible personage except Moses. The book bearing his name, therefore, provides a template for studying aspects of God's character. It ends with Job's healing, his silence, and an additional time (possibly totaling 140 years) of family and financial blessings—time enough to ponder how better know God through his remarkable self-revelation. God, most graciously, is scrutable and knowable to Job—but on his own terms and within his own time schedule.

This chapter shows several character traits the Lord reveals about himself in the book of Job. Though not exhaustive, the list is individualized to one person, Job. Other traits like mighty deliverer and lawgiver are more fully developed in other books and other encounters.

The Lord gears this self-revelation individually to Job's life, past experience, and present circumstances. Furthermore, as a result of this new, corrected knowledge, God seeks ongoing and improved relationships with Job and the book's three or possibly four other characters.

While Job wanted a trial in which the Lord was cross-examined, the Lord answered Job's persistent demands for a hearing in an unexpected way: the Lord questioned Job!

The Lord's method, his presence, and the encounter changed and reassured Job. While Job's initial queries about why horrible losses and sudden suffering came upon him are not specifically addressed, the encounter arguably addressed Job's deeper needs. The encounter calmed Job. The book's tone, volume, and words shift from stridency to reverence. The book of Job ends with Job's silence, a literary tool that arguably shows a satisfied Job—and that should satisfy us as readers and hearers. Job confesses, sighs, and worships with this phrase, "my eyes have seen you . . . and I repent" (Job 42:5–6).

Put another way, the book of Job and Job himself present one man's experience of suffering and of getting to know God. These two themes serve as templates, broad guidelines to readers and hearers. This chapter views getting to know God as the more important of the two.

Consequently, this chapter advocates reading the book of Job from the Lord's viewpoint. He corrects Job thusly, "Who is this that darkens my counsel with words *without knowledge*?" (38:2, italics added). The Lord states that Job first and later three or possibly four others do not speak accurately of him. All five have spoken from incorrect knowledge. This is a serious charge. The Lord arrives in a storm—a vehicle that may reflect both urgency and anger—to set aright their viewpoints and theologies. A later Scripture enlarges this theme of God's jealously over his word and name (Ps 138:2).

The Lord seeks to correct this lack of knowledge in the book's concluding five chapters (Job 38–42). Via two long monologues, he lets Job (and probably Eliphaz, Bildad, Zophar, and Elihu) get to know him. He shares his interests and character. The Lord either interrupts and silences Elihu's long monologue or arrives at its finish. A textual reading of Job 37:24–38:1 indicates that five human beings watch a storm, know it heralds the Lord's arrival, and wait silently as greeters. The Lord signals out Job (38:2) but does not dismiss the other four. Therefore, I assume they listened to the Lord's monologues in silence—perhaps grateful they were not the ones called out!

This chapter argues that the book of Job's primary theme should not focus on the suffering of the innocent—a creditable sub-theme—but on God's perspective, specifically correct knowledge of God. This chapter follows the shift Job himself experienced. Job's concentration shifted from unhealthy self-absorption to delightfully learning about the Lord's character.

The Lord gives Job a direct tutorial (Job 38–41). Job soon agrees he has not known the Lord and puts his hand over his mouth (40:3–5). Readers and hearers for generations have eavesdropped, so to speak, thereby also receiving direct knowledge of the Lord.

Readers and hearers identify with the book of Job because it is about empathy and emotional progression; they recognize the bodily suffering of another.[1]

Yes, unmerited suffering is a secondary theme and one developed more fully in New Testament texts. That is significant. Indeed, the Lord seems to honor Job's suffering and publicly promote him—but much later, more fully, and in a most unexpected way.

---

1. Van der Zwan, "Pathology and Pain," Conclusion.

OTHER VIEWS ON THE BOOK OF JOB'S THEME

The standard view of the book of Job is that it is a treatise on unjust suffering.[2] D. A. Carson writes that "Job is in the position of a man who is suffering even though he does not deserve it."[3]

Marcia Webb, a psychologist, notes that the book of Job examines "unmerited suffering in a universe guided by a loving, all-powerful and all-knowing God."[4] She states that "Job's experiences qualify as traumatic stressors."[5] Lance Hawley sees the book's plot as revolving around the loss of life.[6]

Textual evidence certainly supports these complementary themes. Yes, for thirty-seven chapters, Job's destruction, the babble about it, and Job's laments dominate. The intense focus on Job—his feelings, sufferings, and possible reasons why he suffers—overwhelms both the characters and subsequent generations of readers and hearers.

METHODOLOGY

The chapter combines a literary approach and canonical insights. A canonical methodology is broad but can include this premise, namely that the canon is not so much a product but a process.[7] I favor that approach; Job himself undergoes the process of change.

As I have stated elsewhere,[8] a canonical approach does the following:

- Uses the text's final form and recognizes it as authoritative
- Acknowledges the earlier work of editors and councils that possibly took generations
- Offers a valid paradigm for interpretation, reading, study, hearing, and writing about the Bible
- Honors the text's inherent historical and theological aspects and contributions[9]

---

2. Fee and Hubbard, *Eerdmans Companion*, 306.
3. Carson, *Collected Writings*, 261.
4. Webb, "Book of Job," para 4.
5. Webb, "Book of Job," para 5.
6. Hawley, "Life in Job," 143.
7. Klein et al., *Introduction to Biblical Interpretation*, 119.
8. Branch, "Gender Balance: Part 1," 3–4.
9. Cf. Gignilliat, "Brief History," 158–67.

A canonical approach sees the biblical books as the authoritative writings of the Jewish and Christian communities; canonical criticism analyzes the editorial design of the present form of the text.[10]

The lens of looking at the canon as a whole melds nicely with literary tools. Literary tools include character, setting, time, diction, plot, conflict, inclusion, tone, point of view, narration, repetition, and dialogue.[11] These literary elements can be considered the surface structure of a specific text.[12]

The book of Job indeed presents real human anguish, analyzes why it happens, and answers some questions but bypasses even more.[13] However, this chapter takes its cue from the hero, Job himself. He remains satisfied with the Lord's words—and by extension, so should we as readers and hearers.

Literary criticism and its subset narrative criticism help readers to identify with a character as a positive influence and to avoid imitating another character because of negative personality traits.[14] Likewise, the book of Job can be seen as a template for how to face or how not to face suffering.

Literary criticism identifies characters as flat, stock, or round, as agents or types or full characters.[15] Job is a round character because of the emotions he experiences, his failures, and his successes. By the end of the book, Job has changed, grown, and is recognizably different.

The book of Job reflects poetry typical of that throughout ancient Mesopotamia. The region's ancient poetry points to the implicit conviction that a deserving ruler (or person) "although seemingly forgotten by the gods, is bound to be restored to grace"; this holds true for Job and Sargon of Akkad.[16] Furthermore, Ezek 14:14–23 states that only Noah, Daniel, and Job emerged "unscathed from universal catastrophes."[17] In the long run, the difficulties besetting Noah, Job, and Daniel made them heroes.

TWO INCLUSIONS FRAME THE BOOK OF JOB

Inclusions are biblical markers indicating a literary unit to a reader and hearer; typically, a word or phrase is given at the beginning and repeated

10. Klein et al., *Introduction to Biblical Interpretation*, 61.
11. Cf. Lostracco and Wilkerson, *Analyzing Short Stories*, 1–60.
12. Klein et al., *Introduction to Biblical Interpretation*, 70.
13. Carson, *Collected Writings*, 23.
14. Cf. Klein et al., *Introduction to Biblical Interpretation*, 65.
15. Klein et al., *Introduction to Biblical Interpretation*, 68.
16. Mazar, *Patriarchs: Volume II*, 7.
17. Mazar, *Patriarchs: Volume II*, 8.

at the end of a passage. Inclusions give clues on how to read the chapters in between.

Job's initial and concluding prosperity forms one inclusion (1:1–3; 42:12–15). The Lord doubles Job's bank account.[18]

A second inclusion is the Lord's designation of Job as "my servant" (1:8; 2:3; 42:7–8). This endearing, enduring compliment verifies the changelessness of Lord's view. Its designation is perhaps the Old Testament's highest praise. Other designees are Moses (Num 12:7) and someone very special in Isaiah (Isa 42:1). Often other biblical characters recognize this specialness; King Darius called Daniel "a servant of the living God" (Dan 6:20). Church father Chrysostom notes that God constantly calls Job his servant and thereby justifies him.[19]

The book of Job presents Job's story as an unexpected free fall from worldwide prominence to street-wide ridicule. Job's circumstances plummet from prosperity to loss, health to oozing sores, high social standing to residence on an ash heap. Arguably his life's single constant was his rank as God's servant. Arguably, the Lord's opinion was the only view that mattered. The Lord's appositive for Job stands like a silent pillar throughout Job 3–37, the chapters detailing Job's self-absorption,

Significantly, the Lord names Job as "my servant" four times in his discussion with Eliphaz. The emphasis hammers. Noticeably, the Lord does not extend the appositive to Eliphaz. Significantly in the Lord's hierarchy, Job outranks Eliphaz. The Lord informs Eliphaz that he and his two friends have not spoken of him rightly "as my servant Job has" (42:7).

Background, Book of Job

The church fathers write that Job lived before Moses, the events in the book of Job actually happened, and Moses wrote the first five books of the Bible and the book of Job while in the wilderness.[20] I accept those statements as a reasonable, believable tradition. I think it is significant that the book of Job (perhaps the Bible's first written book) presents the story of a non-Israelite, a believer in God but outside the covenant line of Abraham, Isaac, and Jacob. Like the priest Melchizedek (Gen 14:24) and Ruth (who like Job has a whole book in her name), Job is a righteous gentile. Others

---

18. Branch, *Space for Joy*, 404.
19. Simonetti and Conti, *Ancient Christian Commentary*, 218.
20. Simonetti and Conti, *Ancient Christian Commentary*, 220–22.

include Balaam the son of Beor (Num 22:5); Agur the son of Jakeh (Prov 30:1) and Lemuel (Prov 31:1).[21]

I acknowledge there is a time interval between when the events in Job happened and the writing and editing of the book. The book may also reflect the later editing of one who crafted it with the oral tradition and the patriarchal period in mind.[22] Other scholars, noting the book's beautiful poetic language and narration, may date it to what is called the Silver Age (500 to 63 BCE).[23]

If the book of Job opens when Job was around seventy, and he lived 140 more years or lived total of 140 years, those figures make Job either 140 years old or 210 years old when he died. Ephrem the Syrian, another church father, writes that Job lived 255 years; seven of these are not included in the total of 248 and represent his time of suffering.[24]

ASPECTS OF THE LORD'S CHARACTER IN THE BOOK OF JOB

The book of Job not only is a deeply human book about one man's sufferings but also a chronicle giving "a coherent character portrayal of God."[25] Consider these fifteen aspects:

Able Administrator

The book of Job opens with a new insight: the Lord holds regular council meetings. Chapters 1 and 2 give the first glimpse of a heavenly routine. Later gatherings are mentioned in 1 Kgs 22:19–24 and Ps 89:5–7. Job never learns of the council meetings nor of his prominence in two.

Attendance seems mandatory and participants seem plentiful.[26] The Lord is presented as an able, courteous, well-informed administrator. In a pre-meeting mingle, the Lord circulates and welcomes in particular one called the Satan, seemingly singling him out.

Although the readers and hearers know the Lord is omniscient, all knowing, the Lord courteously asks questions. He asks about the Satan's

21. Mazar, *Patriarchs: Volume II*, 234.
22. Cf. Fee and Hubbard, *Eerdmans Companion to the Bible*, 306–7.
23. Mazar, *Patriarchs: Volume II*, 112, 115.
24. Simonetti and Conti, *Ancient Christian Commentary*, 222.
25. Cf. Ham, "Gentle Voice of God," 528.
26. Cf. Miller, *Divine Warrior*, 66–67.

activities since, presumably, the last meeting. He specifically mentions one human being, "Have you considered my servant Job?" (Job 1:8). Although the Bible does not give the tone of voice, it would seem that the Lord's voice is pleasant because his words are pleasant.

Then the Lord describes Job's various virtues: upright, blameless, like no one on the face of the earth, a man who fears God and turns away from evil; the direct speech echoes the narrator's introduction (1:8, 1). Actually, the Lord's description, heavy-laden with accolades, is possibly the most elaborate in all Scripture. Repetition, a literary tool, signals importance. The echo establishes Job's exemplary character and emphasizes the Lord's esteem.

Satan seemingly snarls an answer; he complains that the Lord has put a protective fence around Job and all his possessions (1:9–10). Then the Satan issues a challenge: "Stretch out your hand now and touch all he has and Job will curse you to your face" (1:11).

The Lord corrects neither the Satan's tone nor his reply's malevolent content. Instead, the Lord, accepts the challenge! He gives the Satan the go-ahead to smite Job's possessions—but with the caveat to spare his life (1:12). The Satan hurriedly leaves the council meeting, brings sudden, complete destruction on all Job's possessions, and masterminds multiple deaths.

Translations for "the Satan" include attacker and adversary. However, Ryan E. Stokes advocates for "executioner."[27] The Satan clearly mounts a vicious attack on Job's property and incites the deaths of his servants and children (1:13–19).[28] "Executioner" also applies to the Satan in Zech 3, 1 Chr 21, and Num 22.[29]

A second council meeting mirrors the first (Job 2). Satan/the executioner attends it and repeats his earlier prediction that Job will curse the Lord "to your face" if the Lord permits Satan to attack Job's body (2:1–5). The Lord permits it but adds the caveat to spare Job's life.

The challenge, though inflicted on Job, is really a challenge to the Lord.[30] The remainder of the book of Job plays out the wager.

Gambler

The exchanges between the Lord and the Satan show interesting characteristics. The Lord is a gambler, the Satan, a fool!

27. Stokes, "Satan, YHWH's Executioner," 267.
28. Stokes, "Satan, YHWH's Executioner," 268.
29. Stokes, "Satan, YHWH's Executioner," 268.
30. Fee and Hubbard, *Eerdmans Companion to the Bible*, 307.

The Lord gambles that Job will not curse him. The Lord accepts the Satan's challenge in a public conversation seemingly heard and observed by the most elite of his creation, the heavenly host. The Lord opens himself to the possibility of public shame. I think it is an amazingly courageous choice.

The Lord gambles in the sense that he wagers Job will not curse him. Council members serve as witnesses for the wager and as onlookers while it plays out.[31]

Here's a (limited) human parallel. My mother was well-known as an expert in bridge, a competitive card game. Here are some rules she followed and taught:[32]

- Know the game
- Give it your full attention
- Remember the bids
- Memorize the cards mentioned
- Observe and assess all players
- Listen intently
- Be pleasant
- Practice, practice, practice
- Learn from mistakes made
- Play the hand you're dealt

The difference here, however, between any human being and the Lord is that the Lord is omniscient; he knows everything. Satan shows his stupidity by forgetting that. An old saying about poker from the American West—a time of land grabbing, lawlessness, cheap liquor, and frequent death—likewise applies to the Satan's stupid wager: don't play a man at his own game.

Satan is a fool for at least two reasons. Firstly, Satan believes he can win. He forgets the Lord's all-knowingness. Additionally, this all-knowingness seems to include a knowledge of love. The Lord knows Job loves him. The Lord wagers that love holds through suffering, even prolonged suffering.

John Calvin adds this brilliant insight: Satan wanted to drive Job to madness by despair.[33] I agree but think he primarily wanted to shame the Lord publicly.

---

31. Branch, "Space for Joy," 396.
32. Gwen Gallaher, private conversations with the author, 2010–2018.
33. Calvin, *Institutes of the Christian Religion*, 136.

The concept of the Lord as a gambler appears elsewhere in Scripture. For example, the heavenly council possibly held its breath awaiting Mary's reply to the angel about her upcoming, unexpected pregnancy. She replied, "Behold the handmaid of the Lord. Be it done to me according to your word" (Luke 1:38). Yet another time was when Jesus asked that the cup of suffering be passed from him (Matt 26:39). It was not. When arrested, Jesus knew he had the power to call twelve legions of angels to his defense (Matt 26:53). He did not.

Listener

Perhaps the highest compliment one person can receive is another's undivided attention, another's active listening. As evidenced by his entry statements and questions to Job in chapter 38, the Lord had actively listened from chapters 3–37.

Gary Chapman writes on active listening. Perhaps he thought of the Lord's seeming silence as he compiled tips.[34] Consider the following advice that applies on a human-to-human level:

1. Maintain eye contact. Give the gift of your full attention
2. Don't do something else simultaneously
3. Listen to the words, but listen as well for feelings
4. Note the voice tone
5. State what emotion you think you are hearing—fear, disappointment, joy, frustration, etc.
6. Look at body language: clinched fist, slumped shoulders
7. Repeat what you think you have just heard
8. Ask for clarification
9. Do not interrupt
10. Consider having this motive: My goal is to understand you

Job thinks the Lord's silence indicates absence (23:8–9) It does not. Instead, it signals listening, courtesy, care, and concern. How so? Because he uses the format Job used. In a series of questions copying Job's learning style, the Lord takes charge.

---

34. Chapman, *Five Love Languages*, 63–63.

One Who Likes Grand Entrances

The Lord's arrival in a storm (Job 38:1) produces no fear in Job, the three friends, or Elihu, the final speaker. Other entrances by the Lord or his representative (see Luke 1:12, 30; 2:9) produce fear. In contrast, Job awaits the Lord's arrival in the swirling clouds in silence and steps forward when summoned. Upon reflection, the Lord's arrival also shows his humility: The Lord condescends to engage in a discussion with a mortal man.[35]

One Exhibiting Good Manners

Good manners are a collection of traits marking someone as pleasant company. Good manners make others feel at ease and treat others with respect. The Lord exhibits good manners throughout the book of Job.

Good manners cover what is said and what is not said. For example, Job looks awful (2:12)—but the Lord makes no mention of that. Perhaps Job's deteriorating condition as the tale progresses made him what we now call disabled.[36] Here's a working description of how Job looked for the most important interview of his life:

> He suffers from a skin disease that seems to spread all over his body; he has infections and darkened skin (38:28); he scratches himself with a potsherd (2:8); his skin has pustules (7:5b) and peels (30:30); he may be both anorexic and emaciated (19:20); he may be feverish (20:30b); others may notice his bad breath and rotting teeth (19:17, 20).[37]

Good manners acknowledge all present. The text does not dismiss Elihu, Eliphaz, Bildad, and Zophar. It would seem that they all hear the Lord's two monologues. Indeed, Eliphaz, representing himself and his two friends, is summoned at the end of the second monologue (42:7).

Good manners are always associated with ethical patterns and open, upright, moral behavior.[38] The Lord certainly is associated with righteousness.

Speech indicates good manners. For example, the exemplary wife in Proverbs has "the law of kindness son her tongue" (Prov 31:26b).

---

35. Ham, "Gentle Voice of God," 540.
36. Van der Zwan, "Pathology and Pain," para 6.
37. Branch, "Space for Joy," 392–93.
38. Cf. Post, *Etiquette*, 683.

God does not ridicule Job, make fun of him, or "dispense wholesale criticism."³⁹ The Lord immediately seems to praise Job in public in front of the other four speakers. He begins his monologue with a courteous word, *Na*, please. Then he seems to commend Job by using the word *geber*, which is which often signifies a mighty man.

Granted, Job in his bedraggled state and illness may not look like a mighty man, but the Lord recognizes and decrees him as such.

Good manners allow for a rest. A break happens between the Lord's two discourses. Job 38–39 and 40–42. A brief narration introduces each section.

Two Examples of Good Manners

It would seem that the five men are lined up waiting for the Lord. Silence prevails. For once, the humans do not talk. Noticeably absent in the Lord's arrival is a response of fear.

The Lord's two monologues begin kindly with the word *Na*, a particle which I translate as "please" or "I ask you" and the public declaration that the Lord considers Job a *geber*, a mighty man (Job 38:2–3, 40:7). I do not think the tone is harsh, impatient or abrupt; however, I acknowledge that other readers may hear it as such.

I suggest this translation for both verses: "Please (*Na*) brace yourself like a mighty man (*geber*); and I will question you."

This translation illustrates two traits of good manners: respect and encouragement. If *Na* is translated "please," it indicates courtesy, respect—and maybe in this case a twinkle in the Lord's eye showing kindness. *Geber* differs from other common words for man like *adam*, *ish*, and *enosh*.

Granted, *Na* often means "now," or "I pray thee."⁴⁰ Sometimes translators omit it altogether. The particle is translated "please" in 2 Kgs 2:9 (NKJV). Just before the chariot came for Elijah to be taken up into heaven, he turned to his successor Elisha and said, "Ask! What may I do for you, before I am taken away from you?" Elisha said, "*Please* let a double portion of you spirit be upon me" (italics added).

In the context of the two monologues, *geber*, mighty man, is a compliment, for bedraggled, destitute, whining, ill, sore-oozing Job neither looks nor acts like a champion. Yet the Lord sees him that way! The Lord calls him up instead of putting him down!

---

39. Haupt, *Seventeen Book of Etiquette*, 8.
40. Harris et al., "Na," 2:541.

The Lord later kindly repeats his first assessment, a further emphasis that Job already is or will be a mighty man. The Lord thereby shows Job (and generations of readers and hearers) that the Lord not only creates via the spoken word as in Gen 1 (vv. 3, 6, 9, 14, 20, 24, 26) but also by the spoken word to Job.

One Who Asks Questions

The Lord does not follow modern psychology models of asking how Job feels about his life; additionally, the Lord ignores Job's list; the Lord ignores Job's list of his righteous actions (Job 31). Instead, the Lord diverts and directs by asking simple questions that must honestly be answered. "No." Like Fred Gottlieb,[41] I do not hear the Lord's tone as sarcasm. Like T. C. Ham,[42] I hear the Lord speaking with compassion and comfort.

Lord asks Job if he was present when the Lord laid the earth's foundation (38:4), or if he has journeyed to the springs of the sea (v. 16) or seen the gates of death (v. 17)? Does Job know the way to "the abode of light" (v. 19) or has Job entered into the storehouses of the snow (v. 22)? Does Job go hunting with the Lord and the lioness (v. 39)?

Perhaps Job and the others laughed when the Lord asked if the rain has a father (v. 28). All answers must be no.

The Lord's speech, in the form of questions, is planned, and serves as a way to move Job toward a new level that the Lord both requires and desires.[43] The Lord clearly separates Creator from created. That humbling marks the beginning of Job's healing.

To the surprise of both Job and the readers, "God answers Job in terms of creation rather than covenant. Amazingly, the Lord becomes a tour guide. The radically non-anthropocentric theology of the divine speeches is at odds with creation theology as it is articulated by the various speakers in the first thirty-seven chapters."[44]

Talking about creation rather than condemnation gives Job (and readers and hearers) a chance to listen to the birds sing, see the ostrich run, and marvel at the mountain goats as they leap and show off for their Creator. The tour gives Job time to undergo a "change or transformation of ego."[45]

41. Gottlieb, "Creation Theme in Genesis 1," para 21 and following.
42. Ham, "Gentle Voice of God," 527.
43. Cf. Simonetti and Conti, *Ancient Christian Commentary*, 195.
44. Davis, "Out of the Whirlwind," 152–53.
45. Venter, "Wealth, Poverty and Mutual Care," 6.

Teacher

Perhaps during the Lord's encounter, Job does not immediately realize this fact: the Lord is teaching him. His classroom has been suffering. The Lord now uses a teaching method—questions—Job suggested with his own monologues. Becoming and being a great teacher can be learned. The Lord gives one model in Job 38–41. God shows his teaching skill in the "homework" of suffering and in the "lecture" mode of a tour, and in a practical activity.

To many generations, the Lord's monologues reveal him as the maker of the universe and its sustainer.[46] The monologues manifest a wondrous God whose name could be Here I Am.[47]

The Lord continues his magnificent discourse on creation in chapter 39 with talking about specific animals. The Lord knows the gestation time of a goat and is present when she bears her kids. Indeed, perhaps the Lord's nickname could also be Midwife and Nanny because the Lord watches as the young kids "grow strong in the wilds" (39:4).

David Clines notes that the deity does not necessarily take part in the birth and is not a midwife.[48] However, I think the text leaves that open as a possibility. Assisting in a birth certainly is in keeping with the attention to detail of creation the Lord shares with Job. The imagery would indicate a hands-on presence rather than an unseen presence, I believe.

The Lord knows the wild donkey, the wild ox, and the joyful ostrich, and seems to delight in their abilities. The wild donkey "laughs at the commotion of a town" and prefers the hills (vv. 7–8). The wild ox is so strong-willed it cannot be tamed to bear a yoke and work the threshing floor (vv. 9–12). The ostrich, while not endowed by the Lord with wisdom or good sense, can outrun a horse and rider (vv. 14–18). A warhorse fears nothing and a battle excites him (vv. 19–25). The eagle builds a high nest and its young feast on blood (vv. 27–30).

The Lord's itemization of his creation shows his care. The Lord is creator and sustainer. Perhaps Job slowly begins to realize that the Lord cares also for him. The lack of comment from Job and the four others may indicate their rapt attention and their knowledge that they are in the presence of one who deserves awe.

---

46. Pretorius and Lioy, "Religion and Natural Science."
47. Ham, "Gentle Voice of God," 541.
48. Clines, "Alleged Female Language," 13.

Here are some hallmarks of a good teacher that are emphasized in education classes at Southern New Hampshire University:[49]

- Strong communicator
- Listens well
- Focuses on collaboration
- Is adaptable
- Engages students with humor and creativity
- Shows empathy
- Has patience
- Emphasizes the real world

From a complementary perspective, here are additional signs of a good teacher that apply to the Lord in the book of Job; the Lord gives Job a personal demonstration of effective teaching in the following ways[50]

- Knows his subjects
- Believes in them
- Is excited about them!
- Anticipates teachable moments
- Keep lessons short
- Communicates qualities of excitement and openness
- Loves Job, his student
- Realizes that each learner needs individual instruction

The Lord's discourses in Job 38–41 seem to offer guidelines for teaching. One definition of a Christian teacher is the person giving constant instruction in daily life for believers.[51] God is a teacher in the sense that he has come in response to Job's questions and is providing insights.

And Job's possible reaction? The Lord's speeches give Job room to start the process of repenting—and repenting without public shame. These two wonderful, amazing gifts serve as templates for generations of readers and hearers.

---

49. Gagnon, *Ten Qualities*, paras 1–11.
50. Cf. Capehart, *Become a Treasured Teacher*, 11–70.
51. Carpenter, "Minister, Ministry," 148.

Firstly, Job's answer (40:3–5) indicates his knowledge of his unworthiness to even try to reply and hence he puts his hand over his mouth and adds, "I spoke once, but I have no answer—twice, but I will say no more" (40:5). He is beginning the change from self-absorption and self-righteousness.

Perhaps Job's tone carries the mood the Lord set, that of lightheartedness, instruction, and compassion. Perhaps his tone indicates respect, humility, and wry humor about himself. I sense that unlike his conversations with the three friends and Elihu, he's now free to poke fun at himself and not take himself so seriously. After all, Job was used to being listened to and respected because of his wealth and society position; it is a new experience to listen to one more knowledgeable and one with more authority than him.

Job shows he views himself a bit differently and is learning submission. Job needed to be reminded that his is the created, and always will be, and God is the Creator, and always will be.

On a humorous note, and continuing with the professor analogy, both prof and students abide by the ten-minute rule, that is, that a class is cancelled if a prof arrives eleven minutes late. The Lord in Job 38ff proves to be a prof well worth waiting for. He awards waiting Job with new material; models the contagious excitement of one who loves his students and concludes with an assignment for Job: teaching others regarding repentance.

The Lord Speaks in a Love Language Job Understands

Psychologist Gary Chapman has identified five ways we humans receive and give love. He calls them love languages. While considered a major tool for marriages, his model also offers insights on biblical characters like Job. Chapman's five languages are Encouragement/Affirmation, Quality Time, Receiving Gifts, Acts of Service, and Personal Touch.[52]

Using this model, the love expression Job receives most from the Lord is Quality Time. The Lord gives Job his focused, undivided attention. Quality Time gives support rather than solves a problem.[53] Perhaps Job needed assurance that he was loved rather than explicit answers to his strident questions.

The Lord's monologues shift the book's focus from Job's self-absorption and the dominance of his insistence of innocence and self-righteousness to the Lord's creation and the Lord as Creator. The shift refreshes both Job and readers and hearers. The book goes from harping to hallelujah, from

---

52. Chapman, *Five Love Languages*.
53. Chapman, *Five Love Languages*, 62.

woebegone despair to delightful knowledge, from small thinking to magnificent insights.

Undoubtedly after listening to God's monologues and going on a tour of creation with God as tour guide, Job felt loved. Job understood a foundation of Quality Time, namely that the Lord had earlier listened to him.

Throughout chapters 3-37, Job's friends argued he must have done something terribly wrong because of the terrible suffering he obviously endures. They pounded him to confess his wrongdoing. Their arguments and monologues showed that they believe him or trust him and that their opinions of him were negative. Although they had known him for decades, they now saw him as a man who had lied to them for years.

Job declined to agree with them. The Lord agreed with Job. However, the Lord graciously put Job in his place as a member of creation and not the center of it.[54]

Tour Guide

One way to get to know a person is to listen to that person talk about a favorite area of expertise. The Lord's encounter with Job in two monologues (38:1—42:6) provides that opportunity. The Lord lets himself be known via a personalized tour of creation.

It is as if Job has won a sweepstakes! The prize is a worldwide tour with the best tour guide ever! The Lord shows both knowledge and excitement about his creation. He shares its details like the morning stars sing (38:7) and its secret places like the storehouse for the snow and the gates of death (38:22, 17). He thereby expresses his ongoing presence in creation. The Lord openly delights in the work of his hands

The tour seems to take place during both day and night. Together the Lord and Job look at the constellations, with the Lord pointing them out by name—the beautiful Pleiades, the cords of Orion, the Bear and its cubs, (38:31-33).

The Lord and Job seem to watch the Behemoth feeding among the grasses and hidden in the reeds of the marsh. The Lord mentions Behemoth's powerful belly muscles and the strength of his loins (40:15-24). Can such an animal be captured or trapped? The Leviathan (Job 41) is similarly magnificent in power. Can he be caught with a fishhook or tamed with a rope? The Lord praises the Leviathan as a creature without equal on earth, a creature without fear, one who is king over all that are proud (41:33-34).

---

54. Davis, "Out of the Whirlwind," 152-53.

During the tour, several things seem to unfold. Job gradually is healed; he seems fully healed by the time of his repentance and new job assignment of bringing his three friends to the Lord for their repentance. The book ends with evidence of his long life, and the Lord's gift of letting him see his children and children's children to the fourth generation (42:16).

For much of the tour, Job remains silent. Perhaps he is speechless. Perhaps his vocabulary cannot match the wonder he experiences. Perhaps hymnwriter Charles Wesley thought of Job's tour when he wrote "lost in wonder, love and praise."[55]

The chapters with the Lord describe two different realities within the creation: the visible and the invisible portions,[56] both what is seen and what is unseen—namely the changes happening to Job.

Humorist

Job and the Lord exchange nicknames. Early on, Job calls the Lord "Watcher of Men" (7:20); the Lord God returns the nickname by calling Job a "faultfinder" and "one who contends with the Almighty" (Job 40:2). Nicknames on a human level often indicate a solid friendship, one that has lasted for years. I think that's a good take-away from this exchange.

One Requiring Repentance before Restoration

The book of Job presents an example of the biblical model of restoration. The process includes the following:

- Naming the offense
- An acknowledgment of an offense
- The offender asking the offended for forgiveness
- The offended granting forgiveness
- Restoration of the friendship/relationship

Jesus more fully examines the concept of repentance/forgiveness/restoration in his teaching that if someone comes to you seven times a day asking for forgiveness, you must give it (Matt 18:22). However, forgiveness is not only the responsibility of the one offended. The offender must acknowledge the misdeed and ask for forgiveness.

---

55. Wesley, "Love Divine All Loves, 657.
56. Edgar, *Truth in All*, 133.

The Lord creates an open atmosphere of teaching in which Job sees his errors and knows to seek forgiveness. Repentance is a gift from God.[57] Job accepts it and repents—of what, we readers and hearers are not sure. It would seem to me that he acknowledges the truth of the Lord's charge—that you have not spoken of me rightly—and repents of that. The Lord accepts his repentance. The relationship is restored.

Once Job had repented, and the Lord had accepted it, the Lord gave Job an assignment. Now that he was restored, he must help in the restoration of fellowship of others with the Lord. The Lord directs Job to officiate in a worship service of burnt offerings and sacrifices brought by Eliphaz and Bildad and Zophar.

One Who Restores

Things happen quickly in the concluding narrational verses in Job 42. God restores, promotes, and assigns a job to Job.

Evidence that the Lord accepts Job's repentance comes immediately. For example, the Lord refers to his designation of Job as "my servant" four times in Job 42:7–8. This designation is a high honor, and was part of the Lord's introduction of Job in his discussion with the Satan (Job 1:8; 2:3).

The book of Job shows that God desires right relationships. Right relationships start with a right knowledge of God. Right relationships can involve correction; correction involves instruction.[58]

The Lord summons Eliphaz. As mentioned, it would seem that Eliphaz, Bildad, and Zophar and maybe Elihu have witnessed the exchange between the Lord and Job. Elihu, however, is written out of the drama after his monologue ends (37:24).

The exchange with Eliphaz is terse and short. Yes, the Lord seeks restoration, but the offenses of Eliphaz, Bildad, and Zophar are greater than those of Job. A heavy investment of animals for sacrifice is required. Restoration is to extend vertically to the Lord and horizontally among the three and Job. The Lord honors Job publicly as the one designated to lead the worship. The Lord hammers with quadruple emphasis Job's status as "my servant". Furthermore, the Lord calls Job "my servant" four times (42:7–8) in the Lord's directions to Eliphaz.

I am sure Eliphaz gets the point!

The Lord gives repentant, restored, forgiven Job the chance to walk in his forgiven, restored status by officiating at the restoration and forgiveness

---

57. Richardson, "Repent, Repentance," 191.
58. Snaith, "Correct," 54.

worship for Eliphaz, Zophar, and Bildad. Just like council meetings, attendance is required! The Lord accepts the sacrifice, thereby clearing the way for the three to receive forgiveness and be restored to fellowship with the Lord.

It would seem that these three—all silent during God's encounter with Job in chapters 38 through 41, may have been listening all the while. They also were learning. They also perhaps were seeing areas in which they needed to repent. It was not just Job who needed to have a right relationship with God. They did, too.

Job 42 is important; it emphasizes reconciliation. The Lord graciously wants Eliphaz and his friends to be reconciled to him the way he and Job are reconciled; the reconciliation must extend horizontally among the four men as well. The Lord wants to restore his relationship with Eliphaz, Bildad, and Zophar. He directs Eliphaz on how to do that. Eliphaz is to take seven bulls and seven rams and "go to my servant Job and sacrifice a burnt offering for yourselves. *My servant Job will pray for you*, and I will accept his prayer and not deal with you according to your folly" (42:8) (italics added).

One Who Promotes

The book of Job illustrates that repentance and restoration of fellowship may bring a promotion, indeed another command from the Lord to be obeyed.

Chrysostom writes that Job now becomes a priest, and that Job is devoid of resentment against God and against his friends.[59] Gregory the Great, another church father, observes that Job is preferred in the divine judgment rather than his friends.[60] In other words, Job is promoted, but the text only mentions that the three friends (if they obey the Lord in terms of sacrifice) are only restored to fellowship.

However, Chrysostom sees a serious warning to Job's friends that exponentially applies to the book's subsequent readers and hearers. It is this: who accuses the righteous will have to expiate a serious fault.[61]

The Lord tells Eliphaz, "My servant Job will pray for you."

The Lord places Job in a spiritual hierarchy over the three. Job will pray for them and the Lord will accept his prayer. That the duty of Job is prayer may indicate Job's promotion to prophet. The chief job of a prophet is prayer.

---

59. Simonetti and Conti, *Ancient Christian Commentary*, 219.
60. Simonetti and Conti, *Ancient Christian Commentary*, 219.
61. Simonetti and Conti, *Ancient Christian Commentary*, 220.

The biblical background is this. Abraham and Sarah are in Gerar; they both claim a brother/sister relationship and not a husband/wife relationship. Sarah is a beautiful woman. Abimelech, the king of Gerar takes her but does not molest her. The Lord visits Abimelech, king of Gerar, in a dream and tells him to release Sarah, who is Abraham's wife. Abimelech is told to release Sarah, Abraham's wife. The Lord says that Abraham "is a prophet and he will pray for you and you will live" (Gen 20:1–7).[62]

One Who Honors Job Posthumously

The Lord avoided answering Job's big question of why he suffered. Job had concluded for himself that he had done nothing to merit the magnitude of his suffering; surely others, in terms of their conduct and words, merited the Lord's rebuke much more than he!

The Lord's silence leaves some commentators, readers, and hearers feeling let down, discouraged, and perhaps even resentful. However, I present another view based on God's changeless characteristic of goodness.

I believe the Lord's silence on why Job suffered points later to a larger honor: Job's sufferings serve as a template for the future sufferings of the Messiah.

In the Christian tradition, Jesus did not deserve the ignominious, cruel, horrible death on a cross. Although convicted in a sham trial and placed between two thieves and left to hang until dead through slow suffocation, Jesus was innocent.

Perhaps Job and his suffering served as a template for that of Jesus. In literary terminology, Job functioned as a type, a precursor, one who foreshadowed. That statement is all the more interesting and relevant when it was not manifested for millennia.

Clearly, the Lord allowed Job's losses and sufferings. It would seem that the "why" was larger than his audience (the Satan, the host of heaven, Job, and his four friends) knew.

The larger purpose, disclosed slowly, shows the Lord's salvific purpose. It publicly honors Job. It vindicates Job's losses. It answers Job's questions.

The surprise honor, which is revealed progressively throughout the canon, is this: Job's sufferings were not a response to Job's sins. Instead, the Lord allows Job's life and his story to serve as a template for the unmerited, unjustified sufferings of one greater than he, the Son of God, Jesus. A major contrast however, exists between Job and Jesus.

---

62. Branch, "Genesis 20," 217, 222, 225.

Job whined and justified himself. Chapters 3–37 become an overwhelming statement of self-absorption. Instead, the African-American spiritual hymn captures Jesus's attitude:

> He Never Said a Mumbalin' Word[63]
> They crucified my Lord
> They nailed Him to a tree
> They pierced him in the side
> The blood came trickalin' down
> He bowed his head and died,
>
> And He never said a mumbalin' word
> Not a word. Not a word. Not a word.

CONCLUSION: THE JOY OF KNOWING YOU, LORD

Carson makes me grin when he calls the Bible's sixty-six books "astonishingly human documents."[64] He's right! The book of Job fits that description; it is an astonishingly human book because of Job's self-absorption.

Larry Crabb, a noted Christian psychologist and counselor, writes about a universal characteristic that is often overlooked in troubled marriages: self-centeredness.[65] It applies to both parties in marriages called either traditional (male headship) or egalitarian (husband/wife co-equality).

I believe self-centeredness likewise applies to the book of Job and to Job himself. Chapters 3–37 are largely Job's views on his losses. They become a tedium of self-righteousness. Job, obsessed with himself, whines, sulks, lashes out. The Lord, through his monologue (38–42:9), presents the only sure cure and ready antidote to self-centeredness: worship.

Through tone, story, anecdotes, examples, focused diction, and the sheer, palpable delight of his presence, the Lord changes the energy and direction of Job's memorized woes. Through a prolonged tour of creation, the Lord creates a healthy climate of love and acceptance that enables Job to confess and repent without shame. Truly, repentance clears the air.

Instead of winning an argument (which, obviously, the Lord can do!) he seeks the restoration of a cherished relationship. Quite possibly during the long silence of Job's suffering, the Lord has missed Job's friendship and

---

63. "He Never Said." The hymn is part of the corporate American songfest, which does not have a specific author, and is in the public domain.

64. Carson, *Collected Writings*, 23.

65. Crabb, *Men and Women*, 49.

fellowship; the Lord, in short, has missed Job himself. What a wonderful thought!

To use Crabb's terminology for broken communication in a marriage,[66] the Lord addresses Job's fatal disease of self-centeredness and his assumption of self-sufficiency. Job becomes aware of his need for forgiving grace.[67] The spouse who addresses his or her core of self-centeredness may well see "a *desire* to do right develop."[68] Because Job faces his self-centeredness and addresses it with repentance, he is set free to worship.

The book of Job presents worship as the only lasting cure for self-centeredness. Worship addresses attention away from self and toward the Lord. Psalm 100 gives one liturgy for worship: entering his gates with thanksgiving, coming before him with praise and thanksgiving, praising him with shouts, acknowledging that he made us and that we are the sheep of his pasture.

A person directs worship toward the Lord and enjoys worshiping as an equal among others.

The book of Job presents restoration as a team effort. It provides a broad template which generations of readers and hearers can ponder and apply to themselves. These generations learn from Job. The narrative summary of Job's life after the restoration lacks the book's heavy prevalence of dialogue and monologue. Perhaps that indicates that Job enjoyed silence. Perhaps a hallmark of a good relationship is the choice to say nothing—for instance to sit and watch together a beautiful sunset. What silence may indicate is the deep enjoyment of another, the foundation of mutual respect, an understanding and acceptance of one another, and the certain knowledge of ongoing love.

Perhaps Paul connected Job with Jesus when he penned this prayer: "That I may know him and the power of his resurrection, and may share his sufferings" (Phil 3:10).

Perhaps Graham Kendrick, a contemporary psalmist, likewise thought of Job when he penned "Knowing You," a hymn to Jesus.[69] Consider verse 1 and the chorus; they perhaps summarize the triumphant theme of the book of Job:

"Knowing You"

Verse 1
All I once held dear, built my life upon

---

66. Crabb, *Men and Women*, 53.
67. Crabb, *Men and Women*, 54.
68. Crabb, *Men and Women*, 55, italics original.
69. Kendrick, "Knowing You."

All this world reveres and wars to own;
All I once thought gain I have counted loss
Spent and worthless now compared to this

Chorus
Knowing You, Jesus
Knowing You
There is no greater thing
You're my all, You're the best
You're my joy, my righteousness,
And I love You, Lord.

BIBLIOGRAPHY

Branch, Robin Gallaher. "Gender Balance: A New Lens for Reading and Studying the Bible, Part 1." *In Die Skriflig* 58.1 (2024) a2978. https://indieskriflig.org.za/index.php/skriflig/article/view/2978.

———. "Genesis 20: A Literary Template for the Prophetic Tradition." *In Die Skriflig* 38.2 (2004) 217–34.

———. "Space for Joy: Another Look at the Book of Job and Job Himself in Light of Some Principles of Wisdom Literature." *Journal for Semitics* 14.2 (2005) 384–412.

Calvin, John. *Institutes of the Christian Religion*. Translated by Henry Beveridge. Peabody, MA: Hendrickson, 2008.

Capehart, Jody. *Become a Treasured Teacher: Practical Strategies for Making a Lasting Difference in Young Lives*. Wheaton, IL: Victor Books, 1992.

Carpenter, H. J. "Minister, Ministry." In *A Theological Word Book of the Bible*, edited by Alan Richardson, 146–52. New York: Macmillan, 1950.

Carson, D. A. *Collected Writings on Scripture*, Wheaton, IL: Crossway, 2010.

Chapman, Gary. *The Five Love Languages: The Secret to Love that Lasts*. Chicago: Northfield, 2015.

Clines, David J. A. "Alleged Female Language About the Deity in the Hebrew Bible," *Journal of Biblical Literature* 140 (2021) 229–49. https://www.researchgate.net/publication/353328484_Alleged_Female_Language_about_the_Deity_in_the_Hebrew_Bible.

Crabb, Larry. *Men and Women: Enjoying the Difference*. Grand Rapids: Zondervan, 1991.

Davis, Ellen F. "Out of the Whirlwind: Creation Theology in the Book of Job." *Shofar* 28.1 (2009) 152–53.

Edgar, William. *Truth in All Its Glory: Commending the Reformed Faith*. Phillipsburg, NJ: P&R, 2004.

Fee, Gordon D., and Robert L. Hubbard, Jr. *The Eerdmans Companion to the Bible*. Grand Rapids: Eerdmans, 2011.

Gagnon, Danielle. *Ten Qualities of a Good Teacher*, 2024. https://www.snhu.edu/about-us/newsroom/education/qualities-of-a-good-teacher.

Gignilliat, M. S. *A Brief History of Old Testament Criticism: From Benedict Spinoza to Brevard Childs*. Grand Rapids: Zondervan, 2012.

Gottlieb, Fred. "The Creation Theme in Genesis 1, Psalm 104, and Job 38–42." *Jewish Bible Quarterly* 44.1 (2016). https://jbqnew.jewishbible.org/index/books-of-the-bible/genesis/creation-theme-genesis-1-psalm-104-job-38–42/.

Ham, T. C. "The Gentle Voice of God in Job 38." *Journal of Biblical Literature* 132.3 (2013) 527–41.

Harris, R. Laird, et al. eds. "Na." In *Theological Word Book of the Old Testament (TWOT)*, 2:541. Chicago: Moody, 1980.

Haupt, Enid A. *The Seventeen Book of Etiquette and Entertaining*. New York: David McKay Company, 1963.

Hawley, Lance, "Life in Job." In *Biblical Theology of Life in the Old Testament*, edited by Albert J. Coetsee and Francois P. Viljoen, 143–57. Reformed Theology in Africa Series, 5. Cape Town: AOSIS, 2021.

"He Never Said a Mumbalin' Word." In *Worship and Rejoice*, 280. Carol Stream, IL: Hope Publishing Company, 2001.

Kendrick, Graham. "Knowing You." 2011. https://gccsatx.com/hymns/knowing-you/.

Klein, William W., et al. *Introduction to Biblical Interpretation*. Nashville: Thomas Nelson, 2004.

Lostracco, Joseph, and George Wilkerson. *Analyzing Short Stories*. Dubuque, IA: Kendal/Hunt, 2008.

Mazar, Benjamin. *Patriarchs: Volume II*. New Brunswick, NJ: Rutgers University Press, 1970.

Miller, Patrick D., Jr. *The Divine Warrior in Early Israel*. Atlanta: Society of Biblical Literature, 2006.

Post, Emily. *Etiquette: The Blue Book of Social Usage*. New York: Funk & Wagnalls Company, 1936.

Pretorius, Mark, and Dan T. Lioy. "What Do Religion and Natural Science Each Have to Say About Origins, Creation and Evolution?" *HTS Teologiese Studies* 77.3 (2021). https://www.scielo.org.za/scielo.php?script=sci_arttext&pid=S0259-94222021000300003.

Richardson, Alan. "Repent, Repentance." In *A Theological Word Book of the Bible*, edited by Alan Richardson, 191–92. New York: Macmillan, 1950.

Simonetti, Manlio, and Marco Conti, eds. *Ancient Christian Commentary on Scripture, Old Testament, VI: Job*. Downers Grove, Illinois: InterVarsity, 2006.

Snaith, N. H., "Correct, Correction, Reprove." In *A Theological Word Book of the Bible*, edited by Alan Richardson, 54. New York: Macmillan, 1950.

Stokes, Ryan E. "Satan, YHWH's Executioner." *Journal of Biblical Literature* 133.2 (2014) 251–70. https://www.jstor.org/stable/10.15699/jbibllite.133.2.251?seq=1.

Van der Zwan, Pieter. "Pathology and Pain, Disease and Disability: The Burdens of the Body in the Book of Job Peering Through a Psychoanalytic Prism." *HTS Teologiese Studies* 78.4 (2022). http://dx.doi.org/10.4102/hts.v78i4.7409.

Venter, Phillip P. "Wealth, Poverty and Mutual Care: Towards a Reconstructive Reading of the Book of Job." *Verbum et Ecclesia* 36.3 (2015). http://dx.doi.org/10.4102/ve.v36i3.1473.

Webb, Marcia. "The Book of Job: A Psychologist Takes a Whirlwind Tour." *Christian Scholar's Review* 44.2 (2015) 155–74. https://christianscholars.com/the-book-of-job-a-psychologist-takes-a-whirlwind-tour/.

Wesley, Charles, "Love Divine, All Loves Excelling." In *The 1982 Hymnal*, 657. New York: Episcopal Church, 1985.

Chapter 4

Incomprehensibility of God as Zest of Life: Proverbs 30

—Frédérique D. Dantonel

Goethe Universität Frankfurt am Main, Germany

ABSTRACT

The traditional distinction between the different forms of knowledge is proposed as a key that could decipher the motif of "understanding" in the book of Proverbs. First, a classical distinction between propositional and perspectival knowledge is drawn upon. Then the occurrences of the concept of "understanding" in the Proverbs are identified. Using meaningful examples, key passages are examined in order to shed light on how "understanding" can be captured in the Proverbs.

INTRODUCTION

Understanding, i.e., the ability to perceive and discern insightfully with the senses, is considered throughout the book of Proverbs to be an essential prerequisite for knowing God and experiencing the fear of YHWH (e.g., Prov 1:2, 6; 2:5, 9; 7:7; 14:15; 19:25; 28:5; 30:2).

At the beginning of the book of Proverbs, namely in chapter 2, the wisdom teacher gives the wisdom student an instruction. With three protasis beginning with "if," the wisdom teacher explains to the wisdom student which prerequisites make it possible for the fear of God to be understood, knowledge of God to be found, and wisdom to be attained.

Prov 2:1–6

בְּנִי אִם־תִּקַּח אֲמָרָי וּמִצְוֺתַי תִּצְפֹּן אִתָּךְ׃

לְהַקְשִׁיב לַחָכְמָה אָזְנֶךָ תַּטֶּה לִבְּךָ לַתְּבוּנָה׃
כִּי אִם לַבִּינָה תִקְרָא לַתְּבוּנָה תִּתֵּן קוֹלֶךָ׃
אִם־תְּבַקְשֶׁנָּה כַכָּסֶף וְכַמַּטְמוֹנִים תַּחְפְּשֶׂנָּה׃
אָז תָּבִין יִרְאַת יְהוָה וְדַעַת אֱלֹהִים תִּמְצָא׃
כִּי־יְהוָה יִתֵּן חָכְמָה מִפִּיו דַּעַת וּתְבוּנָה׃

1 My son, if you accept my words
And my commandments you store up with you,
2 by making your ear attentive to wisdom,
Inclining your heart to understanding,
3 indeed, if to insight you call,
To understanding you raise your voice,
4 if you seek it like silver
And as for (hidden) treasures you search for it,
5 then you will understand the fear of YHWH
And knowledge of God you will find,
6 for YHWH gives wisdom,
From his mouth (come) knowledge and understanding;[1]

In the penultimate chapter of the book, chapter 30, the author has the character Agur say in verses 2 and 3 that he does not have the understanding of human beings:[2]

Prov 30:1–4

דִּבְרֵי ׀ אָגוּר בִּן־יָקֶה הַמַּשָּׂא נְאֻם הַגֶּבֶר לְאִיתִיאֵל לְאִיתִיאֵל וְאֻכָל׃

כִּי בַעַר אָנֹכִי מֵאִישׁ וְלֹא־בִינַת אָדָם לִי׃
וְלֹא־לָמַדְתִּי חָכְמָה וְדַעַת קְדֹשִׁים אֵדָע׃
מִי עָלָה־שָׁמַיִם ׀ וַיֵּרַד מִי אָסַף־רוּחַ ׀ בְּחָפְנָיו
מִי צָרַר־מַיִם ׀ בַּשִּׂמְלָה מִי הֵקִים כָּל־אַפְסֵי־אָרֶץ
מַה־שְּׁמוֹ וּמַה־שֶּׁם־בְּנוֹ כִּי תֵדָע׃

1 The words of Agur, the son of Jakeh. The pronouncement.
The prophetic utterance of the man to Ithiel, to Ithiel and Ucal.
2 Surely, I am the most brutish of men

---

1. Translation by Bernd U. Schipper; Schipper, *Proverbs 1–15*, 101.

2. Own translation relying on the commentaries of Michael Fox and Bruce Waltke. Fox, *Proverbs 1–9*, 106; Waltke, *Book of Proverbs*, 454–57.

And do not have the understanding of a human being.
3 And I have not learned wisdom,
And I do not know the Holy One.
4 Who has ascended the heavens and come down?
Who has collected the wind in his fists?
Who has gathered the waters in his robe?
Who has established all the ends of the earth?
What is his name and what is his son's name?
Surely, you know!³

The Hebrew root for "understanding" is בין with the meaning "to understand, perceive, consider" in the Qal and "to have insight, to comprehend, to bring to insight" in the Hiphil.⁴ Since "understanding" is a prerequisite for knowledge, the question arises as to whether the difference between the different Hebrew terms for "understanding" and "comprehending" can be explained by the difference between propositional knowledge and perspectival knowledge.⁵ This article attempts to answer this question. For this purpose, a contemporary division of knowledge is taken up.

"DISCERNING," "UNDERSTANDING," AND "COMPREHENDING" IN THE BOOK OF PROVERBS

In the tradition of Kantian concepts of perspectival knowledge, there are many contemporary approaches to the classical division of knowledge. One of them was proposed by Job Y. Jindo.⁶ His approach offers the concise and precise way of getting to the heart of the difference between propositional and perspectival knowledge.

> Propositional knowledge here refers to a descriptive knowledge about beings, conditions, or events, whether they may be observable or imaginary, factual or hypothetical. Perspectival knowledge, on the other hand, refers to ways of seeing and thinking, or particular modes of cognition, whereby people perceive and experience such beings, conditions, or events. In other words, the knowledge we communicate—and we live by—involves not

---

3. Translation by the author of this article.
4. HALOT, 122.
5. For discussion of the difference between propositional knowledge and perspectival knowledge see, for example, Jindo, "On the Biblical Notion," 433–53.
6. Christopher B. Ansberry refers to Jindo's definition in his commentary on Proverbs. The author of this article became aware of the definition of Jindo by reading Ansberry's commentary.

only *what* we know or experience, but also *how* we conceive of, and orient ourselves toward what we know or experience.[7]

The decisive point is the *how*. The *how* is equated with the path of understanding, of comprehending. In order to answer this question, at least to some extent, the passages in the book of Proverbs where the Hebrew terms for "understanding" and "comprehending" occur will first be systematically identified in the form of a table. Then individual exemplary passages are examined.

The following table shows the distribution of the lexemes בין, בינה and תבונה in the 915 verses of the book of Proverbs, verse by verse and systematically according to the corresponding corpora that make up the book of Proverbs. In the first column, there is the root as an infinitive or finite verb; in the second column, the participle and, in the third and fourth columns, the nouns that derive from the root. Similarly, all verses in which either the tetragram or the term of God Eloha/Elohim occurs are also noted. In this way, verses can be recorded in which both a lexeme of comprehension and a term for God occur and relate to each other. In the first part of the article these verses are examined and in the second part conclusions are drawn regarding the statements of Agur in Proverbs 30.

Table 2: Distribution of the lexemes בין, בינה and תבונה in the 915 verses of the Book of Proverbs

	בִּין as verb. inf, or fin.	בִּין as verb pt. The discerning understanding, intelligent person	בִּינָה noun: *intellectus*; understanding	תְּבוּנָה Noun: *intelligentia*; understanding, cleverness, skill.	יהוה אֱלוֹהַּ אֱלֹהִים
Prov 1:1—9:18	1:2.6; 2:5.9; 7:7; 8:5;	1:5; 8:9;	1:2; 2:3; 3:5; 4:1.5.7; 7:4; 8:14; 9:6.10;	2:2.3.6.11; 3:13.19; 5:1; 8:1;	1:7.29; 2:5; 2:6; 3:5.7.9.11. 12.19.26.32. 33; 5:21; 6:16; 8:13. 22.35; 9:10; [2:5.17; 3:4];

---

7. Jindo, "On the Biblical Notion" 438–39.

10:1—22:16	14:15; 19:25; 20:24	10:13; 14:6.8; 14:33; 15:14; 16:21; 17:10; 17:24; 17:28; 18:15; 19:25;	16:16;	10:23; 11:12; 14:29; 17:27; 15:21; 18:2; 19:8; 20:5; 21:30;	10:3.22.27.29 11:1.20; 12:2. 22; 14:2.26.27; 15:3.8.9.11.16. 25. 15:26.29.33; 16:1.2.3.4.5.6. 7.9. 16:11.20.33; 17:3.15; 18:10. 22; 19:3.14.17.21. 23; 20:10.12.22.23. 24. 20:27; 21:1.2. 3. 21:30.31; 22:2.4.12.14;
22:17—24:22	23:1 (2x); 24:12;		23:4; 23:23;	24:3;	22:19.23; 23:17; 24:18.21;
24:23–34					
25:1—29:27	28:5; 29:7.19;	28:2.7.11;		28:16.	25:22; 28:5.25; 29:13.25.26; 25:2
30:1–33			30:2;		30:9; [30:9]
31:1–31					31:30.

Considering the distribution of the Hebrew lexemes for "understanding," namely the root בין and the two derived nouns בינה and תבונה, it becomes clear that they are unevenly distributed. They do not occur at all in chapters 24:23–34 and 31.

Instead, they occur very frequently in chapters 1 to 9 and 10 to 22. Chapters 1 to 9 are considered the introduction to the book of Proverbs. Chapters 10 to 22 are dated as the oldest chapters. In chapter 30, such a lexeme from the semantic family of "understanding" appears only once, in negated form. The same applies to the tetragram, as can be seen in the last column of the table. There are also verses in which both a term of understanding and a term for God, be it the tetragram, be it *eloha* or *elohim*, occur. The verses in which a term for God occurs are the following: 2:5.17; 3:4.9. There are a total of seven verses in which both a term of "understanding" and a term for God occur: 2:5.6; 3:5.19; 9:10; 20:24; 21:30. Compared to the 915 verses in the book of Proverbs, and compared to their respective occurrences, these are only a few verses. With these seven verses, it can be observed that five of them are found in chapters 1 to 9, which are considered young, later compositions. Two are in the earlier composition, chapters 10:1—22:16.

EXAMPLES OF KEY JUNCTIONS

Prov 2:4–6

אִם־תְּבַקְשֶׁנָּה כַכָּסֶף וְכַמַּטְמוֹנִים תַּחְפְּשֶׂנָּה׃

אָז תָּבִין יִרְאַת יְהוָה וְדַעַת אֱלֹהִים תִּמְצָא׃
כִּי־יְהוָה יִתֵּן חָכְמָה מִפִּיו דַּעַת וּתְבוּנָה׃

> 4 If you seek it like silver
> and as for (hidden) treasures you search for it,
> 5 then you will understand the fear of YHWH
> and knowledge of God you will find,
> 6 for YHWH gives wisdom,
> From his mouth (come) knowledge and understanding.[8]

The imperfect forms of the verbs introduced by the conjunction אִם in the protasis and the following apodosis express on the one hand the irrealis—or the not yet realis—and on the other hand the unambiguous.[9] In the conditional protasis v. 4, which is introduced with "if," wisdom is compared to silver and treasures. The motif of searching for silver is a very old motif which, as Schipper highlights, can be found, for example, in ancient Egyptian literature from the Ptolemaic period, specifically in the book of Toth.[10] Also, the search for silver is not a search for finished objects such as jewelry or jewels, but rather a search for the "raw material."[11] The same applies to the search for hidden treasures. In verse 5, which is part of the conditional apodosis v. 5–8, the poet solves the metaphors of silver and treasures (v. 4). Seeking silver and treasures means understanding the fear of YHWH. Understanding the fear of YHWH means finding knowledge of God. It is

---

8. Schipper, *Proverbs 1–15*, 101.

9. For the form and functions of the imperfectives see Cook, *Biblical Hebrew Verb*, 196–214.

10. Schipper, *Proverbs 1–15*, 109.

11. Phrasing by Schipper, *Proverbs 1–15*, 108–9. He also refers to Job 28. See the commentary by Witte, *Das Buch Hiob*, 406, 423.

noteworthy that in the first colon the tetragram is used and in the second colon the appellative for God. According to verses 2:4–8, the searching for wisdom leads to a perspectival understanding of the fear of YHWH. The fear of YHWH is the result of the process of understanding: Within verse 5, the lexeme for understanding is chiastic to the lexeme for finding. In the middle of the chiasmus and parallel to each other are the fear of YHWH on the one hand and the knowledge of God on the other. It arises from this that, according to these two verses, wisdom only comes from God and that the student of wisdom should submit to a process of understanding if he wants to acquire insight into the fear of YHWH.

This statement is then substantiated in verse 6. The justification is introduced by the particle כִּי: YHWH is the source and creator of wisdom, knowledge and understanding. At this juncture and in this context, God is placed both as the source and giver of wisdom. This is a key aspect of wisdom literature.[12] The verse refers to an anthropomorphic idea, namely the idea that knowledge and understanding come from the mouth of YHWH. This anthropomorphic idea is often found in priestly, deuteronomic and prophetic texts. It clearly expresses the fact that the human being reaches its limits where wisdom is more than just education imparted through teaching and instruction.

Prov 3:5.19

Prov 3:5

בְּטַח אֶל־יְהוָה בְּכָל־לִבֶּךָ וְאֶל־בִּינָתְךָ אַל־תִּשָּׁעֵן׃

> Trust in YHWH with all your heart,
> But do not rely on your own understanding.[13]

As Bernd Schipper notes in his commentary,

> Proverbs 3:5 is the only verse in the book of Proverbs in which the word בִּינָה ('insight') has a suffix. Thus, בִּינָה ('insight') is unique in describing that which a person can acquire through reflection and discovery.[14]

---

12. For discussion, see Melton, "That I Knew Where," 205–16. Melton gives further examples, such as Eccl 2:26 and Job 28:20, 23.

13. Schipper, *Proverbs 1–15*, 130; Fox, *Proverbs 1–9*, 149.

14. Schipper, *Proverbs 1–15*, 131.

The negative instruction in 5b functions as a negative offset to the positive instruction in 5a.[15] Proverbs 3:5 suggests that human insight is not the wisdom of God. Rather, human insight and wisdom are far apart because in his effort to seek, humankind reaches the limits of understanding. However, this does not mean that rapprochement is perspectival impossible. The first step is "trust." This is the first word of the verse. בטח is a term of essential importance in the Old Testament. It expresses the quality of the relationship between people and God as it is or should be.[16] The second step is antithetically parallel to the first colon. It is about being careful of self-insight. Here, with the second colon, a negative emphasis is placed on human reason, human insight, as opposed to trust in YHWH, which should come from the heart. This is a warning.[17]

Prov 3:19

יְהוָה בְּחָכְמָה יָסַד־אָרֶץ כּוֹנֵן שָׁמַיִם בִּתְבוּנָה׃

By wisdom Jhwh founded the earth,
By understanding he established the heavens.[18]

Prov 3:19–20 is, along with Prov 8:22–31, one of two poems in the first part of the book of Proverbs addressing the motif of creation.[19] 3:19 is set in the context of the memory of the garden of Eden, which is echoed in 3:18 with a tree of life. In this context, a cosmic quality is ascribed to wisdom in 3:19.[20] This quality is reinforced by the parallel to "understanding" in 19b. 3.19 constitutes a synonymous parallelism. "Understanding," בִּתְבוּנָה, is placed in parallel with wisdom. The bicolon focuses on the function of wisdom and the function of "understanding" during the founding of the earth and the establishing of heaven at the beginning of time. Surprisingly, however, the verb from the first creation account Gen 1:1, ברא (*to* create), is not used, but rather יסד *to found* (19a) and כון *to establish* (19b). This is all the more remarkable as this is not about human "understanding," but about "understanding" as an attribute of God, just as wisdom is an attribute of God.

Wisdom therefore turns out to be an attribute of God, namely "understanding."

15. Ansberry, *Proverbs*, 184.
16. See Moberly, "בטח," 644–49.
17. See Fuhs, *Das Buch der Sprichwörter*, 72–73.
18. Schipper, *Proverbs 1–15*, 138; Fox, *Proverbs 1–9*, 156.
19. The other poems in the book in which the creation motif appears are Prov 14:31; 16:4, 11; 17:5; 20:12; 22:2; 29:13. See here Boström, *God of the Sages*, 48–89.
20. Ansberry, *Proverbs*, 199.

This is emphasized by the fact that the cosmological elements earth, heaven and primordial water (in verse 20) are mentioned. With the two verbs used, "founded" and "established," the proverb also suggests that "understanding" and wisdom are assigned to the act of creation. At this point and in this context, God is portrayed both as the creator of the world and as the source and giver of wisdom.

The sages sought wisdom as a means to experience the divine presence. As a result, wisdom and understanding are treated as almost equivalents.[21]

Prov 9:10

תְּחִלַּת חָכְמָה יִרְאַת יְהוָה וְדַעַת קְדֹשִׁים בִּינָה׃

The beginning of wisdom is the fear of Jhwh,
And knowledge of the Holy one is understanding.[22]

This bicolon is significant for several reasons. Firstly, it expresses the motif of the fear of God in an interactive way, namely as the equivalent of the beginning of wisdom (10a). Secondly, this motif is in synonymous parallel with "understanding," which is declared to be equivalent to knowledge of the Holy One (10b).

The plural term קְדֹשִׁים can be understood as an elative plural or "plural of excellence," that means the highest degree of holiness. The verse repeats the idea of chapter 2, verses 5 and 6. This is also a leitmotif of the book of Proverbs.

The Holy could refer to divine knowledge that may be approachable by those who live in the fear of YHWH. It might be YHWH's word, i.e., the Torah?

"The fear of YHWH is the beginning of wisdom" (10a). Remarkable is the fact that it remains only "the beginning." The implication of this may be that humans cannot reckon with fully "understanding" the purposes of YHWH.[23] The wise one should and can continue to practise this wisdom. This wisdom can only be regarded as genuine wisdom when it is connected to the perspectival understanding of the relationship with God.

Prov 20:24

מֵיְהוָה מִצְעֲדֵי־גָבֶר וְאָדָם מַה־יָּבִין דַּרְכּוֹ׃

---

21. For a discussion see Melton who regards God and Wisdom as "referred to interchangeably." Melton, "That I Knew Where," 206.

22. Schipper, *Proverbs 1-15*, 332–33; Fox, *Proverbs 1-9*, 296.

23. See Lucas, "Book of Proverbs," 43.

From Jhwh are the steps of a man
And a human—how can he understand his way?

Proverbs 20:24, as well as Prov 21:30; 27:1 and 30:2–4, is one of the texts that emphasize how limited human understanding can be.

The bicolon compactly summarizes the theme of incomprehensibility as an attribute of God: Jhwh has endowed human beings with the ability to perceive, to learn, and thus to acquire knowledge and skills. Since these senses and faculties were created by God, their acquisition is not hidden from God himself. The wise man who acquires understanding with his "God-given senses"[24] would stray from the very "beginning of wisdom" if he imagined that his knowledge and "understanding" could develop independently of God. On the one hand, there is human responsibility for one's own actions, for one's own path in life; the teacher of wisdom wants the student of wisdom to take this responsibility seriously—even and especially when it is difficult to recognize the path (16:2; 21:2) and to follow it. On the other hand, God is the one who is involved in everything that happens. In the second part of the bicolon, the unfathomable is emphasized by a question that points to the limits and incomprehensibility of wisdom.

In Prov 30, Agur also asks himself such a question in a way that gives the impression that he is in despair.

However, the bicolon in no way contrasts with Proverbs, which convey that humankind can at least approach the beginning of wisdom by "understanding" the relationship with YHWH, such as Prov 9:10. Although humankind reaches a limit of understanding, God gives the ability to behave ethically and morally responsibly. God also provides humankind with the capacity to learn and develop responsible character. Thus, the teachings of Proverbs are in accordance with the commandments of the Pentateuch and with the teachings of the Prophets.[25]

Prov 21:30

אֵין חָכְמָה וְאֵין תְּבוּנָה וְאֵין עֵצָה לְנֶגֶד יְהוָה׃

There is no wisdom and there is no understanding
And there is no counsel in front of Jhwh.

---

24. Frydrych, *Living Under The Sun*, 128–29.

25. For discussion of the connection between wisdom and Torah, see Schipper and Teeter, *Wisdom and Torah*. For discussion of the connection between wisdom and "covenantal Yahwism," see Adams, *Wisdom in Transition*, 80–82.

The power of Jhwh is emphasized. This verse reinforces the statement of 20:24, first with the alliteration of the negative existential particle *'ên* ("*there is none*," cf. 13:4; 17:16) at its beginnings and second the assonance of the feminine /a/ at its ends: *ḥokmâ* (wisdom, cf. 1:2), *tᵉbûnâ* (insight, cf. 2:2) and *'ēṣâ* ("counsel," cf. 1:25; cf. 2 Sam 16:23). The third segment merges into the B bicolon, creating a strong anaphora. The human beings should assume their behavior and actions before God. Since God has given them the means and the ability to act, they must be held accountable for their actions. Humans are responsible to God because divine wisdom surpasses human wisdom.

"UNDERSTANDING" AND PROVERBS 30

The book of Proverbs is characterized by an inherent didactic process.[26] The book is structured in such a way that Prov 30 and 31 describe figures whose characters and behaviors correspond to the instruction given in the different corpora of the composition.[27] Thus, Prov 30 and 31 function as a realization of what was announced in the preamble Prov 1:1–7 and prologue of the book Prov 1–9: The search for wisdom leads to the knowledge of God and qualifies for experiencing and living the fear of YHWH. However, understanding is a prerequisite. It is not just about understanding what is described in the instructions. Rather, understanding is a question of cognitive and empathic perception, of comprehending with all the senses, of internalizing reality in a new way, of perceiving. There is therefore a major difference between propositional understanding and perspectival understanding, just as there is a major difference between propositional knowledge and perspectival knowledge. The images and metaphors from the animal world used in Prov 30 refer to knowledge that is not merely propositional. Only a perspectival understanding can provide the key to unlocking these images and metaphors. Without this understanding, the realization of what is at stake remains closed.

Implications of "Understanding"

The first part of Prov 30 contains a reflection on the theme of the relationship of humans to God with the motives of understanding and knowledge

26. For the discussion of the didactic process in Proverbs, see Ansberry, *Be Wise, My Son*.

27. For the discussion of the book of Proverbs as a composition, see Schipper, *Proverbs*.

with its implications (vv. 1–4), followed by wise counsel (5–6) and prayer (vv. 7–9). Words to God (vv. 1b–3) are followed by a reflection on human understanding, knowledge, the unfathomability of God, (v. 4), then words about God (vv. 5–6), and finally a prayer, i.e., words to God again (vv. 7–9). Verses 10–14 take up the theme of the relationship of human beings to other human beings.

Agur is the figure who experiences first-hand the unfathomable and incomprehensible nature of God, which is summarized abstractly in Prov 20:14.

His assertion, Prov 30:2–3, sounds as if he were desperate, even weary of life:

כִּי בַעַר אָנֹכִי מֵאִישׁ וְלֹא־בִינַת אָדָם לִי׃
וְלֹא־לָמַדְתִּי חָכְמָה וְדַעַת קְדֹשִׁים אֵדָע׃

> 2 Surely, I am the most brutish of men
> And do not have the understanding of a human being.
> 3 And I have not learned wisdom,
> And I do not know the Holy One.

Nevertheless, in v. 4, he immediately asks the questions that bring him back to life and take him out of despair:

Prov 30:4

מִי עָלָה־שָׁמַיִם ׀ וַיֵּרַד מִי אָסַף־רוּחַ ׀ בְּחָפְנָיו
מִי צָרַר־מַיִם ׀ בַּשִּׂמְלָה מִי הֵקִים כָּל־אַפְסֵי־אָרֶץ
מַה־שְּׁמוֹ וּמַה־שֶּׁם־בְּנוֹ כִּי תֵדָע׃

> Who has ascended the heavens and come down?
> Who has collected the wind in his fists?
> Who has gathered the waters in his robe?
> Who has established all the ends of the earth?
> What is his name and what is his son's name?
> Surely, you know!

These rhetorical questions, which focus on the cosmological elements of creation, show him his limits as a living being before God.

"Understanding" the Incomprehensibility of God

By acknowledging his limits and professing his faith in God, he emerges from despair and turns to life. He does this first with a graded numerical saying in which he once again expresses his astonishment, but no longer out of despair, but as pure observation: Prov 30:18–18.

Prov 30:18–19

שְׁלֹשָׁה הֵמָּה נִפְלְאוּ מִמֶּנִּי וְאַרְבָּעָה לֹא יְדַעְתִּים׃
דֶּרֶךְ הַנֶּשֶׁר ׀ בַּשָּׁמַיִם דֶּרֶךְ נָחָשׁ עֲלֵי צוּר
דֶּרֶךְ־אֳנִיָּה בְלֶב־יָם
וְדֶרֶךְ גֶּבֶר בְּעַלְמָה׃

> Three things are wonderful for me, and four things I cannot understand,
> The way of an eagle in the sky,
> the way of a snake upon the rock,
> the way of a ship on the high seas,
> and the way of a man with a young woman.

This riddle challenges the reader and the listener to understand the common element underlying the phenomena described. Four things are compared with each other that do not seem to pass on their way. The motive of the path/way is brought to light. The images expressed can be understood and interpreted on different levels and in more than one conceivable mode, so that they are ambiguous.

Three cosmological elements are referred to: heavens, water, and rock, i.e., earth. These three cosmological elements are used to refer to creation. On the other hand, the addition of the ship after the motifs of the eagle and the snake is very striking and somewhat surprising. While the eagle and the snake represent nature and possibly divine creation, the ship stands for human culture.

Verse 18 introduces the four visions expressing they have in common something that transcends human understanding. However, it is not the behavior of the eagle, serpent, ship, or young man that goes beyond human understanding, it is their *way*. In all four cases, neither the starting point nor the destination is known.[28] None of these four paths can be retraced. The paths are not understandable. Human beings's propositional knowledge is not sufficient to ensure that the four paths are comprehended. On the other hand, if the reader or listener follows the epithet "wonderful/wondrous"[29] and tries to understand it from a perspectival point of view, they can then recognize what is intended by this riddle.

---

28. Roland E. Murphy already draws attention to this. See Murphy, *Proverbs*, 235.
29. For a discussion on this motif see Fox, *Proverbs*, 870–872.

This numerical saying Prov 30:18–19 formally forms a bridge to the second part of the chapter, in which other elements of creation—this, in this case, living beings, animals—are considered.

Agur focuses his attention on the smallest, lively animals to describe their behavior and contrast it with that of humans.

Small animals can do what humans can't do. Famine often occurs among the people. Nothing like that among ants: they ensure their food supply during the harvest season. Among the people there are homeless people and people who live in very miserable accommodation. Nothing like that among the rock badgers. The badgers ensure appropriate accommodation in the sun. Unlike humans, locusts and wall lizards do not need a king, a ruler or palaces. They are organizing themselves and each of them is living proof that humans have forfeited their mission to have dominion over the earth and over all life. These creatures know nothing of God and yet are very wise. Human beings, on the other hand, presume to want to know everything about God and his creation and do not even respect other living beings, but instead take away their living space, kill them, and destroy the earth. With mockery and irony, the poet shows that the wisdom disciple Agur becomes aware of his limitations as a human being and thereby acquires a certain wisdom and can take on responsibility.

He makes it clear to the Ithiels and Ukals that the ants—here as representatives of all animals—have even more understanding of life and the works of creation than humans. God's creations remain unfathomable to humans. This topic is a main topic of wisdom also found in Eccl 3:11; 7:13, in Job 38–42 and, for example, in the book of Sirach. It is important for the wisdom teacher to convey to the disciples that they should learn to become aware of their limits and possibilities and to behave responsibly toward their fellow human beings, other living beings and God. Learning this is the first step to understanding that the beginning of all wisdom is the fear of God.

CONCLUSION

The traditional distinction between the different forms of knowledge can provide a key to unlocking the motif of "understanding" in the book of Proverbs. "Understanding" can be propositional and perspectival. In contrast to other living beings, humans are gifted not only with propositional but also with perspectival "understanding." To this end, humans should learn to behave ethically and morally responsible toward their fellow human beings, other living beings and God. They should also shape their character accordingly. When they do this, they can understand that their relationship with God is a special one, but that God's wisdom remains wonderful. With this "understanding," the person is at the beginning of the path of wisdom.

BIBLIOGRAPHY

Adams, Samuel L. *Wisdom in Transition. Act and Consequence in Second Temple Instructions.* JSJSup 125. Leiden: Brill, 2008.

Ansberry, Christopher B., *Be Wise, My Son, and Make My Heart Glad: An Exploration of the Courtly Nature of the Book of Proverbs.* BZAW 422. Berlin: De Gruyter, 2011.

_____. *Proverbs. The (Trans)formation of Character in Accord with WISDOM and Virtue.* Zondervan Exegetical Commentary on the Old Testament. Grand Rapids: Zondervan, 2024.

Boström, Lennart. *The God of the Sages. The Portrayal of God in the Book of Proverbs.* Coniectanea Biblica. Old Testament Series 29. Stockholm: Almqvist & Wiksell International, 1990.

Cook, John A., *The Biblical Hebrew Verb. A Linguistic Introduction.* Grand Rapids, Michigan: Baker Academic, 2024

Fox, Michael V. *Proverbs 1–9. A New Translation with Introduction and Commentary.* The Anchor Bible 18A. New York: Doubleday, 2000.

Frydrych, Tomáš. *Living Under the Sun. Examination of Proverbs and Qoheleth.* VTSup. XC. Leiden, Boston, Köln: Brill, 2002.

Fuhs, Hans F. *Das Buch der Sprichwörter. Ein Kommentar.* Forschung zur Bibel 95. Würzburg: Echter Verlag, 2001.

Jindo, Job Y., "On the Biblical Notion of the 'Fear of God' as a Condition for Human Existence," *BibInt* 19 (2011) 433–53.

Koehler, Ludwig, and Walter Baumgartner. *The Hebrew and Aramaic Lexicon of the Old Testament.* Revised by Walter Baumgartner and Johann Jakob Stamm. Study Edition. Leiden: Brill, 2001.

Lucas, C. "The Book of Proverbs: Some Current Issues." In *Interpreting Old Testament Wisdom Literature,* edited by David G. Firth and Lindsay Wilson, 37–59, Downers Grove, IL: IVP Academic, 2017.

Melton, Brittany N. "'Oh, That I Knew Where I Might Find Him': Aspects of Divine Presence in Proverbs, Job and Ecclesiastes." In *Interpreting Old Testament Wisdom Literature,* edited by David G. Firth and Lindsay Wilson, 205–16. Downers Grove, IL: IVP Academic, 2017.

Moberly, R. Walter L. "בטח." *NIDOTTE* 1:644–49.

Murphy, Roland E. *Proverbs.* WBC 22. Nashville: Thomas Nelson, 1998.

Schipper, Bernd U. *Proverbs 1–15. A Commentary on the Book of Proverbs 1:1–15:33.* Translated by Stephen Germany. Minneapolis: Fortress, 2019.

Schipper, Bernd U., and D. Andrew Teeter, eds. *Wisdom and Torah. The Reception of 'Torah' in the Wisdom Literature of the Second Temple Period.* JSJSup 163. Leiden, Boston: Brill, 2013.

Waltke, Bruce K. *The Book of Proverbs. Chapters 15–31.* NICOT. Grand Rapids: Eerdmans, 2005.

Witte, Markus. *Das Buch Hiob.* Das Alte Testament Deutsch. Band 13. Göttingen: Vandenhoeck & Ruprecht, 2021.

Chapter 5

The Incomprehensibility of God in LXX Psalm 102

—GERT J. STEYN

Theologische Hochschule Ewersbach, Germany and Extraordinary Professor of the Faculty of Theology and Religion, University of Pretoria, South Africa

ABSTRACT

LXX Ps 102 belongs to Book IV of the Greek Psalter. This group of psalms portray the attributes of God in a very distinctive way. Especially four categories of divine attributes can be identified here. Firstly, God is portrayed as *Divine Creator and Sustainer*, holy and glorious, eternally in existence and the Most High above all that exists. Secondly, God is portrayed as the *Great and Majestic King*, who is the ultimate protector and rescuer. Thirdly, he is portrayed as a *Righteous Judge*, who is merciful, gracious and patient, yet does not tolerate injustice and lawlessness. Fourthly, God is portrayed as a *Wisdom Teacher*, who teaches and instructs, yet disciplines and chastises to guide believers on their way.

Where most of the psalms in Book IV briefly refer to several of these attributes, Ps 103 (LXX 102), however, distinguishes itself by describing comprehensively a broad range of attributes that portray an exceptional picture of a compassionate Father and his child—especially in contrast to LXX Psalms 85, 88 and 104 where the relationship is referred to in terms of a slave. LXX Ps 102 portrays an exclusive picture of the Lord (ὁ κύριος) who is Holy, Creator, Sustainer, Ruler, Revealer, Healer, Redeemer, Reconciler,

Consoler, Compassionate Father, Merciful, and Righteous. These attributes are framed with a double "Bless the Lord, O my soul" at the beginning and four-fold repetition of "Bless the Lord" at the end of the psalm.

This contribution explores the composition of the psalm and how these attributes create a distinctive picture of a divine entity within a compassionate parent-child relationship.

INTRODUCTION

The Hebrew Ps 103 can be found in its Masoretic Text version (MT) as well as in 4Q82 (4QPs^b),[1] which dates from the second half of the first century BCE. I stated elsewhere that this fragment "is stichometrical and contains Pss 91–118—with Ps 112 which follows Ps 103, and with Pss 104–111 missing."[2] The first eleven verses of Ps 103 are also to be found in 2Q14 (2QPs) and a remnant of its opening line occurs in 11Q5 (11QPs^a).[3] The psalm belongs to Book Four of the Psalter, which consists of Pss 90–106 (LXX Pss 89–105). This group of psalms share several common characteristics in style, wording, and theology. Although debatable, Ps 103 itself might probably be situated contextually within post-exilic times[4] and connected with the temple.[5] Scholars suspect that the psalm was probably sung in a liturgical setting and meant to inspire others.[6]

In this contribution, the focus of attention will be exclusively on the ancient Greek translation of the psalm, namely the Septuagint (LXX) Ps 102 (MT 103), as a version in its own right.[7] The oldest Greek translation of this psalm can be found in manuscripts from the third to the fifth

---

1. García Martinéz and Tigchelaar, *Dead Sea Scrolls*, 278; Lehnardt, *Bibliographie*, 202; Ulrich et al., *Qumran Cave 4*, 45; Dahmen, *Psalmen- und Psalter-Rezeption*, 109.

2. Steyn, *LXX Vorlage*, 369. See Skehan, "Psalm Manuscript," 313–22; Flint, "Psalters at Qumran," 40–41.

3. Hossfeld and Zenger, *Psalms*, 38.

4. Dahood, however, is sceptical and reckons that a post-exilic date of composition appears very unlikely. Dahood, *Psalms*, 24.

5. Weber, *Werkbuch Psalmen*, 176; Burden, *Psalms*, Ps 103.

6. See Ross, *Commentary*, 228; Weber, *Werkbuch Psalmen*, 176; Burden, *Psalms*, Ps 103. Cf. also Longman: "The psalmist begins the hymn with a *call to worship*. Usually, this call is extended to other worshipers, but occasionally (as in Ps 103) it is a call to the psalmist himself to worship the Lord" (Longman, *How to Read Psalms*, 24). Hossfeld and Zenger cautions: "A clear cultic association is not particularly evident," but they do consider vv. 1–2 as "liturgical-priestly thanksgiving—whether spontaneous or in a cultic-ritual praise of YHWH." Hossfeld and Zenger, *Psalms*, 31, 34.

7. Unless otherwise specified, this contribution uses for the Greek text Rahlfs, *Psalmi cum Odis*.

centuries CE, such as Papyrus Bodmer XXIV (Rahlfs 2110), as well as in codices Sinaiticus, Alexandrinus, and Vaticanus. The psalm is clearly intended as a praise psalm to the LORD (יְהוָה / κύριος). This becomes clear from the repetition of the verb εὐλόγει, which runs through as a key word (*Stichwort*) throughout the psalm. The phrase εὐλόγει, ἡ ψυχή μου, τὸν κύριον occurs three times—at the beginning in v. 1 and v. 2, as well as in the closing line of the psalm (v. 22b).[8] Another three occurrences with "Praise the LORD"— now with the imperative, second person plural εὐλογεῖτε—are to be found in the closing section of the psalm. These include in the plural:

- all his angels (εὐλογεῖτε τὸν κύριον, πάντες οἱ ἄγγελοι αὐτοῦ, v. 20)
- all his hosts / powers (εὐλογεῖτε τὸν κύριον, πᾶσαι αἱ δυνάμεις αὐτοῦ, v. 21)
- and all his works (εὐλογεῖτε τὸν κύριον, πάντα τὰ ἔργα αὐτοῦ, v. 22a).

The name of Israel's covenantal God, יְהוָה,[9] surfaces eleven times in this praise psalm and has been translated consistently by the Greek translator with κύριος.[10] This high frequency and repetition of the LORD's name—which is usually sparingly used or rather avoided—is a prominent feature of the psalm.[11]

THE LORD'S DIVINE ATTRIBUTES IN LXX PSALM 102

The psalm can be divided into three parts, namely the opening strophe of vv. 1–5, where the psalmist himself praises the LORD; the central strophe consisting of vv. 6–18, where the psalmist reflects on the LORD's covenantal relationship; and the concluding strophe with vv. 19–22, where the praise peaks into a triumphant conclusion, calling all of creation to bless their LORD.[12]

---

8. The *inclusio* has been noted by others as well. Cf. Allen, *Psalms*, 29; Burden, *Psalms*, Ps 103; Day, *Psalms*, 112; Dahood, *Psalms*, 25.

9. "The holy Name corresponds to YHWH's holy nature." Hossfeld and Zenger, *Psalms*, 34.

10. Cf. Ps 102:1, 2, 6, 8, 13, 17, 19, 20, 21, 22a, 22b.

11. Cf. also Allen: "The actual divine name also plays a dominant role, occurring no fewer than eleven times, twice in the first strophe, four times in the second, and five in the third." Allen, *Psalms*, 29.

12. Ross, *Commentary*, 230; Allen, *Psalms*, 29; Burden, *Psalms*, Ps 103.

Five Descriptors of the Lord's Divine Nature (vv. 3–5)

The first five verses of this psalm focus on an individual self-exhortation to praise the Lord.[13] He rehearses the mercies of God granted to him with deep gratitude.[14] Like counting with five fingers on one hand, the author presents five descriptors in vv. 3–5 by which the divine nature of the Lord (יְהוָה) κύριος is further qualified.[15] These are all introduced by using a present participle accusative masculine singular form:

- who is very conciliatory (τὸν εὐιλατεύοντα) toward all your acts of lawlessness (v. 3a)[16]
- who heals (τὸν ἰώμενον) all your diseases (v. 3b)[17]
- who redeems (τὸν λυτρούμενον) your life from corruption (v. 4a)
- who crowns (τὸν στεφανοῦντά) you with mercy and compassion (v. 4b)[18]
- who satisfies (τὸν ἐμπιπλῶντα) your desire with good (v. 5)

These descriptors elaborating on the divine nature of the Lord, portray imagery of a merciful *judge*, a caring *healer*, an able *redeemer*, a compassionate

---

13. Allen, *Psalms*, 27.

14. Ross, *Commentary*, 230.

15. Hossfeld and Zenger also noted "the series of five so-called hymnic participles that function as reasons for the introductory self-exhortation." Hossfeld and Zenger, *Psalms*, 31. Dahood, too, identified five blessings for which the psalmist employed five participles in the Hebrew text. "The forgiveness of sins, the healing of illnesses, rescue from Sheol, admittance to a blessed afterlife, the eternal enjoyment of God's beauty in heaven." Dahood, *Psalms*, 24. Burden, however, includes v. 6 in this list and identified six verbs in vv. 3–6 that the psalmist used in the Hebrew text to convey the message that all previous distracting or disorienting factors belong to the past. Burden, *Psalms*, Ps 103. They tell a story of restoration, of reorientation without providing all the details: (sin) *forgiven*, (sickness) *healed*, (sickness) *saved* (from the grave), (with love and mercy) *crowned*, (abundance) *made to enjoy*, and he who *does* (justice and right).

16. Hossfeld and Zenger observed, "What is striking in the description and care here is the forward position of the forgiveness of sins" (*Psalms*, 34). It should be noted, however, that the LXX substitutes the term "lawlessness" (ἀνομία) for the Hebrew "sin" or "iniquity" (עָוֹן)—cf. Hossfeld and Zenger, *Psalms*, 37.

17. Cf. Hossfeld and Zenger: "Sickness is here explained theologically and evokes speculation on guilt as the cause, as exhibited in the psalms of sickness, Psalms 6 and 38." Healing, on the other hand, is God's privilege in the Old Testament. Hossfeld and Zenger, *Psalms*, 34.

18. Burden draws attention to the fact that the terms "love" and "mercy" in v. 4 of the Hebrew text, are two covenant terms that, as key words, provide the key to the interpretation of the psalm and that these two words are fundamental to the saving acts of the Lord. Burden, *Psalms*, Ps 103.

ruler, and a reliable *sustainer*. Those who are the objects benefitting from these qualities of the LORD, are listed in all five descriptors in the second person singular:[19] "*your* acts of lawlessness" (πάσαις ταῖς ἀνομίαις σου, v. 3a); "*your* diseases" (πάσας τὰς νόσους σου, v. 3b); "*your* life from corruption" (ἐκ φθορᾶς τὴν ζωήν σου, v. 4a); "*you* with mercy and compassion" (σε ἐν ἐλέει καὶ οἰκτιρμοῖς, v. 4b); "*your* desire" (τὴν ἐπιθυμίαν σου, v. 5).

The first three descriptors picture the LORD as Savior in dire circumstances. He is merciful in *all* acts of lawlessness (πάσαις ταῖς ἀνομίαις), heals *all* diseases (πάσας τὰς νόσους), and redeems[20] life from corruption (ἐκ φθορᾶς τὴν ζωήν). The Greek translation chose here φθορά ("corruption," NETS;[21] "Verderben," LXX.D[22])—a state of transience—abstractly translating "corruption"[23] for the Hebrew שַׁחַת ("pit" or "grave").[24] The last two descriptors picture the LORD as a rewarder who graciously bestows mercy and compassion, and who satisfies desires with good things. The act of being "crowned" (στεφανοῦντά) with these qualities, should probably be understood within an eschatological context.[25] *Summa*: Verses 3–5 lists the LORD's "beneficent deeds for every individual petitioner suffering distress."[26]

---

19. Unless otherwise specified, this contribution orientates itself on the NETS-translation of Pietersma and Wright, *New English Translation*, whilst existing English Bible translations (such as the NRSV etc.) are all based on the Hebrew version of the psalm.

20. The Lord is pictured as "Redeemer" (τὸν λυτρούμενον). So, also, Hossfeld and Zenger, *Psalms*, 34.

21. Pietersma and Wright, *New English Translation*.

22. Karrer and Kraus, *Septuaginta Deutsch*. Cf. Bauer, "Verderben, Vernichtung, Untergang," in *Griechisch-Deutsches Wörterbuch*, s.v. φθορά.

23. So also, Hossfeld and Zenger, *Psalms*, 37.

24. Dahood draws attention to the fact that "'the Pit' (is) a key word in Psalms (7:16, 9:16, 16:10, 30:10, 35:7, 49:10, 55:23, 94:13)" and that its first nonbiblical appearance is in Ugaritic literature. He elaborates further, "Like the author of Ps 16:10, 'Since you will not put me in Sheol, nor allow your devoted one to see the Pit,' the psalmist is confident that he will be removed from the Pit and transferred to Yahweh's eternal abode." Dahood, *Psalms*, 25–26.

25. See Dahood: "The mention of šaḥat, 'the Pit,' in the first colon and the use of three eschatological terms in the following verse show that the psalmist is describing the afterlife wherein Yahweh will place crowns on the heads of the just admitted to Paradise." Dahood, *Psalms*, 26.

26. Hossfeld and Zenger, *Psalms*, 33.

Deeds of a God-in-Action (vv. 6–8)

This list is enhanced in vv. 6–8 with further qualities that point to the deeds of a God-in-action.[27] Here, at v. 6, the psalm develops into a communal hymn of praise, describing the LORD's self-revelation to Israel.[28] The LORD is portrayed as not being static, but dynamic, living, and active. These acts are vividly described with a choice of verbs and adjectives that portray the character of a divine being who is deeply involved in the lives of those who are being oppressed and marginalized. In doing so, the psalmist relates the divine attributes to history:[29]

- He performs acts of pity (ποιῶν ἐλεημοσύνας),[30] and judgment for all who are being wronged (κρίμα πᾶσι τοῖς ἀδικουμένοις) (v. 6).

- He made his ways known (ἐγνώρισεν τὰς ὁδούς) to Moses and his will to the Israelites (v. 7).

- He is compassionate (οἰκτίρμων) and merciful (ἐλεήμων), slow to anger (μακρόθυμος) and abounding in mercy (πολυέλεος) (v. 8).[31]

These qualities portray the LORD mainly in his function as a *judge*, who communicated his expectations to Moses and to his people. This observation connects closely with the salvation and covenantal history of God with his people.[32] As he reviews the facts of history, the psalmist realizes that the covenant relationship that the LORD has made with frail sinners, gives

---

27. Cf. Weber: "Der ausgedehnte Mittelteil (Corpus) ist gefüllt und gerahmt mit hymnischer Darbietung von Gottes Heilswirken in Geschichte und Gegenwart." Weber, *Werkbuch Psalmen*, 176.

28. Allen, *Psalms*, 27.

29. Ross, *Commentary*, 236.

30. Kim has drawn attention to the frequent choice of ἐλεημοσύνη as LXX translation equivalent for the Hebrew צְדָקָה (e.g., Deut 6:25; 24:13; Ps 24[23]:5; 33[32]:5; 35[34]:24; 103[102]:6; Isa 1:27; 28:17; 59:16; Dan 4:24[27]; 9:16). Kim poses the question, "Aus welchem Grund soll man mit den Armen Erbarmen haben bzw. ihnen ein Almosen geben, um צדקה im Leben zu erweisen?"—and answers with reference to Ps 103(102): "Das ist deswegen, weil Gott selbst צדקה tun, indem er sich mit den Armen und Schwachen Erbarmen hat." (Kim, "Zur Wiedergabe," 516–17.)

31. Cf. Ross: "The attributes listed refer to the ways that God deals with his sinful people. Such descriptions have been a comfort and relief to all subsequent sinners in their guilt and fears." Ross, *Commentary*, 236.

32. Weber states that the artfully constructed Ps 103 draws on wisdom and salvation history, but especially on the core statements of the renewal of the covenant at Sinai (Exod 32–34) and aims at the kingship of YHWH (Weber, *Werkbuch Psalmen*, 176). Brueggemann, too, draws attention to the fact that "the poem lyrically identifies YHWH with a characteristic cluster of covenantal adjectives." Brueggemann, *Introducing the Psalms*, 46.

hope.³³ By looking back into the historical trajectory and reflecting theologically about the qualities of their Lord God, the psalmist and his community are able to identify the Lord's guidance, sustenance and presence as it unfolded during his revelation to his people. Not only does he execute his judgment in a just manner, but is portrayed particularly as a compassionate judge, who is pitiful, merciful, and patient. The objects of this compassionate judge are "all who are being wronged" (πᾶσι τοῖς ἀδικουμένοις, v. 6).

The chain of Greek adjectives in v. 8 "evokes the stereotypical formula of confession which recurs with slight variations in various texts."³⁴ It is, therefore, no wonder that v. 8 is considered by some scholars to be the center of the psalm and understood as the "graciousness formula"³⁵ from Exod 34:6, which is the Lord's second self-declaration after Exod 3:14—"a description of God that is highly regarded today for its important influence and widespread reception."³⁶

Statements about the Patience and Mercy of the Lord (vv. 9–14)

The latter list of qualities continues in vv. 9–12 where the psalmist switches to four statements in the negative form to express the patience and mercy of the Lord.

- He will *not* be totally angry, *nor* will he keep his wrath forever (v. 9)
- *Not* according to our sins did he deal with us, *nor* according to our acts of lawlessness did he repay us (v. 10).³⁷

The four statements consist of two pairs of perfect parallelisms:

> Verse 9a = οὐκ | εἰς τέλος | ὀργισθήσεται
> Verse 9b = οὐδὲ | εἰς τὸν αἰῶνα | μηνιεῖ·
> Verse 10a = οὐ | κατὰ τὰς ἁμαρτίας ἡμῶν | ἐποίησεν ἡμῖν
> Verse 10b = οὐδὲ | κατὰ τὰς ἀνομίας ἡμῶν | ἀνταπέδωκεν ἡμῖν·

---

33. Ross, *Commentary*, 230.

34. Bons, "Psalter Terminology," 437. Bons refers to Exod 34:6; Num 14:18; Neh 9:17; Ps 85:15; 102:8; 144:8; Joel 2:13; Jonah 4:2.

35. Cf. Hossfeld and Zenger: "It is related to a Ugaritic formula about 'the Gracious One, El, the Merciful' and may have been taken over from the cult and then expanded. In the Psalter it is included also in Pss 25:10; 86:15; and 99:8." Hossfeld and Zenger, *Psalms*, 35.

36. Hossfeld and Zenger, *Psalms*, 35.

37. Cf. Ross: "God's anger and discipline is tempered by his grace and mercy." Ross, *Commentary*, 236.

The tone becomes intensely personal in v. 10, when the psalmist switches to the first person plural personal pronoun: "*our* sins (ἡμῶν) . . . *us*" (ἡμῖν) and "*our* acts (ἡμῶν) . . . *us*" (ἡμῖν). This expresses a very special and close relationship between the psalmist and his community, on the one hand, and their covenantal God, on the other hand. The more general second person singular of vv. 3–5 or the general plural form of vv. 6–8, have now changed to the first person, with which the psalmist identifies himself as part of the in-group who experiences the patience and mercy of the Lord.[38]

These qualities—especially the Lord's mercy—are further intensified and qualified by means of two comparisons (or similes: "as . . . is"), in which stark geographical or spatial contrasts are used as analogy. These are presented as evidence of the Lord's great patience and mercy and connected by means of the conjunction ὅτι at the beginning of v. 11:

- *because*, as (κατά) the sky is high above the earth (11a) → *above-below spatial simile*[39]
- the Lord strengthened his mercy (ἐκραταίωσεν) toward those who fear him (11b)
- as (καθ') far as east is from west (12a) → *east-west geographical linear simile*[40]
- he has removed (ἐμάκρυνεν) from us our acts of lawlessness (12b).

The psalmist again applies the first-person plural—"from our acts of lawlessness"—thereby including himself within the in-group who benefits from the Lord's great mercy.

In the last two verses of this section (vv. 13–14), the psalmist creates an intensification and climax. It follows the confessional statements as expressed in vv. 9–10 (in the first-person plural) and climaxed with the analogy of a father in vv. 13–14 (again connected with "*our* makeup" in the first-person plural). In these two latter verses, he draws a comparison (καθώς) between "the Lord, who has had compassion (οἰκτίρησεν κύριος) for those who fear him" (v. 13b) and "a father who has compassion (οἰκτίρει

---

38. "The petitioner allies himself with the 'we' group in his confession of sins. He knows that he is a sinner as part of the collective Israel, and he has the catastrophe of the exile before his eyes. But God's exercise of anger ends in his forgiveness." Hossfeld and Zenger, *Psalms*, 35.

39. "The first comparison describes the cosmic expansion of YHWH's love from a vertical perspective." Hossfeld and Zenger, *Psalms*, 35.

40. "The second comparison, from a horizontal perspective, in v. 12, involves both space and the (spatial) category of time, more precisely the visible extent of a twenty-four-hour day." Hossfeld and Zenger, *Psalms*, 35.

πατήρ) for his 'sons' (children)" (v. 13a).⁴¹ The expansion of the LORD's qualities of patience and mercy—as elaborated upon in vv. 11–12⁴²—continues here with another analogy, this time, however, not spatial, but relational on a personal level. The psalmist, again, substantiates his observation, or rather, confession, being evidenced with a ὅτι conjunction in v. 14a:

- "*because* (ὅτι) he knew our makeup" (αὐτὸς ἔγνω τὸ πλάσμα ἡμῶν).⁴³

This knowledge of humanity's Creator leads the psalmist to an important reminder for his audience in v. 14b—"Remember that we are dust!"⁴⁴—expressed by means of μνήσθητι (an aorist imperative⁴⁵ passive second person singular) with the first-person plural ἐσμεν, by which the psalmist addresses his in-group as audience, including himself. There is a clear difference here between the possible Hebrew *Vorlage* and the Greek translation. Whereas the Hebrew ascribes the idea that humanity is dust as continuation of the fact that "the LORD knows how we were made—he remembers (זָכוּר) that we are dust," the LXX translator vocalized the word differently (זְכוֹר) and interprets it with the imperative that we should "remember that we are dust!"⁴⁶

Statements About the Mercy, Righteousness, and Kingdom of the LORD (vv. 17–19)

The psalmist highlights again three key attributes of the LORD in vv. 17–19: his mercy, righteousness, and kingship. The first two attributes highlight the LORD as a merciful and righteous *judge*. These first two are, furthermore,

41. Ross draws attention to the prominence of the word "compassion" in the Hebrew text, which would also apply here to the Greek translation. Compassion is "appropriate in this context; it describes the tender care and nourishing that a parent gives to a child (although often in the analogy of a mother and her child)." Ross, *Commentary*, 237.

42. Weber, too, points to the role of vv. 11–14 as expression of the LORD's mercy: "Es folgt eine Triplette von Vergleichen 'in extremis'" (11–13), die die Gnadenmächtigkeit JHWHs nochmals steigern und mit der Hinfälligkeit des Menschen erklären (14)." Weber, *Werkbuch Psalmen*, 176.

43. The term πλάσμα also occurs in LXX Job 40:19; Isa 29:16; Hab 2:18; Jdt 8:29. Knut Usener elaborates that it could be understood as "das mit all seinen Besonderheiten '(von Gott erschaffene) Wesen, Gebilde." Usener, "Hiob 40 LXX," 58–59.

44. The Greek translation chose the word χοῦς ("dust"/"*Staub*") here for the Hebrew עָפָר. Dahood argues, however, that the conventional translation of the Hebrew should rather be understood here as "clay," as that is the medium with which a potter works. Dahood, *Psalms*, 28.

45. The LXX translator replaces the Hebrew verbal adjective "remembers" in v. 14b with an imperative. Hossfeld and Zenger, *Psalms*, 37.

46. See Seiler, "Psalm 102[103]."

closely connected with two aspects, namely their duration (αἰῶνος ἕως αἰῶνος; υἱοὺς υἱῶν), as well as the obedience of the believers as a condition ("on those who"; "for those who") in order to experience these divine attributes (vv. 17–18):[47]

k. the mercy of the Lord (τὸ δὲ ἔλεος τοῦ κυρίου) is
l. from everlasting even to everlasting (αἰῶνος καὶ ἕως τοῦ αἰῶνος)
m. on those who fear him (ἐπὶ τοὺς φοβουμένους αὐτόν)
n. his righteousness (ἡ δικαιοσύνη αὐτοῦ)
o. on sons' sons (ἐπὶ υἱοὺς υἱῶν)
p. for those who keep (τοῖς φυλάσσουσιν) his covenant and remember (μεμνημένοις) his commandments, to do (ποιῆσαι) them

The third and last attribute (in v. 19) acknowledges and affirms the position of the Lord as Almighty *King* of the universe:

- "The Lord prepared his throne (τὸν θρόνον αὐτοῦ) in the sky, and his kingdom (ἡ βασιλεία αὐτοῦ) rules over all."[48]

Psalm 102 LXX closes with an *inclusio*. The psalm has started in vv. 1–2 with the double call "Bless the Lord, O my soul" (εὐλόγει, ἡ ψυχή μου, τὸν κύριον) and concludes again in vv. 20–22 with a fourfold call to bless the Lord: εὐλογεῖτε τὸν κύριον. It is thus appropriate to note that vv. 19–22 "represent an imperatival hymn, a summons to all Yahweh's creatures and subjects to praise God as king and a figure of authority."[49] The contents of the psalm acknowledge, confirm, and praise the divine attributes of the Lord.

CLUSTERING AND SYSTEMIZING THE DIVINE ATTRIBUTES IN LXX PSALM 102

Ross is correct in observing that "Psalm 103 is filled with solid doctrinal statements of faith, so much so that it would be difficult for the expositor to exhaust this material in one exposition."[50] It became clear from the survey

---

47. Cf. Ross: "The love of God that is described in these verses is only known by those who have received the grace of God." Ross, *Commentary*, 238.

48. "Throne is a symbol of his reign; and its location in the heavens places his reign far above and over all the earth and all mortal beings. The Lord himself established his rightful authority by creation and by redemption. Everything belongs to him; and he rules over it all." Ross, *Commentary*, 238.

49. Allen, *Psalms*, 27.

50. Ross, *Commentary*, 239.

above that LXX Ps 102 presents a high density of divine attributes that are linked to the Lord God of Israel. This image of the Lord clearly differentiates itself from that of the numerous idols who were in circulation within a multi-religious context. The idols of those religions were cruel, impatient, unjust, unfair, and merciless. This stands in stark contrast to the Lord God who acts patiently, mercifully and like a father figure with his followers—those with whom the Lord has a covenantal relationship. The Lord is indeed a merciful judge, a caring healer, an able redeemer, a compassionate ruler, and a reliable sustainer.

When clustering and systemizing these attributes that occur in LXX Ps 102, there are especially four categories of divine attributes that one might identify here. Firstly, God is portrayed as *Divine Creator and Sustainer*, Holy and Glorious, eternally in existence and the Most High above all that exists. Secondly, he is portrayed as the *Great and Majestic King*, who is the ultimate Protector and Rescuer. Thirdly, he is portrayed as *Righteous Judge*, who is merciful, gracious, and patient, yet does not tolerate injustice and lawlessness. Fourthly, God is portrayed as *Wisdom Teacher*, who teaches and instructs, yet disciplines and chastises to guide believers on their way.

God as Divine Creator and Sustainer

LXX Ps 89 as the opening psalm of Book IV of the Greek Psalter already introduced the identity of the Lord as an eternal God, who is the Creator and Sustainer of all. The identity (σὺ εἶ, LXX Ps 89:2)[51] of the κύριος is directly linked with the fact that he existed before the creation of the mountains, the earth, and the residential world (πρὸ τοῦ ὄρη γενηθῆναι[52] καὶ πλασθῆναι τὴν γῆν καὶ τὴν οἰκουμένην, 89:2). This statement is connected with the phrase "you are from *aion* to *aion*" (ἀπὸ τοῦ αἰῶνος ἕως τοῦ αἰῶνος, 89:2). This link to eternity surfaces several times in Book IV: LXX Ps 91:8–9; 92:2; 99:5; 101:13; 102:17.

But the divinity of the Lord is not merely marked by time and the fact that the Lord is eternal and before all creation, it is also marked by space. A clear distinction is made between a heavenly domain "above," an earthly domain "below," and an underworld. The distance between the first two spaces

---

51. "Der MT hat noch אל ('bist du, Gott'), was die LXX offensichtlich als Negation und dann in Verbindung mit V.3 las." Seiler, "Psalm 102[103]," 1758.

52. "Die LXX stellt nur den Werdeprozess als solchen heraus (γίνομαι), während der MT diesen als eine Art Geburtsvorgang darstellt ('geboren wurde'; von qal ילד)." Seiler, "Psalm 102[103]," 1758.

is referred to in LXX Ps 102:11: "as the sky is high above the earth" (κατὰ τὸ ὕψος τοῦ οὐρανοῦ ἀπὸ τῆς γῆς).

The striking and extreme difference between Creator and creature is mentioned particularly in LXX Ps 102:14b. The psalmist draws attention to the fact that the LORD "knows our makeup," on the one hand, and reminds his readers and co-believers: "Remember that we are dust!"

Our psalm presents a clear picture of the Creator God who is intensely involved in his creation and who sustains his people whom he created. Being portrayed as Sustainer, several attributes overlap with the qualities of the LORD as a king, or as a judge, for instance. There are some attributes, however, that portray the LORD as Sustainer as One "who heals all your diseases" (v. 3b), "who redeems your life from corruption" (v. 4a), "who crowns you with mercy and compassion" (v. 4b), "who satisfies your desire with good" (v. 5), and who "performs acts of pity and judgment for all who are being wronged" (v. 6). These qualities present a picture of a unique God, who is strikingly different to those known of the surrounding idols of Israel's neighbors. This striking contrast with of the covenantal LORD God, the κύριος of LXX Ps 102, is incomprehensible against the backdrop of other divine entities, who are distanced, cruel, and uninvolved. LXX Ps 102 portrays a picture of the Divine Creator and Sustainer of the universe, who is holy and glorious, eternally in existence, and the Most High above all that exists.

God as the Great and Majestic King

The anthropomorphic projection of the transcendent Divine LORD God as a great and majestic king is a dominant theme (*Leitthema*) in Book IV of the Greek Psalter. The cosmological image in LXX Ps 102 is analogue to that of a king who sits on his throne and rules: "The LORD prepared his throne in the sky (κύριος ἐν τῷ οὐρανῷ ἡτοίμασεν τὸν θρόνον αὐτοῦ), and his kingdom rules over all" (καὶ ἡ βασιλεία αὐτοῦ πάντων δεσπόζει, LXX Ps 102:19).

The LORD's absolute divinity is marked by the fact that "his Name is holy" (τὸ ὄνομα τὸ ἅγιον αὐτοῦ, v. 1b)—which is stated as the reason why he should be praised at the very beginning of the psalm. The absolute Divinity of the LORD as "King of the universe" is further marked and confirmed by the heavenly beings who are subordinate to him, who worship him, and who are praising him (εὐλογεῖτε τὸν κύριον). They include "all his angels" (πάντες οἱ ἄγγελοι αὐτοῦ, LXX Ps 102:20), "all the hosts (powers) of the LORD" (πᾶσαι αἱ δυνάμεις αὐτοῦ) and "his (cultic) ministers doing his will" (λειτουργοὶ αὐτοῦ ποιοῦντες τὸ θέλημα αὐτοῦ, LXX Ps 102:21).

The psalm paints a picture of a unique God—of the covenantal Lord God, the κύριος—who is strikingly different to the other divine entities, the surrounding idols, who are characterized by their limitations and incompetence. LXX Ps 102 portrays a picture of the κύριος as an incomprehensible great and majestic divine king, who is the ultimate protector and rescuer.

God as a Righteous Judge

The "Lord God" (κύριος ὁ θεός)—is portrayed in Book IV of the Greek Psalter with qualities and functions as a warrior against his opponents, as a saviour of his people, and as a righteous judge of all. His portrayal as a righteous judge in LXX Ps 102 is presented with attributes that describe his "very conciliatory reaction toward all your acts of lawlessness" (v. 3a) and the fact that "he performs acts of pity and judgment for all who are being wronged" (v. 6). A very interesting perspective regarding the Lord's attributes of compassion and mercy, is the fact that these qualities are also being transferred to humanity, when the psalmist states that the Lord "crowns (τὸν στεφανοῦντά) you with mercy and compassion" (v. 4b).

Especially the Lord's qualities of compassionateness and mercifulness are frequently highlighted in vv. 8–13 with keywords or phrases such as "compassionate" (οἰκτίρμων, v. 8; οἰκτίρει πατήρ, v. 13a; οἰκτίρησεν κύριος, v. 13b); "merciful" (ἐλεήμων, v. 8) or "abounding in mercy" (πολυέλεος, v. 8); "slow to anger" (μακρόθυμος, v. 8) or "not be angry until the end" (οὐκ εἰς τέλος ὀργισθήσεται, v. 9); "nor will he keep his wrath forever" (οὐδὲ εἰς τὸν αἰῶνα μηνιεῖ, v. 9); "not according to our sins did he deal with us (οὐ κατὰ τὰς ἁμαρτίας ἡμῶν ἐποίησεν ἡμῖν), nor according to our acts of lawlessness did he repay us" (οὐδὲ κατὰ τὰς ἀνομίας ἡμῶν ἀνταπέδωκεν ἡμῖν, v. 10). These qualities show a progression in intensity. They start, firstly, with positive descriptors that portray the divine reaction (compassionate, merciful, abounding in mercy), before progressing to more intense descriptors that utilize conscious decisions of the Lord *not* to act with impatience, anger, and severe judgment—as would have been expected: "slow to anger," "*not* (οὐκ) being angry until the end," "*nor* (οὐδέ) keeping his wrath forever," "*not* (οὐ) dealing with us according to our sins," "*nor* (οὐδέ) repaying us according to our acts of lawlessness." These descriptors peaked in an intensification with two similes. The first is linked to "the Lord (who) strengthened his mercy (ἐκραταίωσεν) toward those who fear him" (τοὺς φοβουμένους αὐτόν, v. 11b) with the qualification of the simile "as the sky is high above the earth" (v. 11a). The second is linked to "the Lord (who) removed (ἐμάκρυνεν) from us our acts of lawlessness" (τὰς ἀνομίας ἡμῶν, v. 12b) with the qualification of the simile "as far as east is from west" (v. 12a). The anthropomorphic comparison (καθώς) between an earthly father who shows compassion (οἰκτίρει) for his children (v. 13a) and the Lord who has compassion (οἰκτίρησεν) for those who obey (literally, "fear": φοβουμένους) him (v. 13b), creates a powerful link between the Divine Judge and the earthly father. In this manner, the divine attribute of compassion mirrors itself within the personal relationship between parent and child.

Two further attributes in LXX Ps 102 that were pointing to the Lord as a merciful (τὸ δὲ ἔλεος τοῦ κυρίου) and a righteous (ἡ δικαιοσύνη αὐτοῦ) judge, were found in vv. 17–18. Both have emphasized the durative aspect of his mercy and righteousness. The psalmist made it clear that "the mercy of the Lord is from everlasting even to everlasting" (αἰῶνος καὶ ἕως τοῦ αἰῶνος) and that "his righteousness" is passed on from generation to generation—expressed by ἐπὶ υἱοὺς υἱῶν. An interesting qualification to each of these was the fact that the Lord's eternal mercy was linked to "those who obey (φοβουμένους) him" and that his continuous righteousness was linked to "those who keep his covenant and who remember to do his commandments."

LXX Ps 102 portrays a picture of the κύριος as an incomprehensible divine judge, who is soft on our sins and doesn't repay us according to our acts of lawlessness. It portrays a judge who is merciful, gracious, and patient, yet does not tolerate injustice and lawlessness.

God as a Wisdom Teacher?

An interesting attribute of the Lord—almost implicitly portrayed in LXX Ps 102—is that of an instructor, or perhaps even as a wisdom teacher. This aspect surfaces in v. 7, when God reveals himself to Moses and the Israelites. These two revelatory aspects are being spelled out. He, firstly, revealed his divine plan, or in the words of the psalmist, "He made known (ἐγνώρισεν) his ways (τὰς ὁδοὺς αὐτοῦ) to Moses. He also, secondly, revealed "his will" (τὰ θελήματα αὐτοῦ) to his covenant people, to the Israelites.

This revelation could be seen as part of the Lord's presentation as a judge—especially given the historical context in which Moses received the Lord's commandments for the people of Israel. The Lord's "ways" and "will" refer to the law, the Torah. But there is more implied here. Underlying the "way of life" as prescribed by the Lord, it also implies the Lord's *instruction* and *wisdom* to steer the direction of life for his people. The goal is not merely to have a legal code in order to regulate daily life, but a deeper relation between God as divine entity and his people. Its purpose is theologically rooted in the salvation-historical plan of Israel's Lord. The psalm has clearly portrayed the Lord's compassion as a judge—compassion that is being compared with that of a loving parent. Precisely the attributes of "compassionate" and "merciful" in v. 8 are the attributes following directly after this verse (v. 7). But being a compassionate and merciful parent implies obedience, commitment, loyalty, and perseverance from his children. These conditional elements are to be found in vv. 17–18: The Lord's mercy is "on those who obey him" (ἐπὶ τοὺς φοβουμένους αὐτόν) and his righteousness "for those who keep his covenant" (τοῖς φυλάσσουσιν τὴν διαθήκην αὐτοῦ) and who "remember to do his commandments" (μεμνημένοις τῶν ἐντολῶν αὐτοῦ τοῦ ποιῆσαι).

LXX Ps 102 portrays a picture of the κύριος as an incomprehensible divine instructor, a wisdom teacher, who teaches and instructs, yet disciplines and chastises to guide believers on their way.

CONCLUSION

Anthropomorphic views of God dominate the divine ontology of Book IV of the Psalter and define the Lord transcendentally as the "God of the Sky," the Creator of the heavens and the earth, as the ultimate origin of the universe. The Lord is immanently present on a cosmological scale in the universe. Firstly, as *creator*, who is actively involved with his creation. The Lord not only created humanity, the inhabited world, and the heavens, but he is portrayed as continually being an active sustainer of his creation. Secondly, as a calculated God who is involved with his creation through thoughtful planning. As an *instructor*, he reveals his ways and makes his will known to his people. Especially his righteousness and *justice* define the nature of his actions and involvement with his creation. Thirdly, the divine being, the transcended Lord God of the ancient universe is above all anthropomorphically pictured as a *king*, whose throne, glory and name are integral to his identity. On a cosmological scale, the universe is his kingdom.

Where most of the psalms in Book IV briefly refer to several of these attributes, Ps 103 (LXX 102), however, distinguishes itself by describing comprehensively a broad range of attributes that portray an exceptional picture of a compassionate father and his child—especially in contrast to LXX Pss 85, 88, and 104 where the relationship is referred to in terms of a slave. LXX Ps 102, on the contrary, portrays an exclusive picture of an incomprehensible Lord (ὁ κύριος) who is Holy, Creator, Sustainer, Ruler, Revealer, Healer, Redeemer, Reconciler, Consoler, Compassionate Father, Merciful, and Righteous. These attributes are framed with a double "Bless the LORD, O my soul" at the beginning and four-fold repetition of "Bless the LORD" at the end of the psalm. The attributes of the κύριος in LXX Ps 102 portray the picture of an incomprehensible *creator* and sustainer, a majestic *king*, a righteous *judge*, and a wisdom *teacher*.

BIBLIOGRAPHY

Allen, Leslie C. *Psalms 101–50*. WBC 21. Dallas: Word, 2002.
Bauer, Walter. *Griechisch-Deutsches Wörterbuch zu den Schriften des Neuen Testaments und der Frühchristlichen Literatur*. Berlin: De Gruyter, 1988.
Bons, Eberhard, "Psalter Terminology in Joseph and Aseneth." In *Die Septuaginta—Text, Wirkung, Rezeption*, 430–43. Tübingen: Mohr Siebeck, 2014.
Brueggemann, Walter. *From Whom No Secrets Are Hid: Introducing the Psalms*. Louisville: Westminster John Knox, 2014.
Burden, J. J. *Psalms 101–19*. Kaapstad: NG Kerk-Uitgewers, 1991.
Dahmen, Ulrich. *Psalmen- und Psalter-Rezeption im Frühjudentum. Rekonstruktion, Textbestand, Struktur und Pragmatik der Psalmenrolle 11QPsa aus Qumran*. Studies on the Texts of the Desert of Judah XLIX. Leiden: Brill, 2003.
Dahood, Mitchell. *Psalms III: 101–50: Introduction, Translation, and Notes with an Appendix: The Grammar of the Psalter*. Anchor Yale Bible 17A. New Haven: Yale University Press, 2008.
Day, John. *Psalms*. London: T&T Clark, 1999.
Flint, Peter W. "The Psalters at Qumran and the Book of Psalms." PhD diss., University of Notre Dame, 1993.
García Martínez, Florentino, and Eibert J. C. Tigchelaar, eds. *The Dead Sea Scrolls Study Edition*. Volume One 1QI—4Q273. Leiden: Brill, 1997.
Hossfeld, Frank-Lothar, and Erich Zenger. *Psalms 3: A Commentary on Psalms 101–50*. Hermeneia. Minneapolis: Fortress, 2011.
Karrer, Martin, and Wolfgang Kraus, eds. *Septuaginta Deutsch: Das griechische Alte Testament in deutscher Übersetzung*. Stuttgart: Deutsche Bibelgesellschaft, 2009.
———. *Septuaginta Deutsch: Erläuterungen und Kommentare zum griechischen Alten Testament*, Bd. 2. Stuttgart: Deutsche Bibelgesellschaft, 2011.
Kim, Jong-Hoon. "Zur Relevanz der Wiedergabe von צדקה mit ἔλεος / ἐλεημοσύνη." In *Die Septuaginta—Orte und Intentionen*, 510–19. Tübingen: Mohr Siebeck, 2016.
Kraus, Wolfgang, and Siegfried Kreuzer, eds. *Die Septuaginta—Text, Wirkung, Rezeption*. WUNT 325. Tübingen: Mohr Siebeck, 2014.
Kreuzer, Siegfried, et al., eds. *Die Septuaginta—Orte und Intentionen*. WUNT 361. Tübingen: Mohr Siebeck, 2016.
Lehnardt, Andreas. *Bibliographie zu den Jüdischen Schriften aus Hellenistisch-Römischer Zeit*, Bd. IV, VI. Gütersloh: Gütersloher Verlagshaus, 1999.
Longman, Tremper, III. *How to Read the Psalms*. Downers Grove, IL: InterVarsity, 1988.
Meiser, Martin, et al., eds. *Die Septuaginta—Geschichte, Wirkung, Relevanz*. WUNT 405. Tübingen: Mohr Siebeck, 2018.
Pietersma, Albert, and Benjamin G. Wright, eds. *A New English Translation of the Septuagint*. Oxford: Oxford University Press, 2007.

Rahlfs, Alfred, ed. *Psalmi cum Odis. Vetus Testamentum Graecum*, Bd. X. Auctoritate Academiae Scientiarum Gottingensis Editum. Göttingen: Vandenhoeck & Ruprecht, 1979.

Ross, Allen P. *A Commentary on the Psalms (90–150): Commentary*. Kregel Exegetical Library 3. Grand Rapids: Kregel, 2016.

Seiler, Stefan. "Psalm 102[103]." In *Septuaginta Deutsch: Erläuterungen, 1789–1791*. Stuttgart: Deutsche Bibelgesellschaft, 2011.

Skehan, Patrick W. "A Psalm Manuscript from Qumran (4QPsb)." *CBQ* 26 (1964) 313–22.

Steyn, Gert J. *A Quest for the Assumed Septuagint Vorlage of the Explicit Quotations in Hebrews*. FRLANT 235. Göttingen: Vandenhoeck & Ruprecht, 2011.

Ulrich, Eugene, et al., eds. *Qumran Cave 4.XI: Psalms to Chronicles*. DJD XVI. Oxford: Clarendon, 2000.

Usener, Knut. "Hiob 40LXX Als Theologische Interpretation der Hebräischen Vorlage." In *Die Septuaginta—Geschichte, Wirkung, Relevanz*, 50–65. Tübingen: Mohr Siebeck, 2018.

Weber, Beat. *Werkbuch Psalmen: Die Psalmen 73 bis 150*, Bd. II, 2. Stuttgart: Kohlhammer, 2016.

Chapter 6

The (In)comprehensibility of God and His Works: A Re-education of Judah in Isaiah 40:12–31

—P. Chris van der Walt

Unit for Reformational Theology and the Development of the South African Society, Faculty of Theology, North-West University, Potchefstroom, South Africa

ABSTRACT

This chapter delves into Isa 40:12–31, where the prophet addresses misconceptions (40:27–28) about the comprehensibility or incomprehensibility of God and his acts in history. The discourse emerges in response to the erroneous belief among the Israelites that their relationship with God depended on the land and the temple. The capture of Jerusalem and subsequent exile of Judah prompts doubts about God's power and involvement in the lives of Judah, leading to questions about why such humiliation was permitted.

The impatience exhibited by the prophet in the discourse stems from the necessity to re-educate Judah on fundamental truths they should have known. The rupture in their knowledge of Yahweh implicated idols. Counteracting the negative perception expressed in 40:27, the judgmental question in v. 28a challenges Israel's complaint. The response emphasizes that, despite God's incomparability and unsearchability, he reveals himself through prophets, offering perspectives on his character and deeds in history.

The revelation of God's character becomes crucial in determining the fate of his people during exile and their return. Human comprehension falls short due to the vastness of God's existence, thoughts, and actions. The prophet serves as God's agent, guiding the people from complaining about Yahweh to praising him. This study explores the intricate interplay between human understanding, divine revelation, and the prophet's role in shaping the perception of God among his people.

INTRODUCTION

This study explores the theological concept of God's (in)comprehensibly and examines if and how he can be known. Henry[1] provides an overview of the notion of God's knowability, which can be summarized and applied in the following manner: The great creeds of Christianity—Orthodox, Catholic, and Protestant—all affirm that God is incomprehensible, meaning finite humans cannot fully grasp the infinite nature and actions of God. However, this does not mean God cannot be known at all. Mystical, agnostic, and existential philosophies often incorrectly place the supernatural beyond cognitive understanding, but the Bible contradicts such views by asserting that we can know God, even if not exhaustively.

Christian tradition, therefore, affirms that God's infinite nature surpasses human understanding, but it also maintains that he reveals himself in ways that allow for meaningful knowledge of him. Isaiah 40:12–31 serves as a key text in addressing misconceptions among the Judeans (40:27), particularly regarding their relationship with God in the aftermath of Jerusalem's capture and Judah's exile to Babylon. Their displacement led to deep uncertainty about God's presence and ability, prompting Isaiah to challenge these doubts and reaffirm God's self-revelation through creation and prophetic messages.

The study highlights the necessity for Isaiah to re-educate Judah on fundamental theological truths that had been lost or misinterpreted. Their belief that their relationship with God depended on the land and temple contributed to their crisis of faith during the exile. Isaiah confronts these misperceptions by emphasizing God's sovereign nature and ongoing revelation. Though God's incomparability means he cannot be fully comprehended, his self-revelation provides significant insights into his actions, character, and relationship with his people. Understanding God is possible through divine revelation, though not exhaustive; it is sufficient for faith and worship.

1. Henry, *God, Revelation*, 389.

A linguistic theological analysis of Isa 40:12–31 within its canonical setting will examine the interplay between divine revelation, human understanding, and the prophet's role in reforming Judah's perception of God. The passage's historical, linguistic, and theological dimensions will be used to demonstrate how Isaiah guides the people from a state of doubt and complaint toward renewed trust in God. Divine revelation thus functions as a means of bridging the gap between human limitation and the transcendent nature of God, enabling a deeper understanding of his presence and purpose, even in moments of uncertainty and exile.

BACKGROUND TO ISAIAH 40

Isaiah 40 marks the beginning of a new section in the canonical book. Isaiah 40–66 is noticeably different from chapters 1–39 in theme and historical setting. While the earlier chapters focus on warnings and impending judgment, Isa 40 signals a shift toward restoration and hope. At the outset, the political calamity foretold in chapters 1–39 is presented as a past event.

The repetition of "comfort, comfort" [נַחֲמוּ נַחֲמוּ (pi'el impt)] in 40:1 emphasizes the prophet's divine commission to bring relief and reassurance to God's people, alleviating their sorrow and distress.[2] This change did not occur because God's people made a spiritual about-face in response to prophetic warnings but because his chastisement for covenant transgression had ended. In his mercy, he made a new beginning for the remnant from the Babylonian exile and announced the end of the period of discipline in a message of comfort. The essence of the message, however, does not concentrate on the people of God and an earthly blessing to them. Instead, the message focuses on God's greatness, which would become visible in the return of the remnant in a new exodus.[3]

STRUCTURE OF ISAIAH 40

40:1–2: Message of Comfort

40:3–5: A voice crying about God's salvation work

40:6–8: A voice crying about humanity's fleeting nature vs. God's eternal word

40:9–11: The sovereign Lord comes with might

---

2. Swanson, "נָחַם (nā·ḥăm)," 412.
3. Paul, *Isaiah 40–66*, 128.

40:12–20: God is incomparable in his ability

40:21–26: Humanity should have perceived how God is

40:27–31: Assurance to a doubting people that God acts according to his true character

In the structure given above, ideas flow from an announcement of salvation by God to disbelief by the hearers, followed by assurance that the sovereign God has not abandoned his people even though they felt so. The emphasis in the argument that follows is then placed on God's in/comprehensible character. We will thus concentrate on 40:12–31, where the doubt and disbelief of the hearers is addressed.

ISAIAH 40:12–31

The genre of Isa 40:12–31 is a disputation speech used to address Judah's perception and complaint that God was apparently not showing proper concern for them and that he was not treating them justly (40:27).

Isaiah 40:12–20

These verses portray a complex group of oracles and thematically related messages about God's ability in justice, sovereignty, and power. The stimulus for the oracles is that there was no need for Judah to question God's sovereign control over nature and the political history of the nations, including that of his people, Judah. The comforting message to Judah was necessary because they felt weak and helpless in exile, wondering why God was doing to them what he did. While in Babylon, far from the demolished Jerusalem and temple, they doubted whether they would ever return to the promised land.[4]

If we look at the individual ideas in the passage, a group of verbs in 40:12 deserves attention. The verbs to be discussed involve the determination of quantity by Yahweh, who is portrayed as a master craftsman or architect measuring and weighing the elements of creation. In this verse, an interrogative pronoun introduces five rhetorical questions.[5] In a hyperbolic manner, it is asked *who* has measured (מִי־מָדַד), marked off (תִּכֵּן), enclosed (וְכָל) and weighed (וְשָׁקַל) the different elements of creation. The implied answer to each question is that no human has the ability to do it, stressing that

---

4. Smith, *Isaiah 40-66*, 129.
5. Grogan, *Proverbs-Isaiah*, 723.

only Yahweh can. For humans to try and do it would not only be impossible, but the effort would also be ridiculous.[6] These verbs collectively indicate God's ability to gauge and control the entire creation. It further wants to convey that God is unlimited; neither *heaven* nor the *heavenly realm* constitutes a vessel large enough to contain him. In the truest sense of the word, he is incomprehensible, beyond measure or definition.[7]

In 40:13–14, another group of verbs is found in a subsequent rhetorical question inquiring about Yahweh's acquisition of intellectual abilities. The implication is that in self-sufficiency, his spirit receives no direction, neither does he receive counsel nor *need to* consult anyone about mental and judicial affairs. Thus, the message to Judah is that Yahweh's mental and judicial ability is such that they should not expect to grasp it exhaustively.

In 40:15–20 the discourse turns to the international political scene when the prophet compares the nations with weightless dust. Although these nations threatened the future of Judah's history, they carried no weight compared to Yahweh. The impotence of idols, which tend to topple, is also addressed to contrast it with the faithfulness and power of Yahweh.

In summary of 40:12–20, Yahweh is contrasted to all people, the cosmos, and idols, indicating his superiority above all. This then forms the introduction to a foundational proclamation to Judah in verse 21.

Isaiah 40:21–26

In 40:21 the prophet asks, "Have you not known? Have you not heard?"[8] (הֲלוֹא תֵדְעוּ הֲלוֹא תִשְׁמָעוּ)

There is a clear tone of impatience toward the addressed in these questions. Isaiah's impatience stems from the fact that he must once again teach God's *covenant people* fundamental truths they should have known long ago. Yahweh's people should not need to be reminded of his character and actions since their past contained much about Yahweh's saving acts since they were led out of Egypt.[9] However, their spiritual knowledge was disrupted when they turned to idol worship, leading them to lose their appreciation of Yahweh, which required renewed foundational instruction (40:19, 20; 44:8, 9).[10]

---

6. Ogden and Sterk, *Handbook*, 1080.
7. Baumann, כול, 87.
8. All direct Bible quotations in this chapter is taken from the NRSV.
9. Abernethy, *Isaiah and God's Kingdom*, 60.
10. Leupold, *Exposition*, 35.

Isaiah uses the two Qal imperfects (תִשְׁמָע֣וּ & תֵדְע֣וּ) to highlight how Judah habitually acted in ignorance, not knowing and not listening. Their lack of understanding could not be attributed to Yahweh ceasing to reveal Himself during the exile, as he continued to do so through prophets such as Isaiah and Jeremiah (Isa 40:3–5; Jer 29).[11] Because Yahweh remained actively involved, Isaiah proclaims the truth of his nature, emphasizing that, as Creator and Sustainer, he remains concerned for his people (Isa 40:1). Despite prophetic voices consistently reaffirming Yahweh's supremacy, Judah did not fully believe or worship him alone.

Isaiah reintroduces fundamental truths about Yahweh to address Judah's disbelief and lack of trust. The first truth stems from creation, not as a natural theological argument but as a divinely revealed reality. Israel was not solely dependent on creation for knowledge of Yahweh. He continuously provided revelation so they could understand his sovereign rule over history and creation. Yahweh remains unmatched in his reign over the nations, determining the power of their rulers (Isa 40:23–26).

Isaiah 40:21–26 thus expresses frustration over Judah's need for re-education on Yahweh's character and reign, truths they should have understood but neglected due to idolatry. Despite their exile in Babylon, Yahweh remains supreme over all nations, revealing his sovereignty even in a foreign land.

Isaiah 40:27–31

This passage addresses Judah's distorted perception of Yahweh's role in their exile. In v. 27, Isaiah verbalizes their complaint: "Why do you say, O Jacob, and speak, O Israel, 'My way is hidden from the Lord, and my right is disregarded by my God?'" Their failure to grasp Yahweh's power and sovereignty made them question whether he was still actively involved in their lives.

While Isaiah had already reaffirmed Yahweh's supremacy over creation and nations, Judah's situation required revelation on God's use of history. Further revelation was needed because it never happened before that Jerusalem and its temple had been destroyed, and Judah's exile to Babylon was unprecedented. The only comparable event was Assyria's exile of the Northern Kingdom in 722 BC, which resulted in Israel never returning as a nation. Without historical precedent to which they could measure their circumstances, Judah concluded that Yahweh had also abandoned them and that they had no future. However, this conclusion was based on their reasoning rather than their true understanding of Yahweh's plans.

---

11. Westermann, *Isaiah 40–66*, 56.

Verse 28 addresses this flawed perspective, proclaiming Yahweh as the omnipotent Creator with unfathomable wisdom. This declaration was meant to give Judah hope, assuring them that Yahweh's sovereignty remained untouched despite their exile.[12]

Judah's lack of hope stemmed from their unwillingness to listen to Yahweh's prophets. For instance, they resisted Jeremiah's warning that Yahweh had sent Babylon and that they should not resist (Jer 25–26). Similarly, Isaiah's promise of renewal in the latter part of his writings was met with skepticism (Isa 42:20; 59:1). This was due to Judah wrongly believing that their covenant with Yahweh should have protected them from disaster, as seen in Hab 1. Although Habakkuk acknowledged Judah's unrighteousness, he struggled to reconcile Yahweh's decision to allow the Chaldeans to conquer them.[13]

Much like Habakkuk, Judah wrestled with the idea that Yahweh's character did not align with their experience of exile. Their suffering seemed inconsistent with their understanding of him, leading them to believe he was no longer actively involved in their lives. Their complaint in Isa 40:27 that Yahweh had disregarded them stemmed from the belief that their relationship with him was tied to the land and temple. The destruction of both in 586 BC (Lam 2:1; 5:18; Jer 7:4–7) reinforced their perception that Yahweh had abandoned them.[14]

Isaiah counters this belief, emphasizing that Yahweh's faithfulness remains intact despite their loss of land and temple. The prophet's questioning in v. 27 continues into v. 28, linking verbs such as *say* (תֹאמַר) and *speak* (וּתְדַבֵּר) with *known* (יָדַעְתָּ) and *heard* (שָׁמַעְתָּ), recalling earlier reflections in v. 21 which emphasize knowledge that should have been established. By invoking the name Yahweh, Isaiah underscores that Judah's complaint against him is unfounded.[15]

Verse 28 responds directly to v. 27, where Judah, either in self-justification (*How could God do this to me?*) or confusion (*How could my God do this?*), accuses Yahweh of disregarding their right. Following Jerusalem's fall, many Judeans began to doubt Yahweh's power, questioning why he had allowed such devastation. If he were truly powerful, why had he not prevented their humiliation (Isa 59:1–2)? They believed something had gone wrong on Yahweh's part, concluding that the exile should not have happened if Yahweh had acted according to character.

---

12. Motyer, *Isaiah*, 305.
13. Van der Walt, "Rigteous Degrees of Comparison," 73–92.
14. Watts, *Isaiah 34–66*, 627.
15. Koole, *Jesaja II*, 79.

Judah reasoned that since they had maintained the temple cult, it should have protected them (Jer 7:9–11; Isa 1:12–15). As a result, they shifted the blame onto Yahweh. However, despite their doubts, the exile became an undeniable reality. While in Babylon, Judah continued questioning Yahweh's power, wondering whether he could restore them to the promised land after failing to prevent their exile.[16]

Isaiah reaffirms the unmatched nature of the Holy One of Israel, seeking to re-educate the people. The solution to their discontent lies in relearning and reflecting on truths they should have known and reopening their ears to divine revelation. Isaiah reassures the exiles that Yahweh, as the Creator of heaven and earth, is not bound by geography. His sovereignty extends to all spheres, including Babylon, even if he is not acknowledged there.

This passage ultimately seeks to restore Judah's faith by emphasizing Yahweh's continued involvement, his unmatched power, and his faithfulness to his people despite their exile.

To better understand the in/comprehensibility of God, the semantic important elements in Isa 40:28 that directly relate to the concept will now be analyzed for better comprehension of the theological depth of God's character.

KEY CONCEPTS

Through Isaiah's message, the dialogue between God and his disheartened people employs every possible means of persuasion, appealing to both reason and emotion. Isaiah presents arguments and evidence (Isa 43:10) to make God known as clearly as possible, emphasizing his eternal nature, creative power, omnipotence, omniscience, and the unfathomable depth of his understanding.

A particular focus is given to God's eternal nature and the immeasurable depth of his understanding. Isaiah 40:28 highlights two key elements of God's nature: תְּבוּנָה (*understanding*)[17] and חֵקֶר (*fathoming or searching*),[18] with the negation אֵין, meaning *none* or *without*. Together, these terms underscore the incomprehensibility of God's understanding, reinforcing that his knowledge surpasses human grasp.

---

16. Blenkinsopp, *Isaiah 40–55*, 194.
17. Swanson, "תְּבוּנָה (tĕ·ḇû·nā(h)," 9312.
18. Swanson, "חֵקֶר (ḥē·qěr)," 2984.

The Everlasting God

God's eternal nature and his unsearchable understanding go hand in hand. The term "everlasting God" (אֱלֹהֵי עוֹלָם) implies that time is, in effect, hidden with him. Time does not affect him; thus, he is incorruptible and unlimited. When (עוֹלָם) is used concerning God, it signifies his unceasing work, covenant, word, promises, and laws. In other words, the eternity of God himself cannot be tied to time as his actions in the world are. He existed before time existed. Thus, God is not subject to time, although he operates within it through his reign over history.[19] As such, God transcends all human affairs but is not detached from humanity, as the history of humankind is governed by him and his word. Although humanity and its history are fleeting, God operates within this temporal realm, using his word—revealed and fulfilled in prophecy—in stark contrast to the temporary things on which humans depend.[20] From conception to death, humans are inherently bound by time, making it difficult to comprehend a being who operates within time and history yet remains unbound by it.

This character trait of God introduces the following Hebrew terms for discussion, emphasizing God's *unsearchable understanding* (אֵין חֵקֶר לִתְבוּנָתוֹ).

God's Understanding is Unsearchable.

Swanson[21] explains God's *understanding* (תְּבוּנָה) as the capacity to discern a right course or action. Judah failed to grasp this course of action, namely the path Yahweh had set for his covenant people, shaped by his character and understanding. Ringgren[22] further emphasizes the close relationship between God's wisdom and complete understanding, highlighting how it directly influences his actions. These perspectives underscore Yahweh's answers to practical questions, such as Judah's situation in Babylon. His intentional involvement in shaping Judah's history according to his divine plan would eventually lead to the remnant's return (Isa 6:11–13).

Regarding the notion of God's understanding, Westermann states, "Those who have Yahweh as their God: his understanding is illimitable and

---

19. Jenni, "עוֹלָם ôlām Eternity," 859.
20. Keil and Delitzsch, *Isaiah*, 401.
21. Swanson, "תְּבוּנָה (teû·nā(h)," 9312.
22. Ringgren, "בִּין,"106.

therefore unsearchable; his designs infinitely outstrip those possibilities for the future which Israel herself can see."²³

The answer to Judah's complaints against God thus lies in the possibilities that exist for him but remain hidden from their understanding. For Judah, the reign of Cyrus still lay in the future and was unbeknown to them. However, Yahweh would use him as his *anointed* to fulfill his promise of a remnant that will return to the promised land. Thus, Isaiah had to re-educate Judah, not only about events in their past but also about how their future would unfold, a future determined by *their God, Yahweh*. This insight, which they had not comprehended before, could not be grasped as long as they interpreted God solely through the lens of their *circumstances* because his *unsearchable understanding* transcends human comprehension.

This inability to fully grasp God's understanding highlights the distinction between human reasoning, which is shaped by circumstances, gradual learning, and divine knowledge.

Tsevat's explanation of חֵקֶר (fathoming or searching) further indicates it as a purely intellectual and analytical approach to examination and testing. Unlike human understanding, which progresses and often relies on analysis, God's knowledge is characterized by immediacy and completeness. However, due to the anthropomorphic ways in which people tend to conceptualize and discuss divine attributes, certain inconsistencies in terminology are to be expected.²⁴

When applying Tsevat's explanation to the context of Isaiah, the disparity between Judah's understanding and God's knowledge becomes evident. As exile approached for Judah, their analysis of unfolding events was ongoing. They interpreted these developments based on their perception of themselves and their limited understanding of Yahweh. Judah believed Yahweh would protect them from being exiled from the promised land. However, in Yahweh's complete assessment, he knew Israel had persistently transgressed the covenant and repented half–heartedly. Consequently, the curse element of the covenant (Deut 28:36) needed to be enforced, as Yahweh had grown weary of their transgressions (Isa 1:14).

Concluding what has been said about God's *eternity* and *perfect understanding*, his comprehensive and immediate judgment of Judah's history as a nation determined that the covenant curse needed to be enforced despite their belief that Yahweh would protect them from calamity. When their own God delivered them into the hands of the Babylonians, whom he had sent, it clashed with their perception of his righteous character. As a result,

---

23. Westermann, *Isaiah 40–66*, 57.
24. Tsevat, "חָקַר," 149.

their analysis led them to conclude that the problem was with God rather than themselves. Their flawed understanding thus necessitated a process of reeducation.

Despite Judah's perception, God remained actively and dynamically involved with his people, just as he was when he delivered them from Egypt. Just as he fulfilled his promises to Abraham at that time, he also fulfilled his covenantal promises of judgment during the exile. However, he would also fulfill his promise to preserve a remnant, for he remains eternally faithful. Because God is eternal and faithful, his ongoing activity as Lord of history and for the benefit of his people is therefore proclaimed in Isa 40–66. However, due to their circumstances, they were unable to comprehend that the exile served the purpose of strengthening his relationship with his people.

In the final verses of Isa 40, human frailty is contrasted with the strength of those who trust in God and patiently wait for him. As part of his long-term plan, he will lead a faithful remnant back to the promised land from Babylon. Judah lacked this hope for the future because they failed to grasp that God's understanding far surpasses their own. However, through Isaiah, God revealed his wisdom anew to his people, offering them reassurance and a deeper perspective on his divine purpose. The ultimate aim of the return from exile is a return to Yahweh.[25]

CONCLUSION

Isaiah 40 is a transitional chapter in the canonical book. The calamity foretold in chapters 1–39 is prophesied as coming to an end. Judah, however, doubted whether the comfort that Isaiah announced would be realized because they doubted Yahweh's ability and presence in Babylon. Through rhetorical questions and hyperboles, Isaiah reeducated Judah on God's sovereignty, eternity, omnipotence, and omniscience, emphasizing his supreme authority over creation, nations, and idols, affirming his unchanging rule. God's plans and actions in Judah's history transcend human intellectual ability, which may lead to uncertainty and despair because of an inability to comprehend. While his power and knowledge go beyond human understanding, he continues to reveal himself, making his presence known. During their exile, Judah questioned God, but Isaiah corrected their misconceptions, reminding them that their relationship with Yahweh never depended on the land or temple.

This chapter shifts from judgment to restoration, showing how God's revelation sufficiently bridges the gap between limited human

---

25. Blenkinsopp, *Beauty of Holiness*, 57.

comprehension and his divine nature. Judah mistakenly believed their suffering meant God had abandoned their right, but Isaiah reassures them that Yahweh's wisdom, power, and faithfulness remain constant, regardless of their circumstances. Though exile was a consequence of their actions, it ultimately strengthened trust in him because of Isaiah's prophetic reeducation. God's everlasting presence brings renewal, hope, and restoration, reaffirming his covenantal bond with his people. In the end, his self-revelation provides knowledge and strengthens faith and worship, helping Judah recognize his enduring sovereignty and thus ensuring the return of the remnant and hope for the future.

The following quotation from Isaiah is, in all probability, the best conclusion after all has been said:

> Isaiah 55:8–9 (NRSV)
>
> "8 For my thoughts are not your thoughts,
>   nor are your ways my ways, says the Lord.
> 9 For as the heavens are higher than the earth,
>   so are my ways higher than your ways
>   and my thoughts than your thoughts."

BIBLIOGRAPHY

Abernethy, Andrew T. *The Book of Isaiah and God's Kingdom: A Thematic-Theological Approach*. New Studies in Biblical Theology 40. Downers Grove, IL: IVP Academic, 2016.

Baumann, A. "כול." In *Theological Dictionary of the Old Testament*, vol. 7, edited by G. Johannes Botterweck and Helmer Ringgren, Translated by Geoffrey W. Bromiley et al., 7:85–89. Grand Rapids: Eerdmans, 1995.

Blenkinsopp, Joseph. *The Beauty of Holiness: Re-Reading Isaiah in the Light of the Psalms*. London: T&T Clark, 2019.

———. *Isaiah 40-55: A New Translation with Introduction and Commentary*. Vol. 19A of *Anchor Yale Bible*. New Haven: Yale University Press, 2008.

Grogan, Geoffrey W. *Proverbs-Isaiah*. Revised edition. Edited by Tremper Longman III and David E. Garland. Vol. 6 of *The Expositor's Bible Commentary*. Grand Rapids: Zondervan, 2008.

Henry, Carl F. H. *God, Revelation, and Authority*. Vol. 5. Wheaton: Crossway, 1999.

Jenni, Ernst. עוֹלָם (*'ôlām) Eternity*. In *Theological Lexicon of the Old Testament*, edited by Ernst Jenni and Claus Westermann, translated by Mark Biddle, 852–62. Peabody, MA: Hendrickson, 1997.

Keil, C. F., and Delitzsch, Franz. *Isaiah. Commentary on the Old Testament*. Peabody, Massachusetts: Hendrickson, 1996.

Koole, J. L. *Jesaja II, deel 1: Jesaja 40-48*. Historical Commentary on the Old Testament. Kampen: Kok, 1985.

Leupold, H. C. *Exposition of Isaiah*. Vol. 2. London: Evangelical, 1974.

Motyer, J. A. *Isaiah: An Introduction and Commentary*. Tyndale Old Testament Commentaries 18. Leicester: Inter-Varsity, 1999.

Paul, Shalom M. *Isaiah 40-66: Translation and Commentary*. Eerdmans Critical Commentary. Grand Rapids: Eerdmans, 2012.

Ringgren, Helmer. בִּין *bîn;* בִּינָה *bînāh;* תְּבוּנָה *tebhûnāh*. In *Theological Dictionary of the Old Testament*, vol. 2, edited by G. Johannes Botterweck and Helmer Ringgren, translated by Geoffrey W. Bromiley et al., 99–107. Grand Rapids: Eerdmans, 1975.

Smith, G. V. *Isaiah 40-66*. New American Commentary. Nashville: Broadman & Holman, 2009.

Swanson, James. "חֵקֶר *(ḥē·qěr)*." In *Dictionary of Biblical Languages with Semantic Domains: Hebrew (Old Testament)*. Oak Harbor, WA: Logos, 1997a.

———. נָחַם *(nā·ḥǎm)*. In *Dictionary of Biblical Languages with Semantic Domains: Hebrew (Old Testament)*. Oak Harbor, WA: Logos, 1997b.

———. תְּבוּנָה *(te⊠û·nāh)*. In *Dictionary of Biblical Languages with Semantic Domains: Hebrew (Old Testament)*. Oak Harbor, WA: Logos, 1997c.

Tsevat, M. חָקַר. In *Theological Dictionary of the Old Testament*, vol. 5, edited by G. Johannes Botterweck and Helmer Ringgren, translated by Geoffrey W. Bromiley et al., 148–50. Grand Rapids: Eerdmans, 1986.

Van der Walt, C. "Does 'Righteous' Have Degrees of Comparison? God's Righteousness and the Righteousness of Humanity in Habakkuk." In *Biblical Theological Investigations into the Righteousness of God*, edited by A. J. Coetsee and F. P. Viljoen. Cambridge: Cambridge Scholars, 2024.

Watts, John D. W. *Isaiah 34-66*. Vol. 25 of *Word Biblical Commentary*. Dallas, Texas: Word, 2005.

Westermann, Claus. *Isaiah 40-66: A Commentary*. Old Testament Library. London: SCM, 1996.

Chapter 7

Jesus Reveals the Incomprehensible God by Sharing Exclusive Knowledge with Humble Followers: A Biblical Theological Investigation into Matthew 11:25–30 and Luke 10:21–22

—Francois P. Viljoen

    Unit for Reformational Theology and the Development of the South African Society, Faculty of Theology, North-West University, Potchefstroom, South Africa

ABSTRACT

Matthew 11:25–30 describes a situation that seems odd. Jesus and John have been rejected by "this generation," but instead of complaining about this, Jesus thanks God. He thanks God for hiding "these things" for one type of people, while "revealing" them to a different type (Matt 11:25–26 // Luke 10:21). The question arises as to what "these things" refer. It seems that the answer lies in Jesus's declaration (Matt 11:27 // Luke 10:22) and invitation (Matt 11:28–30) that follows. Jesus claims to have exclusive knowledge of God due to his unique relationship as the Son of the Father. God is incomprehensible to all but Jesus. However, Jesus claims to have the gift of revealing his Father to whom he chooses. The Matthean narrative proceeds with Jesus's invitation to all the weary to find rest with him. This invitation contains a paradox. Instead of advising the burdened to escape, he calls them to take up his yoke. In Judaism, taking up the yoke is frequently used as a metaphor for obeying the Torah. The Torah contains the revelation of God and his will for human beings. By carrying this yoke, one is equipped with the knowledge of God to deal with the burdens of life. Matthew identifies Jesus with the Torah, which makes him the full revelation of God and his will. He reveals God with his words (Sermon on the Mount, Matt 5–7) and works (10 miracles, Matt 8–9). Those who arrogantly reject his words and works cannot get to know God. Jesus's invitation follows after Matthew has identified him with "Wisdom" who was rejected (Matt 11:19). Like the invitation of "Wisdom" in Jewish traditions, Jesus extends his invitation to the gentle and humble in heart to gain knowledge.

The chapter investigates the question of what "these things" that are "hidden" and "revealed" precisely entails, and how this relates to the incomprehensibility of God; what Jesus reveals about God; and what qualifies a human to receive such revelation.

INTRODUCTION

Matthew 11:25–30 and Luke 10:21–22 present an intriguing scenario. Despite being rejected by unrepentant cities (Matt 11:20–25 // Luke 10:10–15), Jesus does not complain. Instead, he thanks God for concealing "these things" from one group of people while revealing them to another (Matt 11:25–26 // Luke 10:21). This raises the question of what "these things" refer to. The answer appears to lie in Jesus's assertion that "knowledge" resides in him (Matt 11:27 // Luke 10:22) and the subsequent invitation to find knowledge with him (Matt 11:28–30). This chapter explores what "these things" that are "hidden" and "revealed" specifically entail and how this relates to the incomprehensibility of God. What does Jesus reveal about God, and what qualifies a person to receive such revelation?

The passage opens by setting the scene (Matt 11:25a // Luke 10:21a), then transitions to Jesus's thanksgiving (Matt 11:25–26 // Luke 10:21b). This is followed by his Christological declaration that knowledge resides with him (Matt 11:27 // Luke 10:22), and concludes with his invitation, unique to Matthew (Matt 11:28–30). The parallel between Matthew's and Luke's versions is illustrated in the table below.

Table 3: The parallel between Matthew's and Luke's versions of Jesus's revelations about God

Matthew 11:25–30	Luke 10:21–22
Scene (Matt 11:25a) Ἐν ἐκείνῳ τῷ καιρῷ ἀποκριθεὶς ὁ Ἰησοῦς εἶπεν	**Scene (Luke 10:21a)** Ἐν αὐτῇ τῇ ὥρᾳ ἠγαλλιάσατο τῷ Πνεύματι τῷ Ἁγίῳ καὶ εἶπεν
Thanksgiving (Matt 11:25b–26) **Ἐξομολογοῦμαί σοι**, Πάτερ, Κύριε τοῦ οὐρανοῦ καὶ τῆς γῆς, ὅτι ἔκρυψας ταῦτα ἀπὸ σοφῶν καὶ συνετῶν, καὶ ἀπεκάλυψας αὐτὰ νηπίοις· ναί, ὁ Πατήρ, ὅτι οὕτως εὐδοκία ἐγένετο ἔμπροσθέν σου.	**Thanksgiving (Luke 10:21b)** **Ἐξομολογοῦμαί σοι**, Πάτερ, Κύριε τοῦ οὐρανοῦ καὶ τῆς γῆς, ὅτι ἀπέκρυψας ταῦτα ἀπὸ σοφῶν καὶ συνετῶν, καὶ ἀπεκάλυψας αὐτὰ νηπίοις· ναί, ὁ Πατήρ, ὅτι οὕτως εὐδοκία ἐγένετο ἔμπροσθέν σου.
Knowledge residing in Jesus (Matt 11:27) **Πάντα μοι παρεδόθη** ὑπὸ τοῦ Πατρός μου, καὶ οὐδεὶς ἐπιγινώσκει τὸν Υἱὸν εἰ μὴ ὁ Πατήρ, οὐδὲ τὸν Πατέρα τις ἐπιγινώσκει εἰ μὴ ὁ Υἱὸς καὶ ᾧ ἐὰν βούληται ὁ Υἱὸς ἀποκαλύψαι.	**Knowledge residing in Jesus (Luke 10:22)** **πάντα μοι παρεδόθη** ὑπὸ τοῦ Πατρός μου, καὶ οὐδεὶς γινώσκει τίς ἐστιν ὁ Υἱὸς εἰ μὴ ὁ Πατήρ, καὶ τίς ἐστιν ὁ Πατὴρ εἰ μὴ ὁ Υἱὸς καὶ ᾧ ἐὰν βούληται ὁ Υἱὸς ἀποκαλύψαι.
Invitation to knowledge (Matt 11:28–30) **Δεῦτε πρός με** πάντες οἱ κοπιῶντες καὶ πεφορτισμένοι, κἀγὼ ἀναπαύσω ὑμᾶς. ἄρατε τὸν ζυγόν μου ἐφ' ὑμᾶς καὶ μάθετε ἀπ' ἐμοῦ, ὅτι πραΰς εἰμι καὶ ταπεινὸς τῇ καρδίᾳ, καὶ εὑρήσετε ἀνάπαυσιν ταῖς ψυχαῖς ὑμῶν· ὁ γὰρ ζυγός μου χρηστὸς καὶ τὸ φορτίον μου ἐλαφρόν ἐστιν.	

Matthew 11:25-30	Luke 10:21-22
Scene (Matt 11:25a) At that time Jesus said,	**Scene (Luke 10:21a)** In that same hour Jesus rejoiced in the Holy Spirit and said,
Thanksgiving (Matt 11:25-26) "**I thank you,** Father, Lord of heaven and earth, because you have hidden these things from the wise and the intelligent and revealed them to infants children; yes, Father, for such was your gracious will.	**Thanksgiving (Luke 10:21b)** "**I thank you,** Father, Lord of heaven and earth, because you have hidden these things from the wise and the intelligent and revealed them to infants; yes, Father, for such was your gracious will."
Knowledge residing in Jesus (Matt 11:27) **All things have been handed over to me** by my Father, and no one knows the Son except the Father, and no one knows the Father except the Son and anyone to whom the Son chooses to reveal him.	**Knowledge residing in Jesus (Luke 10:22)** **All things have been handed over to me** by my Father, and no one knows who the Son is except the Father, or who the Father is except the Son and anyone to whom the Son chooses to reveal him."[1]
Invitation to knowledge (Matt 11:28-30) **Come to me,** all you who are weary and are carrying heavy burdens, and I will give you rest. Take my yoke upon you, and learn from me; for I am gentle and humble in heart, and you will find rest for your souls. For my yoke is easy, and my burden is light."	

The chapter begins with an overview of the narrative context of these utterances in Matthew and Luke, followed by a semantic analysis of each. These utterances reveal contrasting parallels between what is concealed from one group and what is disclosed to another. These parallels illuminate the contrast between God's incomprehensibility and his comprehensibility through selective self-revelation.

---

1. Translation in the tables are taken form the New Revised Standard Version (NRSV), but translation in the article text are my own direct translations.

NARRATIVE CONTEXT OF JESUS'S UTTERANCES

Jesus's utterances in Matthew and Luke should be interpreted within their broader narrative contexts. This entails examining the preceding events and observing how elements from these utterances reappear in the subsequent narratives.

The Matthean Context

Despite Jesus's revelations, he is consistently met with misunderstanding and unbelief. Opposition and rejection are recurring themes throughout the narrative. Jesus is misunderstood by various individuals, including the Pharisees and his own family. Even those meant to support him, such as John's disciples, fail to grasp his message. Although some accepted his revelations, he faced significant rejection. His statements of concealment and revelation in Matt 11:25–30 encapsulate the culmination of the rejection and acceptance he experienced.

Revelation and Concealment

REVELATION IN WORDS AND DEEDS

The Matthean Jesus reveals himself through both words and deeds. Significant in Matthew's Gospel are his five teaching blocks:[2] the Sermon on the Mount (Matt 5–7), the Mission Discourse (Matt 10), the Parable Discourse (Matt 13), the Discourse on the Church (Matt 18), and the Discourse on End Times (Matt 23–25).[3] Jesus's teachings in the Sermon on the Mount (Matt 5–7) are complemented by a series of healing miracles and the calming of the storm (Matt 8–9).[4] He responds positively to the inquiry of John's dis-

---

2. The closing formula ὅτε ἐτέλεσεν ὁ Ἰησοῦς τοὺς λόγους τούτους (when Jesus had finished these words) signifies the conclusion of each of these teachings (Matt 7:28, 11:1, 13:53, 19:1, and 26:1).

3. I regard chapters 23 to 25 as constituting the final discourse, given the contrasting parallel between the beatitudes in the Sermon on the Mount and the woe sayings in Matt 23. However, some scholars prefer to limit the final discourse to chapters 24 and 25.

4. The contrast between the ten plagues by Moses and the healings performed by Jesus is striking. The miracle narratives showcase Jesus's compassion and authority over illness, nature, demons, paralysis, disabilities, and death. The early Christian text, Pseudo-Clementine, highlights this similarity and contrast. "As Moses did signs and

ciples by revealing his identity through passages from Isaiah (Matt 11:2–6).[5] These revelations culminate in Jesus's outcry in Matthew 11:25–30.

Revelation continues beyond this scene. Jesus heals many who follow him, instructing them not to reveal their experiences (Matt 12:15–21). He heals a blind and mute man λαλεῖν καὶ βλέπειν (to speak and see, Matt 12:22–30). He imparts τὰ μυστήρια τῆς βασιλείας τῶν οὐρανῶν (the mysteries of the kingdom of heaven) to his disciples (Matt 13:11). Jesus uses parables to disclose hidden truths κεκρυμμένα ἀπὸ καταβολῆς [κόσμου][6] (things concealed since the foundation [of the world], Matt 13:35).[7] He teaches in the synagogue of his hometown, and the people ἐκπλήσσεσθαι (were astonished). They asked from where ἡ σοφία αὕτη καὶ αἱ δυνάμεις (the wisdom and mighty works), though they question him (Matt 13:53–58). At Peter's confession of Jesus as the Christ, the Son of the living God, Jesus declares Peter blessed, as σὰρξ καὶ αἷμα οὐκ ἀπεκάλυψέν σοι ἀλλ' ὁ Πατήρ μου ὁ ἐν τοῖς οὐρανοῖς (flesh and blood did not reveal this to you, but my Father in heaven, Matt 16:17).

The disciples are uniquely privileged to receive Jesus's special revelations, which are not shared with the general crowds. They are entrusted with the secret meanings of Jesus's parables (Matt 13:11–17, 34–35).[8] Among the disciples, Peter is particularly distinguished by the depth of knowledge and revelation he receives, earning him the role of the rock upon which Jesus will build his church (Matt 16:18). Additionally, Peter, James, and John are granted the extraordinary experience of witnessing the theophany on the Mountain of Transfiguration (Matt 17:1–8).

---

miracles, so also did Jesus. And there is no doubt but that the likeness of the signs proves him (Jesus) to be that prophet of whom he (Moses) said that he should come 'like myself'". Pseudo-Clementine, *Recognitiones*, 1.57.

5. Isa 26:19; 29:28–29; 35:5–6 and 61:1.

6. More reliable manuscripts do not have κόσμου.

7. While parables reveal the mysteries of the kingdom, they also conceal them. It seems that parables by nature were enigmatic and required explanation. Hultgren, *Parables*, 456. Jewish leaders commonly used parables as illustrations to clarify their teachings. Keener, *Matthew*, 378. However, if they provided only the illustration without the underlying message, it remained a riddle (Test Abr 12–13A). In the context of Jesus's ministry, this means that only those who knew him could understand his parables. For those who rejected him, such as the Pharisees, the parables remained enigmatic (cf. Matt 12:24–45).

8. The Synoptic Gospels vividly portray the disciples' difficulties in comprehending Jesus's parables, frequently necessitating additional clarification. Jesus employed parables in his public teachings but subsequently explained their meanings in private (cf. Mark 4:33–34; 6:30–31; 7:14–17; 9:28, 33; 10:10). Culpepper, *Mark*, 137. Through this method, Jesus revealed the apocalyptic secrets of the imminent eschatological reign of God. Witherington, *Matthew*, 263.

It is within this broader literary context that Jesus thanks the Father for revealing these things to the little ones (ἀπεκάλυψας αὐτὰ νηπίοις) and to those to whom the Son chooses to reveal them (ᾧ ἐὰν βούληται ὁ Υἱὸς ἀποκαλύψαι, Matt 11:25-27).

Jesus acts as the agent of this revelation. The content of this revelation is both eschatological and apocalyptic. With Jesus, the kingdom of heaven arrives, and a new order is inaugurated.

Concealment

In contrast to his revelations, themes of concealment also appear in the narrative. Jesus emphatically orders the man he healed from leprosy, Ὅρα μηδενὶ εἴπῃς (See not to tell anyone, Matt 8:4). Later, he instructs those he has healed, ἵνα μὴ φανερὸν αὐτὸν ποιήσωσιν (not to make him known, Matt 12:16). In the parable discourse, Jesus states that τὰ μυστήρια τῆς βασιλείας τῶν οὐρανῶν (the mysteries of the kingdom of heaven) are not granted to the crowds (Matt 13:11). He warns his disciples, μηδενὶ εἴπωσιν ὅτι αὐτός ἐστιν ὁ Χριστός (they should say to no one that he is the Christ, Matthew 16:20). The greatest secret remains, Περὶ δὲ τῆς ἡμέρας ἐκείνης καὶ ὥρας οὐδεὶς οἶδεν, οὐδὲ οἱ ἄγγελοι τῶν οὐρανῶν [οὐδὲ ὁ Υἱός], εἰ μὴ ὁ Πατὴρ μόνος (about that day and the hour [of the Son of Man], no one knows, not even the angels in heaven, [nor the Son], but the Father only, Matt 24:36).

It is also within this context that Jesus thanks the Father for ἔκρυψας ταῦτα ἀπὸ σοφῶν καὶ συνετῶν (hiding these things from the wise and learned, Matt 11:25).

Acceptance and Rejection

Acceptance

Equally significant in this Gospel are the themes of acceptance, perception, and understanding. John and his disciples inquire in good faith about the identity of Jesus, asking, Σὺ εἶ ὁ ἐρχόμενος (Are you the one who is to come?, Matt 11:3). In contrast to his disbelieving mother and brothers, Jesus states, ὅστις γὰρ ἂν ποιήσῃ τὸ θέλημα τοῦ Πατρός μου τοῦ ἐν οὐρανοῖς, αὐτός μου ἀδελφὸς καὶ ἀδελφὴ καὶ μήτηρ ἐστίν (whoever does the will of my Father in heaven is my brother and sister and mother, Matt 12:49-50). In the parable discourse, Jesus states that his disciples βλέπετε (see) and ἀκούετε (hear,

Matt 13:17). In his explanation of the parable of the sower, the good soil is compared to ὁ τὸν λόγον ἀκούων καὶ συνιείς (the one who hears the word and understands it, Matt 13:23). Jesus tells the parable of the net, and his disciples respond positively to his question about whether they have understood all these things, συνήκατε ταῦτα πάντα; λέγουσιν αὐτῷ Ναί (have you understood all these things? They answered him, "Yes," Matt 13:51).

Considering these positive responses, Jesus thanks the Father that the νήπιοι (little ones) receive revelation (Matt 11:25).

Rejection

In contrast to the theme of acceptance, rejection is also prominent in the Gospel. This rejection begins in the birth narrative with Herod's suspicion, conspiracy, and cruel infanticide (Matt 2:1–18). The Pharisees criticize Jesus for eating with tax collectors and sinners, asking, διὰ τί μετὰ τῶν τελωνῶν καὶ ἁμαρτωλῶν ἐσθίει ὁ διδάσκαλος ὑμῶν (why does your master eat with tax collectors and sinners?, Matt 9:11). After Jesus has healed a mute man, the Pharisees accuse him, saying, Ἐν τῷ ἄρχοντι τῶν δαιμονίων ἐκβάλλει τὰ δαιμόνια (it is by the prince of demons that he casts out demons, Matt 9:34).

Jesus's words in Matt 11:25–30 follow directly after his pronouncements of woe on the Galilean cities of Chorazin, Bethsaida, and Capernaum[9] (Matt 11:20–24 // Luke 10:13–15). Despite his mighty works (δυνάμεις)[10] among them, they refused to repent,[11] leading to strong expressions of complaint, οὐαί (woe, Matt 11:20–24).

Immediately following these words, the Sabbath controversy between the Pharisees and Jesus is described. Matthew portrays the Pharisees as critical of Jesus's behavior and malicious in their intent. They challenge Jesus for allowing his disciples to pluck grain on the Sabbath (Matt 12:1–8) and for healing a man with a withered hand (Matt 12:9–14). The Pharisees συμβούλιον ἔλαβον κατ' αὐτοῦ ὅπως αὐτὸν ἀπολέσωσιν (held counsel against him how to destroy him, Matt 12:14).

The narrative continues with a Scripture quotation identifying Jesus as God's chosen servant who was fulfilling prophecy (Matt 12:15–21).

---

9. The woe pronounced against Capernaum, the city of Jesus, carries significant weight due to its solemn biblical language and its resemblance in wording to the judgment against Nebuchadnezzar in Isaiah 14:13–15. Luz, *Matthew*, 153.

10. The δυνάμεις (mighty works) refer to Jesus's healing miracles in Matt 7:22; 13:54, 58; 14:2.

11. The traditional biblical values are inverted by contrasting the cities of Israel with gentile cities. Judgment, which was originally directed against foreign nations, is now applied to Israel. Luz, *Matthew*, 153.

However, in the very next scene, the Pharisees accuse Jesus of exorcising ἐν τῷ Βεελζεβοὺλ ἄρχοντι τῶν δαιμονίων (by Beelzebul, the prince of demons) when he healed a blind and mute man who was said to be demon-possessed (Matt 12:22–30). While Jesus is depicted as the embodiment and source of mercy, he is criticized for it. In Nazareth, Jesus is met with skepticism, unbelief, and rejection by his fellow townsfolk, who ἐσκανδαλίζοντο ἐν αὐτῷ (are offended by him) when listening to his parables (Matt 13:57). The Pharisees and scribes confront Jesus because his disciples do not observe the tradition of handwashing (Matt 15:1–20).[12] The Pharisees and Sadducees test Jesus by asking for σημεῖον ἐκ τοῦ οὐρανοῦ (a sign from heaven), but Jesus responds by directing them to τὸ σημεῖον Ἰωνᾶ (the sign of Jonah, Matt 16:1, 4).

While the rejection of Jesus by the Jewish leaders is a recurring theme throughout the Gospel, the conflict reaches its peak during the passion week, culminating in Matt 21–28. Matthew 21:23–22:46 details various challenges posed by the religious leaders to discredit Jesus and contest his authority to teach. They position themselves on a legal and moral high ground, and their challenges become increasingly sophisticated.[13] The conflict begins with the chief priests and elders questioning his authority (Matt 21:23), followed by the disciples of the Pharisees and Herodians challenging him on paying taxes to Caesar (Matt 22:15), the Sadducees questioning him about the resurrection (Matt 22:23), and an expert in the law testing him on the greatest commandment (Matt 22:35).

These episodes clearly illustrate that knowledge is hidden from them.

The Lukan Context

When examining the parallel utterances in Luke 10:21–22, similar motifs can be recognized. Jesus's words follow his Galilean ministry (Luke 4:14–9:50), where he reveals his authority and power through teachings and miracles. In some instances, this leads to positive amazement, understanding, and confession of him. However, in other cases, it results in rejection and opposition. Miracles play a prominent role through which Jesus demonstrates his power and authority.

---

12. Matthew 15:1–20 parallels the handwashing dispute described in Mark 7:1–23. In his more concise account (almost by half), Matthew omits the explanation of the ceremony (Mark 7:2–4) and the declaration that Jesus made all food clean (Mark 7:19). Instead, Matthew includes a parable and condemns the leaders as "blind guides" (Matt 15:4–6). The Pharisees are depicted as being preoccupied with external, man-made rules to ensure purity, while Jesus emphasizes inner purity based on God's word.

13. Simmonds, "Woe to You," 338.

Revelation and Concealment

Jesus's revelation in teachings and miracles

Jesus begins his ministry in Galilee as αὐτὸς ἐδίδασκεν (he taught regularly) in their synagogues (Luke 4:15). The perfect indicative form of the verb indicates a repeating action.[14] When reading from the Isaian scroll (Isa 61:1–2), he identifies himself as the one in whom this prophecy is fulfilled, Σήμερον πεπλήρωται ἡ γραφὴ (today the Scripture is fulfilled, Luke 4:21). Through a series of teachings, he imparts knowledge to the people of Nazareth (Luke 4:32) and declares his mission to preach the kingdom of God (Luke 4:42–44).

In addition to his teachings, Jesus performs a series of healing miracles. He heals a demon-possessed man by rebuking the demon, saying, Φιμώθητι καὶ ἔξελθε ἀπ' αὐτοῦ (be silent and come out of him, Luke 4:35). He heals Simon's mother-in-law, as he ἐπετίμησεν τῷ πυρετῷ (rebuked the fever, Luke 4:39). He heals many suffering from various kinds of sickness by ἑνὶ ἑκάστῳ αὐτῶν τὰς χεῖρας ἐπιτιθεὶς (laying his hands on each of them, Luke 4:40). He heals a man with leprosy by ἐκτείνας τὴν χεῖρα ἥψατο αὐτοῦ (stretching out his hand he touched him, Luke 5:13). Crowds come to hear him and θεραπεύεσθαι ἀπὸ τῶν ἀσθενειῶν αὐτῶν (to be healed of their sicknesses, Luke 5:15). He tells the paralytic, ἔγειρε καὶ ἄρας τὸ κλινίδιόν σου πορεύου εἰς τὸν οἶκόν σου (stand up, take your mat, and go to your home, Luke 5:24–25). He tells the man with the shriveled hand, Ἔκτεινον τὴν χεῖρά σου . . . καὶ ἀπεκατεστάθη ἡ χεὶρ αὐτοῦ (Stretch out your hand . . . and his hand was healed, Luke 6:10). A large crowd comes to hear him ἰαθῆναι ἀπὸ τῶν νόσων αὐτῶν, καὶ οἱ ἐνοχλούμενοι ἀπὸ πνευμάτων ἀκαθάρτων ἐθεραπεύοντο (to be healed from their diseases, and those troubled by evil spirits were cleansed, Luke 6:18). He heals the centurion's servant from a distance (Luke 7:10). He raises the son of the widow of Nain by simply instructing him, ἐγέρθητι (stand up, Luke 7:15). He cures many who have diseases, sicknesses, are troubled by evil spirits, and are blind (Luke 7:22). He heals the demon-possessed man by sending the evil spirits into a herd of pigs (Luke 8:32–33). The bleeding woman ἥψατο τοῦ κρασπέδου τοῦ ἱματίου αὐτοῦ, καὶ παραχρῆμα ἔστη ἡ ῥύσις τοῦ αἵματος αὐτῆς (touches the fringe of his cloak, and immediately her blood flow stops, Luke 8:44). He raises Jairus's daughter by telling her, Ἡ παῖς, ἔγειρε (Child, get up, Luke 8:55). He heals the boy with the evil

---

14. Levine and Witherington, *Luke*, 112.

spirit as ἐπετίμησεν δὲ ὁ Ἰησοῦς τῷ πνεύματι τῷ ἀκαθάρτῳ, καὶ ἰάσατο τὸν παῖδα (Jesus rebuked the evil spirit and healed the boy, Luke 9:42).

In addition to his healings, Jesus demonstrates his power by calming the storm. As it is written, ἐπετίμησεν τῷ ἀνέμῳ καὶ τῷ κλύδωνι τοῦ ὕδατος καὶ ἐπαύσαντο, καὶ ἐγένετο γαλήνη (he rebuked the wind and the raging of the water, and they ceased, and there was calm, Luke 8:24). He also fed five thousand people with five loaves of bread and two fish (Luke 9:16-17).

The culmination of his revelation occurs after his resurrection when he converses with the travelers to Emmaus. Initially, they do not recognize him, but διερμήνευσεν αὐτοῖς ἐν πάσαις ταῖς γραφαῖς τὰ περὶ ἑαυτοῦ (he interpreted to them in all the Scriptures the things concerning himself, Luke 24:27). When he breaks the bread and gives it to them, αὐτῶν δὲ διηνοίχθησαν οἱ ὀφθαλμοί, καὶ ἐπέγνωσαν αὐτόν (their eyes were opened, and they recognized him, Luke 24:31). Later, he appears to the disciples and διήνοιξεν αὐτῶν τὸν νοῦν τοῦ συνιέναι τὰς γραφάς (he opened their minds to understand the Scriptures, Luke 24:45).

Through these revelations, Jesus calls his disciples, awakening their faith and understanding. He warns them of opposition and encourages them to stand firm.

Concealment

Yet the theme of concealment also surfaces. Jesus instructs the man he had cleansed of leprosy αὐτῷ μηδενὶ εἰπεῖν (not to tell anyone), but to show himself to the priests (Luke 5:14), and Jairus and his wife μηδενὶ εἰπεῖν τὸ γεγονός (not to tell what had happened) after raising their daughter (Luke 8:56). Jesus spoke in parables ἵνα βλέποντες μὴ βλέπωσιν καὶ ἀκούοντες μὴ συνιῶσιν (so that [the rest][15] would not see while seeing and not understand while hearing) the secrets of the kingdom of God (Luke 8:10). Jesus παρήγγειλεν μηδενὶ λέγειν τοῦτο (instructed [his disciples] not to tell it) after Peter's confession that Jesus is the Christ of God (Luke 9:21).

15. Jesus distinguishes between the group with him and those on the outside. In Mark, the outside group is clearly defined as "those on the outside" (ἐκείνοις δὲ τοῖς ἔξω). Although Jesus's invitation to listen in Mark 4:3 and 4:9 is addressed to everyone, the secret of God's kingdom is given only to those ready to receive it. Hooker, "Parables," 91. Matthew also refers to "those" (ἐκείνοις) but omits "on the outside." Luke doesn't clearly delineate between insiders and outsiders, instead referring simply to "the rest" (τοῖς . . . λοιποῖς). However, all three Synoptic Gospels distinguish between how Jesus speaks to his disciples and how he speaks to others. It's important to note that God enables the inside group to understand the mysteries of Jesus's teachings, while the rest do not have this ability. Although the disciples don't comprehend everything, they are privileged to receive additional explanations from Jesus.

Acceptance and Rejection

Amazement and Acceptance

When Jesus taught in Capernaum, the people ἐξεπλήσσοντο ἐπὶ τῇ διδαχῇ αὐτοῦ (were astonished at his teaching) because his message was delivered with authority (Luke 4:32). When he drove out an evil spirit from a demon-possessed man, ἐγένετο θάμβος ἐπὶ πάντας (astonishment came upon all, Luke 4:36). Simon Peter προσέπεσεν τοῖς γόνασιν Ἰησοῦ (fell at Jesus's knees) after the miraculous catch of fish (Luke 5:8). When Jesus healed the paralyzed man, ἔκστασις ἔλαβεν ἅπαντας, καὶ ἐδόξαζον τὸν Θεόν, καὶ ἐπλήσθησαν φόβου (amazement seized all, and they praised God and were filled with awe, Luke 5:26). When Jesus called Levi to become a disciple, καταλιπὼν πάντα ἀναστὰς ἠκολούθει αὐτῷ (he left everything behind, stood up, and followed him, Luke 5:28). When Jesus raised the widow of Nain's son, ἔλαβεν δὲ φόβος πάντας, καὶ ἐδόξαζον τὸν Θεόν (fear seized all [the disciples and a large crowd], and they glorified God, Luke 7:16). A sinful woman ἤλειφεν τῷ μύρῳ (anointed him with fragrant oil, Luke 7:38). Peter confessed Jesus to be τὸν Χριστὸν τοῦ Θεοῦ (the Christ of God, Luke 9:20). When Jesus healed the boy with the evil spirit, ἐξεπλήσσοντο δὲ πάντες ἐπὶ τῇ μεγαλειότητι τοῦ Θεοῦ (all were astonished by the majesty of God, Luke 9:43), thus directly linking Jesus's deeds with God's greatness.

Later in the narrative, Jesus heals a blind beggar who, immediately after receiving his sight, ἠκολούθει αὐτῷ δοξάζων τὸν Θεόν (followed him, glorifying God). All who witnessed this ἔδωκεν αἶνον τῷ Θεῷ (gave praise to God, Luke 18:43). Zacchaeus, the tax collector, ὑπεδέξατο αὐτὸν χαίρων (welcomed him [Jesus] gladly, Luke 19:6). During his triumphal entry into Jerusalem, ἅπαν τὸ πλῆθος τῶν μαθητῶν χαίροντες αἰνεῖν τὸν Θεὸν φωνῇ μεγάλῃ (the whole multitude of disciples rejoiced and praised God with a loud voice, Luke 19:38) and blessed him. One of the criminals crucified with Jesus rebuked the other who mocked Jesus and pleaded with Jesus μνήσθητί μου ὅταν ἔλθῃς εἰς τὴν βασιλείαν σου (remember me when you come into your kingdom, Luke 23:42). The centurion at the crucifixion praised God when he recognized Jesus as a δίκαιος (righteous man, Luke 23:47).

The significance of the amazement and acceptance of the travelers to Emmaus, positioned at the climactic ending of this Gospel, should be recognized. Αὐτῶν δὲ διηνοίχθησαν οἱ ὀφθαλμοί, καὶ ἐπέγνωσαν αὐτόν (their eyes were opened, and they recognized him, Luke 24:31). They asked each other, οὐχὶ ἡ καρδία ἡμῶν καιομένη ἦν ἐν ἡμῖν, ὡς ἐλάλει ἡμῖν ἐν τῇ ὁδῷ, ὡς διήνοιγεν ἡμῖν τὰς γραφάς; (was our heart not burning within us while he spoke to us on the road, as he opened to us the Scriptures?, Luke 24:32). This climactic acceptance is complemented by the joy and amazement of the disciples when Jesus appeared to them. Διήνοιξεν αὐτῶν τὸν νοῦν τοῦ συνιέναι τὰς γραφάς (he opened their minds to understand the Scriptures, Luke 24:45).

Misunderstanding and Rejection

However, the narrative is also marked by misunderstanding and rejection. Jesus's opening sermon in the synagogue in Nazareth is met with a hostile reaction (Luke 4:16–30). All the people in the synagogue ἐπλήσθησαν πάντες θυμοῦ (were filled with anger). They got up, ἐξέβαλον αὐτὸν ἔξω τῆς πόλεως (cast him out of the city), and took him to the brow of the hill ὥστε κατακρημνίσαι αὐτόν (to throw him down the cliff, Luke 4:28–29). He is constantly confronted by demonic powers. While teaching in the synagogue in Capernaum, an evil spirit cried out, "What do you have with us?!" Ironically, they knew his identity, crying, οἶδά σε τίς εἶ, ὁ Ἅγιος τοῦ Θεοῦ (we know who you are, the Holy One of God, Luke 4:33–34). Later in the narrative, the demons once again confronted Jesus, yet ᾔδεισαν τὸν Χριστὸν αὐτὸν εἶναι (they knew that he was the Christ, Luke 4:41).

Pharisees and teachers of the law objected to Jesus's association with tax collectors and sinners, questioning his disciples, διὰ τί μετὰ τῶν τελωνῶν καὶ ἁμαρτωλῶν ἐσθίετε καὶ πίνετε; (why does he eat and drink with tax collectors and sinners?, Luke 5:30). They also questioned why Jesus's disciples did not fast and pray like the disciples of John and the Pharisees, οἱ δὲ σοὶ ἐσθίουσιν καὶ πίνουσιν (but they eat and drink, Luke 5:33). When Jesus healed a man with a shriveled hand on the Sabbath, the Pharisees ἐπλήσθησαν ἀνοίας, καὶ διελάλουν πρὸς ἀλλήλους τί ἂν ποιήσαιεν τῷ Ἰησοῦ (were filled with rage and discussed among themselves what they could do to Jesus, Luke 6:11).

Simon the Pharisee objected to Jesus permitting a sinful woman to anoint and touch him, saying, οὗτος εἰ ἦν προφήτης, ἐγίνωσκεν ἂν τίς καὶ ποταπὴ ἡ γυνὴ ἥτις ἅπτεται αὐτοῦ, ὅτι ἁμαρτωλός ἐστιν (if he were a prophet, he would have known who and what kind of woman touches him, for she is a sinner, Luke 7:39). Herod the tetrarch διηπόρει (was perplexed) by Jesus because some were saying that it was John who had been raised from the dead (Luke 9:7). The Samaritan village οὐκ ἐδέξαντο αὐτόν (did not welcome him, Luke 9:53).

In summary, analyzing the narrative context of Jesus's statements in both Matthew and Luke reveals elements of revelation contrasted with concealment, and acceptance contrasted with rejection. It is within this context that Jesus praised God.

JESUS'S PRAISE

Situation (Matt 11:25a // Luke 10:21a)

Both Matthew and Luke set the scene for the circumstances in which Jesus spoke these words.

Table 4: Jesus's praise

Matt 11:25a	Luke 10:21a
Ἐν ἐκείνῳ τῷ καιρῷ **ἀποκριθεὶς** ὁ Ἰησοῦς **εἶπεν**	Ἐν αὐτῇ τῇ ὥρᾳ **ἠγαλλιάσατο** τῷ Πνεύματι τῷ Ἁγίῳ καὶ **εἶπεν**

The praise is tied to a key moment in Jesus's ministry. Both phrases, "Ἐν ἐκείνῳ τῷ καιρῷ" in Matthew and "Ἐν αὐτῇ τῇ ὥρᾳ" in Luke, pinpoint the exact moment Jesus made this declaration within a hostile context.[16]

In the Matthean account, this prayer follows the escalating opposition Jesus faced from Israel in the preceding passages (Matt 11:2–24). The cities of Korazin, Bethsaida, and Capernaum were expected to embrace Jesus and his message. At first glance, it appears that Jesus's revelation was unsuccessful (Matt 11:2–19). These cities rejected both Jesus and John, his messenger (Matt 11:16–19 // Luke 7:31–35), leading to the judgment of the unrepentant Galilean cities (Matt 11:20–24 // Luke 10:13–15).

In the Lukan version, the prayer follows the joyful return of the seventy (two) with the good news that they were able to perform exorcisms, and Jesus exclaiming that he saw Satan falling (Luke 10:17–20). However, in the preceding passage, the rejection of Jesus and John is also reported (Luke 7:31–35 // Matt 11:16–19), leading to the judgment of the unrepentant Galilean cities (Luke 10:13–15 // Matt 11:20–24). The depiction of this precise moment in the Gospels underscores the seriousness of rejection and the subsequent marvel of receiving divine revelation.

Amidst the broader context of revelation and concealment, acceptance and increasing rejection, Jesus offers a prayer of thanksgiving to God. The positive tone of Matt 11:25–30 and Luke 10:21–22 starkly contrasts the growing opposition. At this point, one might expect a complaint. However, Matthew employs neutral language to describe Jesus's response: ἀποκριθεὶς

---

16. Davies and Allison, *Matthew*, 527, aptly note that Jesus employs the message of judgment as a means to lead people toward salvation.

ὁ Ἰησοῦς εἶπεν (answering Jesus said). Conversely, Luke underscores the contrast by using a verb that expresses joy in the Holy Spirit: ἠγαλλιάσατο τῷ Πνεύματι τῷ Ἁγίῳ καὶ εἶπεν (he rejoiced in the Holy Spirit and said). While Matt 11:25 is more succinct, Luke 10:21 provides a fuller expression of Jesus's joy in the Holy Spirit, adding a Trinitarian dimension.

Thanks to the Father (Matt 11:25b–26 // Luke 10:21b)

The oxymoron persists as Jesus thanks God for both concealing and revealing, and for the lack of understanding as well as the positive reception.

Table 5: Jesus's thanks to the Father

Matt 11:25b–26	Luke 10:21b
Ἐξομολογοῦμαί σοι, Πάτερ, Κύριε τοῦ οὐρανοῦ καὶ τῆς γῆς, ὅτι ἔκρυψας ταῦτα ἀπὸ σοφῶν καὶ συνετῶν, καὶ ἀπεκάλυψας αὐτὰ νηπίοις· ναί, ὁ Πατήρ, ὅτι οὕτως εὐδοκία ἐγένετο ἔμπροσθέν σου.	Ἐξομολογοῦμαί σοι, Πάτερ, Κύριε τοῦ οὐρανοῦ καὶ τῆς γῆς, ὅτι ἀπέκρυψας ταῦτα ἀπὸ σοφῶν καὶ συνετῶν, καὶ ἀπεκάλυψας αὐτὰ νηπίοις· ναί, ὁ Πατήρ, ὅτι οὕτως εὐδοκία ἐγένετο ἔμπροσθέν σου.

Jesus addresses God as Πάτερ, Κύριε τοῦ οὐρανοῦ καὶ τῆς γῆς (Father, Lord of the heaven and the earth). He emphasizes his intimate and personal relationship with God, while acknowledging God's supreme authority over all creation.

Jesus joyfully thanks God for hiding knowledge ἀπὸ σοφῶν καὶ συνετῶν (from the wise and learned)[17] while revealing it νηπίοις (to the little ones).[18] In the biblical context, the "wise and learned" are often associated with the proud and arrogant (Isa 29:14; 1 Cor 1:19–21), those who consider themselves spiritually superior and look down on others while basking themselves in self-importance. In contrast, the "little ones" are linked with the humble (Isa 57:15; 66:2), those who recognize their sins and seek help.

Jesus's thanksgiving reflects broader Biblical themes, such as Κύριος ὑπερηφάνοις ἀντιτάσσεται, ταπεινοῖς δὲ δίδωσιν χάριν (The Lord opposes the proud but gives grace to the humble, Prov 3:34 LXX), quoted in Jas 4:6 and 1

---

17. In the Old Testament, the "wise and understanding" are frequently portrayed negatively as proud, arrogant, and self-assured, yet far from possessing true wisdom (e.g., Job 5:13; Isa 5:21; Jer 8:8; 9:23–24; 49:7).

18. In the Septuagint (LXX), "little children" frequently refers to those who are considered weak by worldly standards but are, in fact, the righteous (Pss 18:7; 114:6; 118:30).

Pet 5:5,[19] and ἐταπείνωσας τὸ ὑψηλόν, καὶ ὕψωσας τὸ ταπεινόν (you humbled the high and exalted the lowly, Ezek 21:26 LXX). Additionally, Ὅστις δὲ ὑψώσει ἑαυτὸν ταπεινωθήσεται, καὶ ὅστις ταπεινώσει ἑαυτὸν ὑψωθήσεται (Whoever exalts himself will be humbled, and whoever humbles himself will be exalted, Matt 23:12 // Luke 14:11; 18:14).

In the contexts of Matthew and Luke, the "wise and learned" likely refer to the scribes and Pharisees, while the "little ones" are probably the disciples, who embody humility.

Jesus acknowledges the sovereignty, wisdom, and grace of the hidden God. Several Jewish echoes of this hidden yet revealing God can be identified: "Truly, you are a God who hides himself, O God of Israel, the Savior" (Isa 45:15); "The Lord has made wise the simple" (Ps 19:7); "Wisdom has opened the mouths of the dumb, and made the tongues of the little ones speak clearly" (Wis 10:21); "Many are lofty and renowned, but to the meek he reveals his secrets" (Eccl 3:19);[20] and "The wisdom of their wise men shall perish, and the discernment of their discerning men shall be hidden" (Isa 29:14).

These passages reveal a divine paradox: those who consider themselves high and wise are actually ignorant, while those who recognize their insignificance are granted divine knowledge. Schlatter[21] often emphasizes the contrast between human wisdom and divine wisdom, highlighting that true understanding comes from recognizing one's need for God. He remarks that no one is so great that God needs him and none so little that God cannot reach him.

Jesus's words also align with Jewish eschatological expectations. According to these expectations, the end times would bring exceptional knowledge and wisdom for the elect (Jer 31:34; Hab 2:14). Unlike Jewish apocalyptic texts, where revelation often comes through angels, in this case, the revelation comes through Jesus to the "little ones."[22] Eschatological knowledge is already present in Jesus, who reveals end-time secrets (cf. Matt 13:16–17).

---

19. James and Peter replace "the Lord" with "God" in the quotation: Ὁ Θεὸς ὑπερηφάνοις ἀντιτάσσεται, ταπεινοῖς δὲ δίδωσιν χάριν.

20. The book of Sirach, also known as Ecclesiasticus, contains Jewish ethical teachings and was written by the Judahite scribe Ben Sira of Jerusalem, around 200 to 175 BCE.

21. Schlatter, *Romans*.

22. In Jewish apocalyptic texts, revelation frequently comes through angels (e.g., Zech 5; Dan 8:15–26; 9:22–27; 10:18–12:4; Acts 7:53; Rev 17:7–18). Davies and Allison, *Matthew*, 279.

Gnosis Resides in Jesus (Matt 11:27 // Luke 10:22)

This thanksgiving is followed by a declaration from Jesus, asserting that knowledge resides in him (Matt 11:27 // Luke 10:22).

Table 6: Gnosis resides in Jesus

Knowledge residing in Jesus (Matt 11:27)	Knowledge residing in Jesus (Luke 10:22)
Πάντα μοι παρεδόθη ὑπὸ τοῦ Πατρός μου, καὶ οὐδεὶς ἐπιγινώσκει τὸν Υἱὸν εἰ μὴ ὁ Πατήρ, οὐδὲ τὸν Πατέρα τις ἐπιγινώσκει εἰ μὴ ὁ Υἱὸς καὶ ᾧ ἐὰν βούληται ὁ Υἱὸς ἀποκαλύψαι.	**πάντα μοι παρεδόθη** ὑπὸ τοῦ Πατρός μου, καὶ οὐδεὶς γινώσκει τίς ἐστιν ὁ Υἱὸς εἰ μὴ ὁ Πατήρ, καὶ τίς ἐστιν ὁ Πατὴρ εἰ μὴ ὁ Υἱὸς καὶ ᾧ ἐὰν βούληται ὁ Υἱὸς ἀποκαλύψαι.

Jesus describes his special relationship with the Father in terms of divine mutuality. Not only does the Son know the Father, but he has also received all things from him. The Father entrusts all apocalyptic mysteries to the Son, to be revealed in his earthly ministry. Without Jesus, God's divinity is inconceivable. Without the Father, there is no way to Jesus. They belong together. God becomes perceivable only as the gift of the Son, and only through revelation. Remarkably, the Son is willing and eager to share this entire relationship and its implications with others. Jesus graciously reveals all he knows about the Father to those who are open to him and accept him in faith. Without Jesus, the full understanding of God remains inaccessible.[23] Jesus is presented as the key to divine revelation.[24] One cannot comprehend God apart from Jesus.[25] As Bruner notes, "Without Jesus, God's Godness is unthinkable."[26]

---

23. Davies and Allison, *Matthew*, 534.
24. Davies and Allison, *Matthew*, 530.
25. Hensell, "Yoke," 12.
26. Bruner, *Matthew*, 531. The claim that salvation can only be found in Christ is a challenging one, often referred to as the "offense of the cross" or the "scandal" of exclusivity. While the world and other religions may acknowledge God's existence, from this perspective, true and complete knowledge of God is mediated exclusively by Jesus and brought into the heart by the Holy Spirit. Deuteronomy 29:29 captures this duality: "The secret things belong unto God; but the things that are revealed belong unto us and our children." Jesus's role is unique in both revelation and mediation, as stated in John 1:18 and 14:9. He himself asserts that he alone knows the Father, and that anyone who comes to know God does so through his mediation. Davies and Allison, *Matthew*, 531, 533.

Davies and Allison draw significant parallels between Jesus and Jewish traditions about Moses (Exod 33:12–14).[27] Both figures received and mediated divine knowledge, with Jesus knowing the Father and Moses seeking to know the Lord. Deuteronomy 34:10 highlights the reciprocal knowledge between the Lord and Moses: "There has not arisen a prophet since in Israel like Moses, whom the Lord knew face to face." This mutual knowledge is exclusive to both the Lord and Moses. Additionally, Jesus defines himself as meek, an outstanding characteristic attributed to Moses.[28] Jesus promises rest, much like the Lord promises rest for Moses (Exod 33:14).

Jesus's Invitation (Matt 11:28–30)

The Matthean account continues with Jesus's invitation to find rest and knowledge in him.

Table 7: Jesus's invitation

Invitation to knowledge (Matt 11:28–30)
Δεῦτε πρός με πάντες οἱ κοπιῶντες καὶ πεφορτισμένοι, κἀγὼ <u>ἀναπαύσω</u> ὑμᾶς. ἄρατε τὸν ζυγόν μου ἐφ' ὑμᾶς καὶ μάθετε ἀπ' ἐμοῦ, ὅτι πραΰς εἰμι καὶ ταπεινὸς τῇ καρδίᾳ, καὶ εὑρήσετε <u>ἀνάπαυσιν</u> ταῖς ψυχαῖς ὑμῶν· ὁ γὰρ ζυγός μου χρηστὸς καὶ τὸ φορτίον μου ἐλαφρόν ἐστιν

This passage is unique among the Gospels. Jesus extends his invitation: δεῦτε πρός με (come to me), followed by a promise κἀγὼ ἀναπαύσω ὑμᾶς (and I will give you rest) and then gives instruction ἄρατε τὸν ζυγόν μου ἐφ' ὑμᾶς καὶ μάθετε ἀπ' ἐμοῦ (take my yoke upon you and learn from me) (Matt 11:28–30).[29] Jesus's invitation to come to him is paralleled by his instruction to take up his yoke and learn from him, with both actions accompanied by the promise of rest.[30]

Jesus's invitation is not just to come to God in an abstract sense but specifically to come to him, emphasizing that he embodies truth.[31] The phrase "Learn from me" (ἀπ' ἐμοῦ) highlights a personal relationship with

---

27. Davies and Allison, *Matthew*, 353.
28. Davies and Allison, *Matthew*, 272, 284, 286.
29. Jesus implicitly identifies himself with Wisdom. In Proverbs 1:20–23 and 8:1–36, Wisdom calls out to listeners, inviting them to learn from her with the promise of finding rest. In the book of Ben Sirach, Wisdom is personified, and the student is encouraged to take on her yoke (Sir 6:30–31) to find rest (Sir 6:28).
30. Davies and Allison, *Matthew*, 289.
31. Bruner, *Matthew*, 537.

Jesus, rather than merely learning about him (περὶ ἐμοῦ). This invitation is selective, directed at those who are weary and burdened, reflecting Jesus's empathy for the crowds who were harassed and helpless (Matt 9:36). This compassion led Jesus to send out the twelve disciples with the message that the kingdom of heaven is near (Matt 10).

Jesus promises rest not through escape, but through taking up his yoke. The "yoke" symbolizes guidance and discipline, rather than a burden to avoid.[32] In Jewish teachings, the "yoke" often refers to the Torah (Sir 6:37; 15:1 and 24:1–34.)[33] Judaism regards the Torah as "the full revelation of God and of [God's] will for man." Taking up the Torah implies embracing "all that God has made known of his nature, character, and purpose, and of what he would have man be and do."[34]

While Jewish teachers call followers to take up the yoke of the Torah, Jesus invites them to take up his yoke, essentially identifying himself with the Torah.[35] This makes Jesus the full revelation of God and his will for humanity.[36]

This invitation encourages followers to embrace Jesus's interpretation of God's wisdom and perfect teachings, contrasting with the burdensome interpretation of the scribes and Pharisees.[37] Their interpretation is exhausting, but Jesus's yoke is easy and his burden light, for he is gentle and humble in heart.

In essence, Jesus's call is an invitation to an intimate, transformative relationship, where rest is found in his presence and through accepting his teachings as a guiding yoke. This relationship is not about avoiding responsibilities but being equipped to live according to Jesus's teachings, thereby finding true rest and fulfillment.

CONCLUSION

From this investigation it can be concluded that God is incomprehensible to the natural human mind, yet he reveals himself to humans in a special

---

32. Bruner, *Matthew*, 538
33. Viljoen, *Torah*, 217.
34. Moore, *Judaism*, 1:263.
35. In Matt 28:19–20, Jesus instructs his disciples to teach converts to obey everything he has commanded them (his yoke), while assuring them of his continual presence. This dual directive forges an inseparable connection between Jesus's teachings and his abiding presence.
36. Moore, *Judaism*, 1:263.
37. Viljoen, *Torah*, 218.

manner. This divine revelation is most profoundly demonstrated through Jesus, his Son, who was sent to impart the knowledge of God. Both Matthew and Luke, among other Gospels, depict Jesus's ministry as a means of revealing God and his will.

Matthew and Luke illustrate how Jesus and his messengers were met with both rejection and acceptance. This dual response underscores the theme of revelation and concealment in Jesus's ministry. While Jesus revealed God through his public ministry—his teachings and miracles—this revelation also involved elements of concealment, linked to the acceptance and rejection he encountered.

Jesus's ministry displays that he is the embodiment of God's wisdom. In Matt 11:25–27 and Luke 10:21–22, Jesus thanks God the Father for making himself known to the humble while concealing himself from those who reject his ministry. This act of thanksgiving is striking because it follows scenes of rejection.

Both passages underscore the divine initiative in revelation, showing that God chooses to reveal his truths to the humble. They highlight the dichotomy between the "wise and learned" and the "little children." They emphasize the significance of humility in receiving divine knowledge.

Jesus serves as the mediator in making God known, a role grounded in his intimate relationship with God the Father. The "wise and learned" who reject Jesus's teachings and ministry are characterized by pride and arrogance, seeing themselves as spiritually superior and looking down on others. In contrast, the "little ones," or the humble, recognize their sins and seek help. They accept Jesus's ministry and are privileged to have God and his will be revealed to them.

Matthew uniquely connects Jesus's mediation to the concept of taking up his yoke, which refers to his teaching of the Torah (Matt 11:28–30). Unlike the burdensome interpretations of the Torah by the scribes and Pharisees, Jesus's yoke brings relief to those weary and burdened. His teachings offer a refreshing contrast, being gentle and humble in heart, providing rest and guidance to those who embrace them.

Thus, through Jesus's ministry, the divine incomprehensible nature of God is made accessible to those who approach him with humility, reinforcing the notion that true understanding of God comes through the acceptance of Jesus and his teachings. This relationship between revelation and concealment highlights the dynamic nature of faith and the transformative impact of Jesus's message.

BIBLIOGRAPHY

Bruner, Frederick Dale. *Matthew: A Commentary. Vol. 1, The Christbook, Matthew 1–12.* Grand Rapids: Eerdmans, 2004.
Culpepper, R. Alan. *Mark.* Macon, GA: Smyth & Helwys, 2007.
Davies, W. D., and Dale C. Allison. *Matthew 8–18.* International Critical Commentary, vol. 2. London and New York: T&T Clark, 2004.
Hensell, Eugene. "The Yoke of Discipleship: Unpacking the Wisdom of Christ in Matthew 11:25–30." *Priest* July (2018) 11–16.
Hooker, Morna D. "Mark's Parables of the Kingdom (Mark 4:1–34)." In *The Challenge of Jesus' Parables*, edited by Richard N. Longenecker, 79–101. Grand Rapids: Eerdmans, 2000.
Hultgren, Arland J. *The Parables of Jesus: A Commentary.* Grand Rapids: Eerdmans, 2000.
Keener, Craig S. *A Commentary on the Gospel of Matthew.* Grand Rapids: Eerdmans, 1999.
Levine, Amy-Jill, and Ben Witherington III. *The Gospel of Luke.* New Cambridge Commentary. Cambridge: Cambridge University Press, 2018.
Luz, Ulrich. *Matthew 8–20: A Commentary.* Minneapolis: Fortress, 2001.
Moore, George F. *Judaism in the First Centuries of the Christian Era, The Age of the Tannaim, volume 1,* Cambridge, MA: Harvard University Press, 1927
Pseudo-Clementine. *Recognitiones* [The Recognitions of Clement]. In *Ante-Nicene Fathers*, vol. 8, edited by Alexander Roberts and James Donaldson. Buffalo, NY: Christian Literature, 1886. Repr., Peabody, MA: Hendrickson, 1994.
Schlatter, Adolf. *Romans: The Righteousness of God.* Translated by Siegfried S. Schatzmann. Peabody, MA: Hendrickson, 1995.
Simmonds, Andrew R. "'Woe to You . . . Hypocrites!': Re-reading Matthew 23:13–36." *Bibliotheca Sacra* 166 (2009) 336–49.
Viljoen, Francois P. *The Torah in Matthew.* Zurich: Lit Verlag, 2018.
Witherington, Ben, III. *Matthew.* Macon, GA: Smyth & Helwys, 2006.

Chapter 8

The Unknowability of God in John's Gospel

—Paul J. Creevey
Department of Biblical Studies, University of Divinity, Melbourne, Australia

ABSTRACT

One of the most fundamental questions of theology is whether human beings in our finitude can ever come to know anything about God. In the ninth century John Scotus Erigena wrote, "We do not know what God is. God Himself does not know what He is because He [God] is not any created thing." Jan van Ruysbroeck, a fourteenth century theologian maintained an apophatic approach that "God is immeasurable and incomprehensible, unattainable and unfathomable." Yet, what is at the heart of Christianity is that God revealed God's-self to humanity in the person of Jesus of Nazareth. As such, the question is how scholars and believers can still maintain that God is unknowable in light of the revelation of Jesus of Nazareth. As John states, "No one has ever seen God. It is God the only Son, who is close to the Father's heart, who has made him known" (John 1:18). This chapter will argue, using John's theology, that Paul's initial insight in Gal 4:9 is an interpretive key: It is not that "we have come to know God" but that "we have come to be known by God." First, this chapter will give a brief consideration to the Pauline texts that speak of the "unknowability" of God. Second, this chapter will consider Johannine texts that talk about Jesus making God known. Finally, this chapter will argue that there is an understanding in Johannine theology that God's mystery is unknowable, but God has given humanity a glimpse into God's love for his creation through the life, mission, death, and resurrection of Jesus, the Nazarene.

INTRODUCTION

One of the fundamental questions of theology is whether human beings in our finitude can ever come to know anything about God. In our Christian tradition, we have numerous examples of theologians emphasizing the ultimate unknowability of God, even though through Scripture, specifically the event of the incarnation, we can gain a glimpse into the mystery that is God. As St. Augustine stated, "For us to have the slightest glimpse of God is a great blessing, but to comprehend God is impossible."[1] Similarly, Gregory of Nazianan implied if we think we understand [who God is], it is not God that we understand.[2] Thomas Aquinas, in the twelfth century stated, "One thing about God remains completely unknown in this life, namely, what God is."[3] This unknowability of God has led to an apophatic strand of theology in response to our knowledge of God: we cannot name what God is, but what God is not.

However, the question of unknowability centers around one's understanding of this term. For these early Christian scholars, it is clear that unknowability reflected that God's essence, radically and paradoxically, are totally beyond human conceptualization due to God's absolute otherness. Human concepts and predicates, including even "existence," can have no literal application to God. Each of these theologians appears to recognize that the biblical text bears witness to the fact that God's nature is ultimately unfathomable, reflecting a long held Christian belief that God can be known only to the extent that God reveals Gods-self. Yet, what is at the heart of Christianity is that we believe that God revealed Gods-self to humanity in the person of Jesus of Nazareth. Accordingly, there is a cataphatic theology strand in Christian Scripture which, given the event of the Incarnation, reflects that there is some degree of knowability about God. Jesus has given us the possibility of knowing God, even though the Incarnation is an event that is fully beyond our limited human comprehension.

The event of the incarnation challenges our thinking as to whether the Old Testament image of God's unknowability can continue to be maintained. We read in John's prologue, "No one has ever seen God. It is God

---

1. Augustine, *Sermon 67*, fn10.
2. See Nazianzen, "Third Theological Oration," fn VIII.
3. Aquinas, *Summa Theogiae* 1.12.11, quoted in Murray, "Unknowability of God."

the only Son, who is close to the Father's heart, who has explained him" (John 1:18). The clear intent is that in some way God has been revealed to humanity through the life, death, resurrection, and ascension of Jesus. Of course, the question is to what extent does the revelation of Jesus "explain" God. For Christian believers, Jesus is God's divine Son-Logos; so, the question becomes how Jesus makes God known fully to humanity or is there still something about God that remains "elusive" and "hidden." As Carabine states, "The Christian theologian who asserts that God cannot be known is forced to take account of the central truth of the NT: the Incarnation."[4] This chapter will attempt to argue that the early church grappled with this contradiction between the ultimate unknowability pertaining to God and the self-revelation of Jesus as the divine Logos. First, it will consider Paul's response to the theme of unknowability, then it will consider the Johannine text. Ultimately, the purpose of this chapter is to offer the suggestion that Paul's insight in Gal 4:9—"It is not that we have come to know God but that we have come to be known by God"—is a possible interpretive key. As such, this chapter will argue that there is an understanding in Johannine theology that God's mystery is unknowable, but God has given humanity a glimpse into God's love for his creation through the life, mission, death, and resurrection of Jesus, the Nazarene, through the gift of the Holy Spirit.

PAUL: UNKNOWABILITY OF GOD

When one reads 1 Cor 1:18–3:23, there are at least six statements that deal with the notion that human beings cannot grasp God's wisdom through their own human wisdom (cf. 1:19, 21; 2:9, 16; 3:19, 20). Further, there is only one way to encounter the secret of God's revelation in Jesus Christ: through God's own πνεῦμα. Paul writes,

> What no eye has seen, nor ear heard, nor the human heart conceived, what God has prepared for those who love him, these things God has revealed to us through the Spirit; for the Spirit searches everything, even the depths of God. For what human being knows what is truly human except the human spirit that is within? So, also, no one comprehends what is truly God's except the Spirit of God (1 Cor 2:9–11).

Here, Paul appears to imply that knowledge of God's wisdom can only come into the world through some other-worldly means: in this case through the gift of the divine πνεῦμα that first rested upon Jesus Christ, his only-begotten

---

4. Carabine, *Unknown God*, 226.

(cf. John 1:18), and was given to humanity after Jesus's earthly existence had ended (cf. John 20:22). One could argue that Paul understands that humanity is not able to understand God in God's wisdom because, as a human being, one has the wrong 'tool': namely, the human capacity for wisdom belongs to this world, the world of flesh. For Paul, clearly, the wisdom of humanity does not belong to the same sphere as the wisdom of God. Paul states, "Has not God made foolish the wisdom of the world?" (1 Cor 1:20) and "For God's foolishness is wiser than human wisdom, and God's weakness is stronger than human strength" (1 Cor. 1:25). This position on the stance on the conditioned knowability of God in Paul is emphasized by Gartner. He states,

> [For Paul], human beings do not possess the quality that would enable them to know God or God's wisdom. Only through the possession of God's own πνεῦμα are human beings open to receive what God reveals. The πνεῦμα is the link between God and humanity. Consequently, the sole being who is able to convey the revelation to humanity and open one's mind to know God is God's πνεῦμα, because the πνεῦμα comes from God. To know God completely is the privilege of God's πνεῦμα. If one truly wants to know God, to have an encounter and insight into God's wisdom, then that person must share the same πνεῦμα.[5]

Before the event of the incarnation the Jewish theologian Philo of Alexandria argued that to enable human beings to know God, God breathed into the creation of human beings a spark of the divine πνεῦμα (cf. Gen 1:27). For Philo, humanity's reason [nous] could not by its own power attain to knowledge of God. God had to reveal himself to human reason.[6] In discussing the work of Philo, Gartner provides the following insight: "Experience of the outer world may enable human beings to acknowledge the existence of a Supreme Being; yet, it is only God's revelations in the soul, made possible by the presence of the divine πνεῦμα, which becomes the only means to gain real knowledge of God."[7] For Philo, there were two paths to know God: the lesser and the greater. The lesser is that of human reasoning, which observes nature and its order. From these works human beings can deduce the existence of God, but this is the path of shadows. The greater path is the mystical path. Here, one must "lift up one's eyes above and beyond creation and obtain a clear vision of the uncreated One, so as from him to apprehend

---

5. Gartner, "Pauline and Johannine Idea," 218.
6. See Philo, *Legum Allegoriae*, 1.38. abr 79f. det. 86.
7. Gartner, "Pauline and Johannine Idea," 214.

both him and his shadow, both the logos and his world."[8] However, this is only possible by a gift from God. For Philo, the Logos is the mediator between God and humanity in relation to the knowledge of God. God is unknowable, but humanity can through its share in the Logos come to understand what God's will is.

Using Philo, and with the ongoing belief in the continuing presence of the divine πνεῦμα after Jesus's resurrection, Paul can locate the event of the incarnation for Christians. For Paul, the event of the incarnation becomes an event that clearly shows that the earthly Jesus shares in the divine πνεῦμα. The arrival of the divine Logos-Son, as pure gift from God, now enables human beings to be open to the gift of the divine πνεῦμα. Belief in Jesus can transform us from a rootedness in worldly things to the invitation to a participation in the ἐπουρανια (heavenly things) through our new connection with the divine πνεῦμα. As Paul declares, "Now, we have received not the spirit of the world, but the Spirit that is from God, so that we may understand the gifts bestowed on us by God" (1 Cor 2:12). We have received the gift of the divine πνεῦμα through the witness of Jesus's life, death, and resurrection, such that we might know what God has given to us. It is not that we will know God, but that we are now known by God because we, too, when we believe, activate the spark of the divine πνεῦμα in us. In the Christian tradition, Jesus's death and resurrection brings to humanity the ongoing gift of the divine πνεῦμα. As we read in John, "Receive the Holy Spirit" (John 20:22; cf. Acts 2:4). This subtle distinction is picked up in Galatians 4:8–9: "Formerly, when you did not know God, you were enslaved to beings that by nature are not gods. Now, however, that you have come to know God, or rather to be known by God, how can you turn back again to the weak and beggarly elemental spirits?"

For Paul, that God remains to some extant unknowable in the face of the incarnation, remains a notion as evidenced in his statement in Rom 11:33: "O the depth of the riches and wisdom and knowledge of God! How unsearchable are his judgments and how inscrutable his ways!" Yet, to some extant God has become knowable through our encounter with the crucified One who is the Risen One. In Acts 17:23–31, reporting on Paul's encounter of an altar in Athens to an "unknown god," Luke clearly states Paul as saying: "What therefore you worship as unknown, this I proclaim to you." Luke appears to reference Paul in subsequent verses explaining how the person of Jesus Christ enables human beings to be known by God. God knows us and invites us into relationship because as human beings we have now inherited, through the church's experience of Pentecost (cf. John 20:19–23; Acts 1:8;

---

8. Philo, *Legum Allegoriae III*, 100.

2:1–4), the divine πνεῦμα that existed on earth in Jesus. It is the continuing presence of the divine πνεῦμα handed over to humanity by God and Christ through Pentecost that brings both the opportunity to be known by God and through that knowing the offer of salvation through the gift of eternal life. It is being transformed by the gift of the divine πνεῦμα that enables human wisdom to grasp something of the mystery of God's wisdom.

Nowhere does Paul explicitly say that a human being can know God, but what the human being can experience is the presence of God in the living out of their belief in Jesus Christ as the agent of God. As Paul states, "It is no longer I who live, but it is Christ who lives in me. And the life I now live in the flesh I live by faith in the Son of God, who loved me and gave himself for me (Gal. 2:20). Also, Paul states in Rom 8:11, "If the Spirit of him who raised Jesus from the dead dwells in you, he who raised Christ from the dead will give life to your mortal bodies also through his Spirit that dwells in you." The scriptural tradition gives plentiful witness to the central importance of the need to one being gifted with the divine πνεῦμα to be open to the experience of God's revelation (cf. Matt 3:11; Luke 24:49; John 14:15–17; 20:22; Acts 2:4; 4:31; 5:32; Rom 5:5; 8:2, 9, 26–27; 1 Cor 3:16; 6:19; 12:13; 2 Cor 5:5; Gal 4:6; 5:18; Eph 2:18, 22; 3:16; 1 John 2:27; 3:24; 4:13).

For Paul, God is mystery (cf. 2 Cor 2:12:2–4) but God is the one who raised Jesus from death (Rom 4:24; 8:11). This event of raising of Jesus discloses not only what God does but, at the same time who God is in love as God desires to know us fully. In God's sending forth of his Son—in Jesus's life, death, resurrection, ascension, and through the gift of the Holy Spirit—God makes it clear that humanity is known and loved by Gods-self and that our purpose is to be reunited with the God who is the giver of all life. As such, belief in Jesus as the one sent by God is integral to any possibility of human beings coming to any understanding of God's own identity.

JOHN: MAKING GOD KNOWN?

In considering the unknowability of God in John, few readers come to the Johannine text without some preconception of what the term "god" signifies or with some notion of who "god" is. These preconceptions are used in the reading of a text, and a reader is aware that "knowledge of God is not understood to be limited to what texts have to say."[9] Indeed, within the Biblical narrative, one of the most fundamental convictions about God is the reliability or faithfulness of God, a God of mercy and justice, who is the bringer of life, and who transcends the human condition.

9. Thompson, "God's Voice," 185.

Regarding the attribute of the unknowability of God, John, like Paul, presents contrasting images to the reader. First, one clearly encounters the notion of the unknowability of God through a number of statements. Some of these are: "He [the Logos] was in the world, and the world came into being through him; yet the world did not know him; He came to what was his own, and his own people did not accept him" (John 1:10–11); "No one has ever seen God" (1:18a); and "His [God's] voice you have never heard, his form you have never seen" (John 5:37); "Though you do not know him" (8:55a); "And they will do this because they have not known the Father or me" (John 16:3); "But the one who sent me is true, and you do not know him" (John 7:28a); and "But they will do all these things to you on account of my name, because they do not know him who sent me" (John 15:21).

In contrast, John makes it clear that in the event of the incarnation, Jesus has come to make the Father known. Again, one encounters a number of statements: "It is God the only Son, who is close to the Father's heart, who has explained him" (John 1:18); "Not that anyone has seen the Father except the one who is from God; he has seen the Father" (John 6:46); "I know him, because I am from him, and he sent me" (John 7:29); "But I know him; if I would say that I do not know him, I would be a liar like you. But I do know him and I keep his word" (John 8:55); "Just as the Father knows me, and I know the Father" (John 10:15); "so that you may know and understand that the Father is in me and I am in the Father" (John 10:38); "If you know me, you will know my Father also. From now on you do know him and have seen him" (John 14:7); "Have I been with you all this time, Philip, and you still do not know me? Whoever has seen me has seen the Father. How can you say, 'Show us the Father'? (John 14:9); "I have made known to you everything that I have heard from my Father" (John 15:15); "Righteous Father, the world does not know you, but I know you; and these know that you have sent me" (John 17:25); "And this is eternal life, that they may know you, the only true God, and Jesus Christ whom you have sent" (John 17:3); and "I have made your name known to those whom you gave me from the world" (John 17:6; cf. 17:26).

Further, throughout the Fourth Gospel, something about God is being revealed by Jesus. Jesus is portrayed as being totally in union with the will of God (John 4:34; 5:30) and doing nothing on his own (John 5:30; cf. 8:28). When Jesus is working, so is his Father (John 5:17), both are givers of life (John 5:21, 26), both can act as ultimate judge (John 8:16) and, ultimately, both are responsible for the sending of the Spirit (cf. John 14:16; 15:26; 16:7). Jesus argued to his disciples, "My food is to do the will of him who sent me and to complete his work" (John 4:34). In his final prayer to God, the Father, Jesus prayed, "I glorified you on earth by finishing the work that you gave me to do" (John 17:4). His final words, at his death on the cross were "It is finished" (John 19:30). Throughout his earthly life, and even in his death, Jesus has acted out his life as making his Father known and loved by his own (cf. John 1:12; 17:6, 26). So, how does one reconcile these apparent contrasting images relating to the unknowability/knowability of God?

In John's Gospel, the character of God, as God, never explicitly appears, and the only words God speaks in the Gospel are words in response to Jesus's life and mission, particularly his forthcoming "hour." God says of Jesus's life, "And I have glorified it, and I will glorify it again" (John 12:28). Yet, those persons present at this significant "intervention" in the story misunderstand God's voice as thunder or an angel speaking (John 12:29). Further, the Gospel holds up both the mystery of God—"His [God's] voice you have never heard, his form you have never seen" (John 5:37)—and God's love for humanity through the sending of his only begotten Son—"God so loved the world that he gave his only Son, that everyone who believes in him might not perish but have eternal life" (John 3:16). This latter statement shows "the world from God's point of view, rather than God viewed from the point of view of the world."[10] Hence, from this perspective, God is characterized, albeit indirectly, in terms that point to originating life-giving actions. As Thompson argues, for Jewish authors of first-century times "the uniqueness of Israel's God was lodged in God's creation of all the world God is the Lord God who gives life to all things."[11]

In the Johannine narrative, human access to God is through the person and agency of Jesus (cf. John 1:18). Thompson nuances this perspective: "It is not so much that Jesus tells us about God but rather it is the words and deeds of Jesus that serve as a characterization of God . . . [the disciples] only access to God is through Jesus, the incarnate Word of God, who speaks so that God is heard, and in whom they see the Father."[12] It is this designation of

10. Thompson, "God's Voice," 199.

11. Thompson, "Living Father," 23. Reinhartz, "Introduction," 1, agrees. "The image of God as father is deeply entrenched in Jewish and Christian Scriptures. God frequently calls Israel God's son (Hos 1:10) or God's first—born son (Exod 4:22)." Further, Reinhartz, "Word Was Begotten," takes Thompson's concern with God as life—giver in a slightly different direction arguing that Greek and Roman theories about the male role in procreation (epigenesis) may have been a significant source of thinking regarding the Johannine presentation of the Father-Son relationship between God and Jesus. Anderson, "Having-Sent-Me Father," 33–57, argues that the Johannine community of believers would have heard the Father-Son relationship against the background of Deut 18:15–22 that promises the return of a Moses-like prophet. Hence, he prioritizes the metaphor of sender to describe God as agent rather than that of creator and life-giver.

12. Thompson, "God's Voice," 188. See also, Culpepper, *Anatomy*, 113. For a summary of the actions of God, made known to the reader by the words of Jesus, see Thompson, "God's Voice," 189–90.

God, as Father, a term that often signifies the source of life and protection, that is most prominent in the Johannine text.[13] Further, it is noted that in John's Gospel, the divine πνεῦμα is bestowed on Jesus at the beginning of his earthly mission (John 1:33), is handed back at the moment of his death (John 19:30), and his given to the whole community after his resurrection (John 20:22). It is this presence of the divine πνεῦμα in Jesus that enables Jesus to know God intimately as his Father. It is Jesus's reception of the divine πνεῦμα that shows that he has come to be fully known by God. This is what Paul argued in Gal 4:9.

Marianne Thompson notes that in the Johannine text "the lack of epithet, adjective, and other kinds of descriptive statements about God stands in contrast both to the other Gospels and to the Old Testament and Jewish narratives."[14] In the Fourth Gospel, there are far more genitive phrases in the form ". . . of God" than there are "God of . . . ."[15] Whereas in the Synoptics one finds genitives such as the God of Abraham or the God of

---

13. See Thompson, *God of John*, 57. Also, Thompson, "Living Father," 19–20. She points out that the most common designation of God in John is "Father." However, the term "father" is not to be considered simply as a substitute for "God." The term "father" is used around 136 times in the Gospel, more than all the other Gospels combined, of which 16 simply refer to the earthly father, the other 120 are predications that relate to God as being Jesus's Father. In the Johannine Letters, the term "father" appears 14 times in 1 John, and twice in 2 John. In comparison, the term "God" appears in John 83 times, 62 times in 1 John, twice in 2 John, and 3 times in 3 John. In the Gospel of John there are 24 genitive constructions, and in 1 John there are 26 genitive constructions. The first references to God, as Father, are found in the prologue (John 1:14, 18), where God is specifically the Father of the only Son. Subsequent references to God, as Father, occur primarily in the words of Jesus. A few are found in the editorial comments, in which God is named as the Father of Jesus (cf. John 5:18; 8:27). Thus, John exemplifies the pattern of the other Gospels in limiting the address of God, as Father, to Jesus. Of the 120 times, 85 times John uses the word "father" in the direct words of Jesus, Jesus speaks of "my father" about 31 times, and he addresses God simply as "Father" nine times. Hence, the noun occurs most frequently in the nominative and accusative cases and so is found in Jesus's speech about, not to, God. As O'Day, "Show Us," 13, states, the term "'Father' belongs primarily to the language of discourse and debate in John, not prayer." Only once does Jesus speak to the disciples of God as "your Father" (John 20:17). There are but one or two exceptions. In John 8, the Jews ask Jesus where his Father is (8:19) and, subsequently, argue that they have God as Father (John 8:41); a claim that Jesus disputes (John 8:42).

14. Thompson, "God's Voice," 195.

15. Frey, *Glory*, 319, points out that "of the 83 attestations to θεός a considerable portion are in genitive constructions, some of which are related to Jesus—Son of God, Lamb of God, Holy One of God and, as such, express Jesus's relatedness to the biblical God. Other genitive connections mark diverse aspects: angel of God (1:51); wrath of God (3:36); the words of God (3:34); the love of God (5:42); the works of God (6:28–29); the kingdom of God (3:3, 5); the bread of God (6:33); or the glory/honour of God (11:4, 40); from the side of God (5:44) or from God (12:43).

Jacob, in the Fourth Gospel one finds genitive phrases such as Son of God (John 1:34, 49; 5:25; 11:27; 19:7; 20:31), lamb of God (John 1:29, 36), gift of God (John 4:10), bread of God (John 6:63), holy one of God (John 6:69), work of God (John 6:29; 9:3), word of God (John 10:35), love of God (John 5:42), kingdom of God (John 3:3, 5), glory of God (11:40), children of God (John 1:12; 11:52) and the gift of God (John 4:10).[16] As Thompson notes, "Most of these genitive phrases serve to characterize Jesus or something that Jesus mediates, brings, or gives. The narrative continues this way, speaking of Jesus in terms of his relationship to God, without defining who 'God' is . . . It is Jesus' prerogative to identify God as his Father."[17] In John, Jesus and God are intimately linked, but the terms "God" and "Father" are not simply interchangeable. As Thompson points out, "Formulations that refer to the Son as being 'sent' belong primarily to the Gospel's 'Father' terminology. It is the Father who sends the Son. Likewise, Jesus is said not to do 'the will of God', but the 'will of the Father.'"[18] Jesus is driven by the intimate friendship that he shares with God, who is Father, but a God who is clearly the God of Israel, the one who alone is God (John 5:44) and is the only true God (John 17:3).[19] Similarly, O'Day points out that for John, "The creator of the world that is Israel's God, and the Father—the one who is relationship with the Son—can only be one and the same God."[20] As Gartner points out,

> All the sayings of Jesus in John that contain the theological conception "to know God" are not descriptions of the status of those who believed during Jesus' earthly ministry. They deal

---

16. The Letters of John, similarly continue this genitive form of construction with the following phrases: word of God (1 John 2:14), will of God (1 John 2:17), children of God (3:1, 2, 10; 5:2, 19), Son of God (1 John 3:8; 4:15; 5:5, 10, 12, 13, 20), born of God (1 John 3:9; 4:7; 5:1, 4, 18), love of God (1 John 3:17), Spirit of God (1 John 4:2), and testimony of God (1 John 5:9)

17. Thompson, "God's Voice," 196. Meyer, "Father," 255, states: "The disconcerting fact that the Gospel never spells out just what it is that the Son has seen and heard from the Father, except by what Jesus says and does, seems all the more to hide the Father behind the Son."

18. Thompson, "Living Father," 20.

19. See Thompson, *God of John*, 228. She states: "More importantly, the actions of God as Father are distinctly and peculiarly concentrated on and through Jesus as the Son." Further, 229, Thompson states: "Given that God is 'Father' in relationship to the Son, that relationship constitutes God's very identity as Father in the Gospel of John. The Father-Son relationship underscores the fundamental portrayal of God in the Gospel of John as the living God and the creator of all life (1:1–3; 6:57)." Further, Thompson, 189, 194–196, argues that the significance of the identification of Jesus as "Son" and God as "Father" lies in the familial relationship it establishes. See, also, Frey, *Glory*, 319.

20. O'Day, "Show Us," 14.

with the conditions of salvation after Jesus had finished his ministry. People could believe, seeing Jesus and listening to him, but "knowledge" of God belonged to the conditions created through Jesus' exaltation.[21]

In the Gospel of John, Jesus is the only-begotten Son who having been sent by the Father, also receives life from his living Father and in turn gives it to others (cf. John 6:57). The only other character in the Johannine narrative sent by the Father is the Paraclete (cf. John 14:26; 15:26; 16:7), another distinct figure who abides now with humanity with the gift of the divine πνεῦμα. Within the Gospel narrative the Evangelist makes it clear that the one who sends is greater than the one who is sent (cf. John 13:16; 14:28). This again reflects a *theo*-centric focus in the narrative as the Father is the source of the life of the Son. As such, "The basic view of God as the one who lives eternally and so is the only source of life for the world fits integrally with John's view of God as the life-giving Father."[22] In John's Gospel, the Father-Son relationship becomes "the theological grounding for the predications of the authority and work of the Father given to an embodied in the Son."[23] Accordingly, the Father has placed all things into the hands of the Son (cf. John 3:35; 13:3; cf. 15:15; 16:15), has given all judgment to the Son (John 5:22), and enjoys the life-giving prerogative of the Father, which allows Jesus to be seen as "equal to God" (cf. John 5:18; 10:30). After Jesus's departure this work will continue under the inspiration of the Paraclete.

Now, scholars see that John's high Christology operates within the central theological framework where the fundamental question is concerned with the nature of revelation: the question of who God is and how is this God revealed to humanity.[24] As James Dunn points out, the primary theological debate that the Fourth Evangelist is engaging in with his Jewish contemporaries is a debate about monotheism, that is, a theological debate about the identity of Jesus.[25] Within the context of the Fourth Gospel, this question becomes one of what is it about God that Jesus reveals. As Thompson opines, "Although Jesus in the Fourth Gospel repeatedly states that he makes the Father known in word and deed, nowhere is it made plain what

---

21. Gartner, "Pauline and Johannine Idea," 226.
22. Thompson, "Living Father," 20.
23. Thompson, "Living Father," 20.
24. Frey, *Glory*, 316–17, argues that, in John, "discussion with the 'Jews' turns on the divine claim of Jesus, the question of the true revelation of God, indeed of God's actual nature, appears to be the ultimately determining factor in Johannine thinking ... It is a Christological *theo*-logy which is at the same time a *theo*-logical Christology."
25. Dunn, "Let John Be John," 318.

it is *about* God that is revealed."[26] Similarly, William Loader argued, "The Evangelist builds, thus, upon the presupposition that God is in some sense known. For all his claims, Jesus does not impart detailed information about God, but speaks on the assumption that God is a word that makes good sense to his hearers."[27] Yet, for the Evangelist "there is no true and fully valid knowledge of God that bypasses the revelation in Jesus Christ."[28] All of Jesus's life-giving works and words are not additional to God: they are the works and words through which God is made known to the world. As Thompson elucidates,

> Jesus is not presented as a second divine being, not a god alongside the one true God, but as the Son who is authorised and even commanded to speak God's words and to do God's work. The identification of Jesus as the Son, and the language of authorisation and command, make it clear that the Son is not the Father, but that the Son always carries out the work of the Father—and he does so by the Father's explicit command and authorisation (cf. 5:19–20, 25–26; 10:18, 32, 37–38). Hence, John's Christology is functional and relational. . . . John's argument for the dependence of the Son on the Father constitutes an argument for their unity.[29]

John's Gospel unequivocally testifies to the unity of the Father and the Son, yet, nevertheless, clearly differentiates between them as distinct entities. As Frey points out in the phrasing of John 10:30, ἐγὼ καὶ ὁ πατὴρ ἕν ἐσμεν, it is configured with the neuter ἕν. Here, "The co-ordination of the Son to the Father . . . is made in a carefully considered manner. On the one hand, it excludes the talk of two gods who stand alongside each other. On the other hand, a simple identification of Jesus with the one God is also excluded, otherwise it would read εἷς ἐσμεν. However, the Son and the Father remain distinct persons."[30] Frey goes on to argue that for the Evangelist "it is ultimately clear that one must not only speak of a oneness of action or even a oneness of will between the Father and the Son, but also a oneness that is grounded in the shared participation in the divine nature."[31] Jesus's identity, as well as his actions and words, originate from God, and his life and

26. Thompson, *God of John*, 9
27. William Loader, *Christology of the Fourth Gospel*, 140.
28. Frey, *Glory*, 339.
29. Thompson, *God of John*, 231.
30. Frey, *Glory*, 336.
31. Frey, *Glory*, 336.

mission point and lead to understanding who that God is.³² As Thompson argues, "The way that Jesus manifests God's presence and work through his signs and in his words, accounts to a large extent for the Gospel's accent on *seeing* the Father in the Son. . . . The hiddenness of the glory of the Father in the Son informs every scene in the Gospel. Even the signs of Jesus are manifestations of the hidden glory of God in Jesus."³³

Within first-century Judaism, the Evangelist is aware that Jewish authors can predicate the notion of "god" to individuals because they have been assigned a particular function or status by God. In Exod 7:1, YHWH said to Moses, "See I have made you like God to Pharaoh." Given, Moses's partnership with God in the exodus event, John is aware of the differentiation between the creator God, and those who have attained an intimate status with God. In John, it appears that the Evangelist has used the concept of Logos as a means to identify and differentiate Jesus from God. It is the use of this term that allows for a dual usage of the term "God."³⁴ As Thompson argues, "Ultimately, the Logos may be called "God' because the Logos derives from God and is an expression of God."³⁵ No clearer evidence is possible of the shared link between the earthly Jesus and the divine Father than Thomas's clear and succinct declaration of the Risen Jesus, "My Lord and my God" (John 20:28). Again, Thompson clearly explains, "In Thomas' confession the reader comes to acknowledge the exclusive and comprehensive revelation of God through the person of Jesus, and the identity of Jesus with God."³⁶

---

32. It is noted that in the opening chapter the reader is confronted with a virtual catalogue of titles that reveal a variety of assertions about Jesus's identity: Logos, Only-Begotten, Messiah, Elijah, Prophet, Chosen One, Lamb of God, Son of God, King of Israel, and Son of Man. For a review of these title see John Ashton, *Understanding the Fourth Gospel*, 253–262.

33. Thompson, *God of John*, 233, 143.

34. See Thompson, *God of John*, 35–37. Here she points out: "Philo can distinguish, at least for heuristic purposes, between God and the second God, the Logos of God. To be clear, this is not two gods, as Philo distinguishes between them with the use of the definite article with theos (see specifically Gen 31:13). Philo argues that the articular denotes the one who is properly called God. The Word is improperly called so not because the manifestations spoken of here is of some deity other than the only true God, but because Philo consistently speaks of the theophanies of God in the Old Testament as appearances of the Logos, not of τὸ ὄν, the God who is. Thus, to call the Logos 'god' expresses the facts: the Logos is not the unknowable high God but nevertheless truly a manifestation of the 'one who is'. Philo assumes a unity between "the one who is" and the Logos since both may be spoken of as God. Philo's discussion largely depends on his Platonism. He is concerned to maintain a distinction between the One who is, who is 'truly' God, and who is immaterial, from the multiple manifestations of the powers of God in the physical world."

35. Thompson, *God of John*, 235.

36. Thompson, *God of John*, 235.

As was noted in the plot of the Fourth Gospel, one key aspect in the Fourth Gospel is that of Jesus's identity, revealed to the reader in the Prologue, but elusive to those who engage with Jesus in narrative time. As Frey points out, "Discussion with the 'Jews' turns on the divine claim of Jesus, the question of the true revelation of God, indeed of God's actual nature, appears to be the ultimately determining factor in Johannine thinking."[37] Jesus's identity becomes a historical issue in the context of Jesus's engagement both with the Jewish religious authorities and the Hellenistic and Roman political power base. As the reader encounters the unfolding story of Jesus, it is clear that "at first the disciples of the earthly Jesus did not understand his words, his true identity, and his fate, and that it was only after his glorification that they could obtain this insight in retrospect (cf. John 2:21–22; 12:16)."[38]

Within the historical context, in the Greek and Roman worldview, "a god who enters into the changeability of history, who not only appears in an 'epiphany' but becomes a real human being, who is mortal and who dies, cannot be a god . . . but can do so only in pretence or as an episode."[39] From the Jewish perspective, "an earthly human being, Jesus, and much more, one who is a crucified one, cannot according to the Biblical Jewish commandment of the oneness and singularity of God, be brought into connection with the eternal God." Accordingly, in the Fourth Gospel there is confusion and uncertainty over Jesus's identity (cf. John 5:18; 10:33; 19:7). Jesus's Judean accusers argue that Jesus has in his words "'usurped' divine dignity, which does not belong to him, but is ultimately an offense against the one God, [an action] that is blasphemous and worthy of death."[40]

Throughout the Johannine narrative, Jesus's humanity is grounded in Jesus's pre-existence as the Logos, such that Ἐν ἀρχῇ ἦν ὁ λόγος, καὶ ὁ λόγος ἦν πρὸς τὸν θεόν, καὶ θεὸς ἦν ὁ λόγος (John 1:1). Further, from the moment of the Incarnation (John 1:14), to his passion and death (John 19:30), the true humanity of Jesus is never in doubt (cf. John 19:5).[41] The language of the Father-Son relationship enhances, for the Fourth Evangelist, the dual nature of Jesus's identity. As O'Day argues, "'Father' is not simply the Fourth Gospel's preferred name for God; it is the Gospel's primary metaphor for

37. Frey, *Glory*, 316.
38. Frey, *Glory*, 336.
39. Frey, *Glory*, 334.
40. Frey, *Glory*, 334.
41. Frey, *Glory*, 280, argues, "The observation that ὁ λόγος is no longer used as a Christological designation in the subsequent course of the Fourth Gospel suggests that this term is reserved for the talk of the 'divine Word before his incarnation. The term, σὰρξ ἐγένετο, becomes the first and last statement about this Logos, Jesus Christ. Even as the crucified and glorified one, he remains the one who became flesh."

shaping theological discourse."[42] Lee concurs. She argues that the symbol of "'Father' is both divinely revealed yet also grounded in human experience: in the 'Word-made-flesh' divine revelation and material reality are fused without losing identity."[43] Accordingly, the symbol of 'father' as it pertains to the Father-Son relationship between God and Jesus holds in tension two theological poles: the mystery and incomprehensibility of God (cf. John 1:18) and that in the event of the Incarnation, God chooses to be revealed in the "flesh."[44] Yet, it is also clear that this understanding of a shared divine nature is from a post-Easter perspective (cf. 2:21–22; 12:16). Through Jesus's resurrection and ascension, and the bestowal of the Spirit, along with reflection on Scripture, the event of the cross has been given a deeper soteriological meaning as a result of Jesus's glorification. This is evident as when the Johannine community of believers first encounters the Risen One; it is as the Crucified One. As Frey points out,

> The Risen One is recognized by the signs of his earthly history. As the definitive place of the revelation of God, Christ is enduringly the Crucified One, and as such he is the eschatological revelation of God. God himself is no longer to be thought without reference to the cross of Christ and thus to a historical event. . . . God himself is no longer to be thought of without reference to the world and to history, to human suffering and human death.[45]

Again, Frey captures the significance of this understanding for Johannine theology and the unknowability/knowability of God:

> Johannine theology has decisively advanced Christian thinking about God and established crucial foundations for all later Christian talk about God. . . . The biblical God involves himself with a human history, indeed the history of humanity such that any image of God that assumes a principled unworldliness and the unhistoricality of God are fundamentally burst open.[46]

---

42. O'Day, "Show Us," 16.

43. Lee, "Divine Fatherhood," 179. In this article, 180–81, she further argues that it is in this notion of "Father" that the transformation of patriarchal fatherhood takes place in John's Gospel as it reflects two keys difference from what one would normally associate with patriarchy. First, the relationship reflects a surrender of power, and second, it restructures patriarchy symbolism through emphasizing the intimacy between the Johannine Jesus and God.

44. Lee, "Divine Fatherhood," 184.

45. Frey, *Glory*, 342.

46. Frey, *Glory*, 344, 324.

CONCLUSION

As this chapter has argued the concept of the unknowability of God was challenged by the event of the Incarnation. Both Paul and John show that the language around the nature of God and the human capacity to know who that God is had to be carefully managed. Both Evangelists used language that maintained the Jewish tradition of God's unknowability and the emerging understanding that Jesus's exaltation and glorification had revealed something of that "unknown" God. It has been argued that for both Evangelists the only way to "know" God is to be filled with the presence of the divine πνεῦμα. It is not that we come to "know God" but we come to know that we are loved and known by God. With Jesus's return to the Father, through his resurrection and ascension, the gift of the divine πνεῦμα was now made available to humanity for all future generations. God's essence remains a mystery, but through an acceptance that we are known by God, and that God invites us into a deeper relationship, we can share in the divine πνεῦμα. As the message the Risen Jesus asked Mary Magdalene to share with the first disciples attests, "I am ascending to my Father and your Father, to my God and your God." (John 20:17). This relationship is deepened when one openly receives the Holy Spirit (cf. John 20:22). Ultimately God remains a mystery, but in the glorification and exaltation of Jesus, human beings have been left with a fleeting glimpse into God's love for each and every human being. This gift is to ensure that we now fully understand that we, too, have been made with a spark of the divine at the beginning of creation, God, through Jesus, has handed over the divine πνεῦμα as a lasting and continued gift. It is participation in this divine πνεῦμα that enables human beings to continually search for an encounter with the mystery that is God's essence and presence in creation. The incarnation continues to imply the unknowability of God but allows human beings to understand that they are known by God and are invited to the mystery of God's love by the gift of the ongoing presence of the divine πνεῦμα breathed into the foundational community through a crucified but resurrected Christ.

BIBLIOGRAPHY

Anderson, Paul. "The Having-Sent-Me Father: Aspects of Agency, Encounter, and Irony in the Johannine Father-Son Relationship." *Semeia* 85 (1999) 33–57.

Augustine. *Sermon 67 on the New Testament*. In *Nicene and Post-Nicene Fathers, First Series*, vol. 6, edited by Philip Schaff, translated by R. G. MacMullen. Buffalo: Christian Literature, 1888.

Carabine, Deidre. *The Unknown God: Negative Theology in the Platonic Tradition Plato to Eriugena.* LTPM 19. Leuven: Peeters, 1995.

Culpepper, R. Alan. *Anatomy of the Fourth Gospel: A Study in Literary Design.* Philadelphia: Fortress, 1975.

Dunn, J. D. G. "Let John Be John: A Gospel for Its Time." In *The Gospel and the Gospels*, edited by Peter Stuhlmacher, 293–322. Grand Rapids: Eerdmans, 1991.

Frey, Jörg. *The Glory of the Crucified One: Christology and Theology in the Gospel of John.* Translated by Wayne Coppins and Christoph Heilig. Waco, TX: Baylor University Press, 2018.

Gartner, Bertil. "The Pauline and Johannine Idea of 'to Know God' against the Hellenistic Background: The Greek Philosophical Principle 'Like by Like' in Paul and John." *NTS* 14 (1968) 209–31.

Lee, Dorothy A. "The Symbol of Divine Fatherhood." *Semeia* 85 (1999) 177–87.

Meyer, Paul W. "The Father: The Presentation of God in the Fourth Gospel." In *Exploring the Gospel of John: In Honor of D. Moody Smith*, edited by R. Alan Culpepper and C. Clifton Black, 255–73. Louisville, KY: Westminster John Knox, 1996.

Murray, Andrew. "The Unknowability of God in Thomas Aquinas." Paper delivered at the Ninth Biennial Conference in Philosophy, Religion and Culture, Strathfield, AU, October 7, 2012. https://andrewmurraysm.wordpress.com/wp-content/uploads/2018/10/murray-unknowabilityofgod.pdf.

Nazianzen, Gregory. "Third Theological Oration (Oration 29)." From *Nicene and Post-Nicene Fathers, Second Series*, vol. 7, edited by Philip Schaff and Henry Wace, translated by Charles Gordon Browne and James Edward Swallow. Buffalo, NY: Christian Literature, 1894.

O'Day, Gail R. "'Show Us the Father, and We Will Be Satisfied' (John 14:8)." *Semeia* 85 (1999) 11–18.

Philo. "Legum Allegoriae (Allegorical Interpretation)." In *Philo*. Translated by F. H. Colson et al., 12 vols. LCL. Cambridge, MA: Harvard University Press, 1929–1962.

Reinhartz, Adele. "'And the Word Was Begotten': Divine Epigenesis in the Gospel of John." *Semeia* 85 (1999) 83–103.

———. "Introduction: 'Father' As Metaphor in the Fourth Gospel." *Semeia* 85 (1999) 1–10.

Thompson, Marianne M. *The God of the Gospel of John.* Grand Rapids: Eerdmans, 2001.

———. "'God's Voice You Have Never Heard, God's Form You Have Never Seen': The Characterization of God in the Gospel of John." *Semeia* 63 (1993) 177–204.

———. "The Living Father." *Semeia* 85 (1999) 19–31.

Chapter 9

"Tightrope Acts": Interpretive Tension, Incomprehensibility and Divine Directive in Acts 1:6–8

—MATTHEW W. WATSON

Instituto Bíblico Português (Portuguese Bible Institute), Portugal

ABSTRACT

Throughout the Scriptures, there is an inherent tension between divine incomprehensibility and knowability. The dialogue presented in Acts 1:6–8 highlights the "theological tightrope" that results from attempting to connect these attributes to one another in a comprehensible and actionable fashion. This chapter seeks to outline the contribution Acts 1:6–8 makes to a biblical theology of divine incomprehensibility by examining the text's structure and content and tracing the literary backdrop of the apostles' query regarding the "restoration of Israel" through Luke's gospel before contemplating different views of Luke's "eschatological tightrope." Strikingly, the incomprehensibility in the text does not appear to result from the human inability to fathom a particular divine mystery. It is, rather, a result of the Father's decision to place the details of eschatological fulfillment "within his own peculiar authority." In would appear that God keeps his people "in the know," albeit on a "need to know" basis. What can be known and acted upon in Acts 1:6–8 is Jesus's outline of a geographically expansive mission in which power from the Holy Spirit enables the apostles to act as effective witnesses. The tension between what is and is not knowable and actionable in this pericope highlights the hermeneutical, theological, and practical "tightrope" which Christians navigate in community in seeking to follow the divine directives of a God whose plans and purposes are only ever partially comprehensible.

INTRODUCTION

It is common for undergraduate theology students to encounter the incomprehensibility and knowability of God addressed together on a spectrum of relative knowability, based on the assumption that God is neither absolutely incomprehensible nor perfectly knowable.[1] In the abstract, it is relatively instinctive to grasp these concepts as logical extensions of both human limitation and divine infinitude. In the concrete context of biblical theology, however, navigating the implications of this relative knowability often requires developing a tolerance for interpretive tension and paradox. This is because the biblical authors frequently seek to help communities of readers struggling to understand their place in the unfolding plan of God and to act accordingly. The questions that arise from such interpretive communities are concrete and situational and, thus, rarely satisfied by abstract formulations.

Acts 1:6–8 is an example of precisely such an interpretive context. Luke-Acts presents the ministries of John, Jesus, and the apostles as the unorthodox fulfillment of the God of Israel's promised plan of salvation, extended beyond national and ethnic boundaries to all peoples.[2] One of the knottier matters of promise and fulfillment addressed in Luke's gospel is the matter of Jewish nationalist restoration. On the one hand, the infancy narrative of the Third Gospel boldly proclaim in texts like Luke 1:30–33 that Jesus, as the object of both angelic and prophetic promise, would go on to become Israel's king. On the other hand, regardless of the date adopted for the writing of Luke and Acts, it is virtually impossible to imagine a scenario in which decades or more had not passed since Jesus's death, with the distinct possibility that the destruction of the Jerusalem temple was already a foregone conclusion. This begs the obvious question: why would Luke deliberately invoke expectations that both author and reader knew could not

---

1. See, for example, Berkhof, *Systematic Theology*, 29–32, and Grudem, *Systematic Theology*, 177–80.

2. For a defense of this view, see Jervell, *Theology of Acts*, 18–25, and Bock, *Luke and Acts*, 121–48.

find fulfillment in the pages of the Gospel? This is a question that does not find a clear answer in Luke's Gospel.[3]

It would seem that Acts 1:6-8, inserted as new material into a narrative summary in Acts 1:1-11 which overlaps with material from Luke 24, represents a deliberate revival of this "unresolved issue" from the Third Gospel. From the internal narrative perspective of the apostles, the question reflects Jewish socio-political sensibility and the revival of hope brought about by the resurrection: surely this was finally "the moment" for Jesus to restore the kingdom to Israel! From the external perspective of the author and reader, with the benefit of decades of hindsight and the knowledge that Jesus had not, in fact, brought about the desired socio-political restoration, the question likely represents an objection or source of uncertainty for the reader.[4] Jesus's paradoxical reply would seem to offer a programmatic answer to both perspectives, making Acts 1:6-8 a fascinating case study in the human interpretation and application of the directives and plans of a God who is only partially comprehensible. To that end, this chapter will examine the structure and content of Acts 1:6-8 and trace the literary backdrop of the apostles' query regarding the "restoration of Israel" through Luke's Gospel before contemplating different understandings of Luke's theological view of the "eschatological tightrope" the apostles and, by extension, future generations of Christians, are called to walk in Acts.

THE STRUCTURE OF ACTS 1:6-8

Acts 1:6 demarcates its introduction of a new development with the discourse marker οὖν.[5] This is reinforced by the way that Acts 1:1-5 progressively traces "from the beginning" (1:1) all that Jesus did and taught, up to the indication of the Holy Spirit's imminent coming "not many days from now" (οὐ μετὰ πολλὰς ταύτας ἡμέρας,[6] 1:5). The sudden occurrence of the

---

3. Some defenders of supersessionism, like Moessner, "Ironic Fulfillment," 35-50, and Brawley, *Centering on God*, 30, would likely disagree with this statement, having posited that Luke's gospel offers an "ironic reinterpretation" of Israel's redemption. While these views will be addressed in depth later in this chapter, the present author sees the disciples' despondent comments on the road to Emmaus in Luke 24:21 and the revival of the matter of nationalist restoration in Acts 1:6-8 as evidence that Luke sees this issue as requiring further clarification.

4. See Luke 1:1-4; for different perspectives on how these verses indicate the gospel's rhetorical objectives, see Yamada, "Preface," 154-72, and Alexander, *Preface*, 187-210.

5. For a discussion of this use of οὖν, especially in narrative contexts, see Runge, *Discourse Grammar*, 43-48.

6. All quotations of the Greek New Testament in this chapter reflect the UBS 5.

ascension "as they were watching" in Acts 1:9 effectively eliminates the opportunity for follow up questions and frames Acts 1:7–8 as Jesus's parting words to the apostles. In terms of internal structure, syntactical correspondence within Acts 1:6–8 creates three neat layers of two-fold structures, in which the second item of each structure can itself be sub-divided into two parts. The following figure summarizes this syntactical correspondence and reflects the author's own translation[7] to bring out elements of syntactical correspondence and exegetical significance:

Figure 2: The syntactical correspondence within Acts 1:6–8

1:6   Οἱ μὲν οὖν συνελθόντες ἠρώτων αὐτὸν λέγοντες,
       They, then, having assembled together, began to ask him, saying,
           Κύριε, εἰ ἐν τῷ χρόνῳ τούτῳ ἀποκαθιστάνεις τὴν βασιλείαν τῷ Ἰσραήλ;
           "Lord, is this the moment for you to restore the kingdom to Israel?"
       εἶπεν δὲ πρὸς αὐτούς,
1:7   He, though, said to them,
           Οὐχ ὑμῶν ἐστιν γνῶναι χρόνους ἢ καιροὺς
           "It is not for you to know the moments or opportune seasons
               οὓς ὁ πατὴρ ἔθετο ἐν τῇ ἰδίᾳ ἐξουσίᾳ,
               which the Father has placed within his own peculiar authority;
1:8   ἀλλὰ   λήμψεσθε δύναμιν ἐπελθόντος τοῦ ἁγίου πνεύματος ἐφ' ὑμᾶς
           instead,   you will receive power when the Holy Spirit comes upon you
                       καὶ ἔσεσθέ μου μάρτυρες ἔν τε Ἰερουσαλὴμ καὶ [ἐν] πάσῃ
                       τῇ Ἰουδαίᾳ καὶ Σαμαρείᾳ καὶ ἕως ἐσχάτου τῆς γῆς.
                       and will be my witnesses in Jerusalem, and [in] all Judea and
                       Samaria and to the end of the earth."

The most obvious two part structure is the μέν . . . δέ construction, which marks the apostles' question in 1:6 and Jesus's reply in 1:7–8. This reply is itself composed of two parts, with 1:7 indicating that the "moments or opportune seasons" (χρόνους ἢ καιροὺς) of eschatological fulfillment should not be the focus of the apostles' energies, and 1:8 pointing to a two-fold injunction: await the imminent coming of the Holy Spirit and "be my witnesses" (ἔσεσθέ μου μάρτυρες) in a geographically expansive mission "to the end of the earth" (ἕως ἐσχάτου τῆς γῆς). Each layer of this structure further develops the tension between human hope and expectation based on divine promise and the need for human action in response to divine directive. The

---

7. All block quotations of Scripture in this chapter use the NRSV. Particular phrases that are referred to within the main text reflect the author's translation and a literal rendering of the Greek for the purposes of exegesis.

remainder of this chapter will address the interpretive and theological issues raised, beginning with the apostles' query in Acts 1:6.

CONTEXTUALIZING THE QUERY: ISRAEL'S RESTORATION IN LUKE AND ACTS

Jesus's reply in Acts 1:7–8 is widely viewed as a form of correction or, at the least, an adjustment of the apostles' perspective as expressed in the question of 1:6. Views diverge, however, as to how and why such a response was required. Some interpreters see a wealth of errors in the apostles' question, resulting from a lack of "perception."[8] Such interpretations generally depend on two assumptions: firstly, that there will be no "restoration of the kingdom to Israel" and, secondly, that Jesus's teachings on the kingdom of God ought to have made this sufficiently clear to the apostles. Luke and Acts, however, do not seem to make a concerted effort to make either of these points clear to the reader. To the contrary, the rich backdrop of Old Testament reference and the use of socio-political language in the Lukan infancy narratives have led many commentators to view the apostles' question as a natural expression of both Jewish messianic expectation and themes from the third gospel.[9]

The infancy narratives of Luke's Gospel have long been recognized as a key hermeneutical feature of the two volumes.[10] Throughout these opening chapters, divine promises spoken by narratively legitimated mouthpieces stimulate precisely the sort of nationalistic, socio-political expectation that is expressed in the apostles' query in Acts 1:6. These promises play a programmatic role, establishing expectations that play out, often in unorthodox or unexpected fashion, in the ministries of John and Jesus in the narratives that follow.[11] A few concrete examples of such language are examined below.

> And now, you will conceive in your womb and bear a son, and you will name him Jesus. He will be great, and will be called the Son of the Most High, and the Lord God will give to him the throne of his ancestor David. He will reign over the house of

---

8. Perhaps the most historically influential defense of this view comes from Calvin, *Acts*, 29. Stott, *Message of Acts*, 41, offers a more nuanced theological analysis while arriving at a similar conclusion.

9. See, for example, Barrett, *Acts*, 77; Witherington, *Acts*, 110; Bock, *Acts*, 62.

10. Brown, *Birth of the Messiah*, 248.

11. For a defense of this view, see Tiede, *Luke*, 39–40, and Bock, *Luke and Acts*, 100–3.

Jacob forever, and of his kingdom there will be no end. (Luke 1:31–33 NRSV)

This is the first use of the term kingdom (βασιλεία) in Luke-Acts and is associated with language that creates a scenario in which it is "difficult to imagine the anticipated redemption will be anything but a nationalistic restoration of Israel."[12] Other themes brought forward in the language of the infancy narratives, such as the inclusion of the gentiles in God's plan of salvation,[13] appear consistently throughout the narrative of Luke before coming to fruition in Acts. While the kingdom of God (βασιλεία τοῦ θεοῦ) is a central focus of Luke-Acts, generations of scholars have debated how to understand its relation to the notion of a restored kingdom for Israel (βασιλεία τῷ Ἰσραήλ), a theme that will be addressed later in this chapter.

> Blessed be the Lord God of Israel, for he has looked favorably on his people and redeemed them. He has raised up a mighty savior for us in the house of his servant David, as he spoke through the mouth of his holy prophets from of old, that we would be saved from our enemies and from the hand of all who hate us. Thus he has shown the mercy promised to our ancestors, and has remembered his holy covenant, the oath that he swore to our ancestor Abraham, to grant us that we, being rescued from the hands of our enemies, might serve him without fear, in holiness and righteousness before him all our days. (Luke 1:68–75, NRSV

The opening portion of Zechariah's prophetic pronouncement (the *Benedictus*) refers to the ministry of Jesus as raising up "a horn of salvation for us in the house of his servant David"[14] before discussing his son John's ministry in the hymn's closing lines. Like the angelic annunciation above, the *Benedictus* is full of Old Testament references and goes even further in its use of language that could hardly have been interpreted by first-century Jews as promising anything other than a nationalistic, socio-political kingdom. To expect a politically repressed people to understand twin references to salvation or deliverance "from the hands" (ἐκ χειρὸς) of enemies, especially when portrayed as "mercy toward our fathers" (ἔλεος μετὰ τῶν πατέρων

---

12. Green, *Luke*, 88.

13. See Simeon's prophetic address in Luke 2:29–32 and private aside to Jesus's parents in 2:34–35. For a synthetic discussion of scholarship on the issue, see Bock, *Luke and Acts*, 291–301.

14. The present author has presented a more literal rendering of the Greek ἤγειρεν κέρας σωτηρίας ἡμῖν ἐν οἴκῳ Δαυὶδ παιδὸς αὐτοῦ in contrast with the NRSV's "mighty savior" cited above.

ἡμῶν) and "covenant remembrance" (μνησθῆναι διαθήκης ἁγίας αὐτοῦ), as anything other than the restoration of socio-political autonomy can only be described as ingenuous.[15]

In light of the deliberate use of such language in the Gospel's programmatic opening narratives and the fact that Luke-Acts does not explicitly cancel the notion of a nationalist Jewish restoration,[16] the present author is hesitant to overly berate the apostles's supposedly "mistaken notions of the kingdom's nature, extent, and arrival."[17] To the contrary, for a first-century reader familiar with Jewish messianic expectations, the fact that Jesus "does not look like a king in Luke"[18] would represent a significant barrier to the sense of security or certainty (ἀσφάλεια) that is laid out as Luke's authorial objective in the gospel's prologue (1:1–4). It is, thus, entirely appropriate for the apostles to return to this unresolved issue in the opening chapter of Acts, in which the incomprehensibility of God's plan and, particularly, its timing is presented as an integral component of the interpretive paradox.

IT IS NOT FOR YOU TO KNOW: DELIBERATE INCOMPREHENSIBILITY

The apostles' query in Acts 1:6 is concrete and focused on the present: "Is this the moment?" (εἰ ἐν τῷ χρόνῳ τούτῳ). Jesus's two-part answer, on the other hand, articulates time in a more complex fashion. The first portion in 1:7 highlights what is not the appropriate focus for the moment by pushing socio-political concerns into the nebulous realm of eschatological fulfillment.[19] The second portion of Jesus's response in 1:8 highlights what is to be

---

15. For a detailed discussion of these issues and their first-century background, see Strauss, *Davidic Messiah*, 130–95.

16. Following Tannehill, "What Kind of King," 50–51. Supersessionist views to the contrary are primarily based on Luke's emphasis on Jewish rejection of Jesus as the Messiah and will be addressed in a following section of the chapter. While rejection is certainly an important element of Luke-Acts, it should not be simplistically equated with a theology of replacement, in which the promises to an "old Israel" are transferred to a "new Israel."

17. Stott, *Message of Acts*, 41.

18. Tannehill, "What Kind of King," 48.

19. The present author agrees with John T. Carroll that "soft-pedaling of imminent future hope is exactly what we should expect to find in Acts" but sees his declaration that "We are left, then, with no passages in Luke-Acts where any hint of Israel's future restoration is to be detected" as extending the theme of rejection in Luke-Acts too far by transforming it into the placement of definite eschatological punctuation where the present author sees Luke as leaving space for more to be written. See *Response to the End*, especially 122; 163–64.

done by placing the present focus on concrete action through the geographically expansive mission of "being my witnesses" (ἔσεσθέ μου μάρτυρες).

Jesus's negative response in 1:7 highlights the incomprehensibility of the Father's plan and, in particular, its timing. By affirming that "it is not for you to know" (Οὐχ ὑμῶνἐστιν γνῶναι), he leaves little room for doubt or misunderstanding; anxiety, speculation, or excessive concern about how and when the desired fulfillment might come are not only cast as inappropriate in light of the incomprehensibility of the divine plan, but also as potentially distracting from the directive at hand, which is explained in 1:8. The use of both Greek terms for time in the plural, with καιρός used in addition to the repetition of χρόνος from the apostles' query in 1:6, would seem to indicate that all such matters of timing are beyond the apostles' purview.[20]

The reason for Jesus's placement of the eschatological fulfillment in the category of "not to be known" is of particular importance for the present study: "the Father has placed (them) within his own peculiar authority" (ὁ πατὴρ ἔθετο ἐν τῇ ἰδίᾳ ἐξουσίᾳ). Lukan use of τίθημι in Acts often carries a sense of placement, the particularity of which is reinforced by the use of ἴδιος. The present author therefore concurs with Barrett that the best sense for the clause is "*reserved for his own decision*, rather than *appointed by his own authority*."[21] Thus, the formulation of the phrase would suggest that the information the apostles are requesting is not classified as a mystery that is unknowable or incomprehensible in the sense of being beyond the limitations of the human mind, but rather as information that, at that particular moment of revelation history, belongs to the exclusive purview of God the Father.

This distinction adds an important facet to the biblical theology of divine incomprehensibility. While it is customary to discuss the incomprehensibility of God in relation to divine transcendence or incommunicable attributes and knowability in relation to God's immanence and communicable attributes,[22] Acts 1:7 takes information that was, presumably, within the realm of human comprehensibility and refuses to divulge it. This refusal is then justified on the basis of God's singular authority over the particulars of eschatological fulfillment and its timing. The present author sees in Acts 1:7 the divine creation of deliberate incomprehensibility or, at the very least, deliberate ambiguity. While it is noteworthy that Jesus does not berate the

---

20. See Jervell, *Die Apostelgeschichte*, 115. On the likelihood that χρόνους ἢ καιροὺς reflects a traditional phrase, see Schneider, *Die Apostelgeschichte*, 220.

21. Original italics, Barrett, *Acts*, 78.

22. For such a discussion, see Berkhof, *Systematic Theology*, 29–32.

apostles for having asked an inappropriate question[23] or resolve their persistent curiosity by explicitly negating all hope for the future restoration of a kingdom to Israel, he likewise refuses to provide the requested clarification. In the present author's thinking, Jesus's response offers invaluable guidance on dealing with biblical ambiguity and theological curiosity, a topic that will be dealt with later in this chapter.

IT IS FOR YOU TO BE WITNESSES: THE REFOCUSING POWER OF DIVINE DIRECTIVE

The initial portion of Jesus's response in 1:7 dealt with the apostles' hope that the coming of the Spirit, indicated in 1:5, was a signal for the imminent socio-political restoration of Jewish independence. In 1:8, Jesus uses "instead" (ἀλλά) to turn the apostles' focus to what the Spirit's arrival would signal: a geographically expansive mission to the ends of the earth. The Spirit's coming is associated with "power" (λήμψεσθε δύναμιν ἐπελθόντος τοῦ ἁγίου πνεύματος ἐφ' ὑμᾶς) and should thus be understood as prerequisite for the supernatural enabling of the apostolic mission described in the narratives that follow. The task for which the Spirit's power was necessary is described by Jesus as "being my witnesses" (ἔσεσθέ μου μάρτυρες). The term μάρτυς is used in Luke-Acts to indicate eyewitness testimony,[24] the positive affirmation of an ideological or behavioral pattern,[25] and, toward the end of Acts, to describe the witness of martyrs.[26]

In light of the ascension which occurs immediately afterward, Jesus's reply seeks to turn the apostles' attention from future possibilities and potentially exclusive Jewish concerns to the ethnically inclusive directive of proclamation in the present. "Instead of worrying about the end of the plan, they are to be equipped to carry the message to the end of the earth."[27] The

---

23. This is an important point of contrast with Jesus's reaction to the despondent description of the disciples on the road to Emmaus in Luke 24:13–35. It should be noted that Jesus's rebuke in this instance seems to be directed toward their inability to understand the scriptural necessity of a suffering Christ, rather than depicting their hope for the redemption of Israel as misdirected.

24. For examples of this sense, see μάρτυς in Luke 24:48, Acts 1:22; 2:32; 3:15; 5:32; 7:58; 10:39, 41; 13:31; 26:16. Within the context, a sense of affirmation and continuity may well be intended in addition to the mere act of serving as eyewitness to the events.

25. The use of μάρτυς in Luke 11:48 clearly precludes eyewitness participation, but accuses the experts in the Law of ideological affirmation and behavioral continuity with "your fathers."

26. The use of μάρτυς in Acts 22:20 would seem to indicate this sense.

27. Bock, *Acts*, 64.

concentric geographical expansion described as "in Jerusalem, and [in] all Judea and Samaria and to the end of the earth" (ἔν τε Ἰερουσαλὴμ καὶ [ἐν] πάσῃ τῇ Ἰουδαίᾳ καὶ Σαμαρείᾳ καὶ ἕως ἐσχάτου τῆς γῆς) has been exhaustively studied and provides a literal and figurative map for the narrative to follow. Regardless of whether one takes "the end of the earth" to refer to Ethiopia, Palestine, diaspora Jews, Rome, Spain, gentiles in general, or the whole world,[28] the thrust of Jesus's instructions point to outward, missionary expansion in direct contrast with a nationalist or parochialist agenda. While Jesus does not explicitly quash all hope of future national restoration, his directive makes it clear that the apostles' sentiments and sensibilities urgently need realignment through the power of the Holy Spirit for the purposes of being instruments of God's plan.

LUKE'S VISION FOR ISRAEL'S FUTURE: MANAGEMENT OF EXPECTATIONS OR IRONIC REINTERPRETATION?

While the focus of this chapter is on the contribution made by Acts 1:6–8 to a biblical theology of God's incomprehensibility, the present author's view that these verses represent a relegation of the issue of a potential Jewish restoration to the ambiguity of eschatological time requires that something be said about Luke's view of Israel in the eschaton. This topic has drawn an enormous amount of scholarly attention and differing views of Israel's future in the eschaton in general and in Luke-Acts in particular have resulted in contrasting interpretations of the pericope at hand. Of particular concern for the present study is whether Acts 1:6–8 serves to indicate Luke's management of the reader's eschatological expectations by directing focus to the ongoing mission to the end of the earth or whether the narratives go further to outline a supersessionist vision in which Israel's future has been the object of ironic reinterpretation.[29]

On this point, it is important to return to the Lukan infancy narratives to demonstrate how Luke 2 serves to manage expectations by providing counterbalance to the nationalistic overtones of Luke 1 by introducing the theme of gentile inclusion in the people of God. This subject was the object of significant debate within Second Temple Judaism, as opinions differed as to whether the promised restoration of Israel would herald judgment or the

---

28. For a discussion of these differing proposals, see Bock, *Acts*, 64–65.

29. For a brief defense of this view, see Moessner, "Ironic Fulfillment," 35–50. For a lengthier analysis of Lukan eschatology that arrives at a similar conclusion, see Carroll, *End of History*.

opportunity for salvation for non-Jews.[30] The angelic announcement to the shepherds made after Jesus's birth begins to tip the author's hand in favor of gentile inclusion.

> But the angel said to them, "Do not be afraid; for see—I am bringing you good news of great joy for all the people: to you is born this day in the city of David a Savior, who is the Messiah, the Lord. This will be a sign for you: you will find a child wrapped in bands of cloth and lying in a manger." And suddenly there was with the angel a multitude of the heavenly host, praising God and saying, "Glory to God in the highest heaven, and on earth peace among those whom he favors!" (Luke 2:10–14 NRSV)

The initial announcement contains little indication that this savior and messiah would bring "great joy" to anyone but the Jews. The term for "people" used here, λαός, is used within Luke-Acts to refer to the Jewish people.[31]

The praise of the armies of heaven, on the other hand, uses language that many understand to be less ethnically exclusive. The term "people of favor/good pleasure" (ἀνθρώποις εὐδοκίας) had a technical force in Jewish contexts that referred to God's elect, but within the preceding context of Mary's *Magnificat*, seems to include non-Jews who would respond favorably to Jesus's coming.[32] As "people of favor/good pleasure" stands in parallel to "God" and "upon earth peace" (ἐπὶ γῆς εἰρήνη) stands in parallel to "in the highest" (ἐν ὑψίστοις),[33] the thrust of the angelic phrase would seem to favor interpretation of the earth in a universal sense, rather than referring specifically to the "land" of Israel.

The angelic chorus's message, then, cracks open the door to gentile inclusion that Simeon's speech opens wide.

> Simeon took him in his arms and praised God, saying, "Master, now you are dismissing your servant in peace, according to your word; for my eyes have seen your salvation, which you have prepared in the presence of all peoples, a light for revelation to the Gentiles and for glory to your people Israel." And the child's father and mother were amazed at what was being said about him.

---

30. Broyles's comparison of Ps 72 with Psalm of Solomon 17 is particularly elucidating on this point, "Psalm 72's Contribution," 33–34. See also Strauss, *Davidic Messiah*, 41, and Bock, *Acts*, 62.

31. Bock, *Luke 1–9:50*, 215–16.

32. See Marshall, *Gospel of Luke*, 112; Fitzmyer, *Luke I–IX*, 411–12; Danker, *New Age*, 60; and Bock, *Luke 1:1—9:50*, 220.

33. See Bock, *Luke 1:1—9:50*, 220.

> Then Simeon blessed them and said to his mother Mary, "This child is destined for the falling and the rising of many in Israel, and to be a sign that will be opposed so that the inner thoughts of many will be revealed—and a sword will pierce your own soul too." (Luke 2:28–33, NRSV)

Simeon's prophetic praise speech (the *Nunc Dimittis*) equates the infant in his arms with divine salvation (τὸ σωτήριόν σου), the key term around which the remainder of the speech revolves.[34] The descriptions that follow leave little doubt that God's program of salvation as realized through Jesus will bring blessing to both Jew and gentile, providing an important counterweight to the nationalistic expectations that were highlighted in the preceding section.[35]

This salvation is presented in 2:31 as "that made ready before the face of all the peoples" (ὃ ἡτοίμασας κατὰ πρόσωπον πάντων τῶν λαῶν), where the term typically used in the singular to refer to Israel (λαός) is used in the plural to refer to all peoples.[36] The remaining descriptions in 2:32, "a light for revelation to the Gentiles and for glory to your people Israel" (φῶς εἰς ἀποκάλυψιν ἐθνῶν καὶ δόξαν λαοῦ σου Ἰσραήλ), flesh out the conclusion that positive outcomes will be offered to both the gentiles and the Jews. Whether or not the respective peoples are willing to respond to the offer is a more complex matter, as Simeon's prophetic aside in 2:34–35 makes clear. The indication in the more private aside in 2:34 that Jesus is "appointed for the fall and rise of many in Israel and as a sign to be opposed/contradicted" (οὗτος κεῖται εἰς πτῶσιν καὶ ἀνάστασιν πολλῶν ἐν τῷ Ἰσραὴλ καὶ εἰς σημεῖον ἀντιλεγόμενον) provides a startling contrasting with the "salvation made ready before the face of all the peoples" in the *Nunc Dimittis*. Implicit in the syntax is the notion that it is God's plan, and not merely human misreaction,

---

34. The use of the relative pronoun ὃ at the beginning of the following clause ensures that "before the face of all the peoples" (κατὰ πρόσωπον πάντων τῶν λαῶν) is directly linked to Jesus as salvation. While there is a semantic ambiguity regarding whether both "light" (φῶς) and "glory" (δόξα) stand in syntactical apposition to "salvation" (σωτήριον), or whether only "light" stands in apposition, with "glory" standing in apposition to "revelation" (ἀποκάλυψις), "salvation" remains the grammatical and thematic linchpin around which the syntax turns. For contrasting interpretations of this ambiguity, see Bock, *Luke 1:1—9:50*, 244–45, and Bovon, *Luke 1*, 103.

35. On this point even authors with divergent viewpoints, like Tiede, "Glory to Israel," 21–34, Tannehill, "Tragic Story," 105–24, and Moessner, "Ironic Fulfillment," 35–50, agree.

36. This language leads the vast majority of interpreters to see this as a clear indication of God's offer of salvation to all. For one of the few contrary opinions, see Kilpatrick, "Laos," 127.

that is leading to the upward and downward motion of inversion.[37] This second speech makes an important contribution to establishing the expectation that the Christ of Luke's Gospel would go on to ruffle feathers and draw ire, in addition to bringing healing and restoration.

There is little doubt that both movements predicted by Simeon play out over the course of Jesus's ministry in Luke and that they continue through the apostles' ministry in Acts. Episodes of blessing and salvation alternate and sometimes even coincide with moments of offense and responses of rejection by other groups present. The question raised by some interpreters is whether this rejection represents a tragic turn in the story of Israel that Luke hopes will be addressed in "the Father's times and seasons"[38] or should be understood to indicate an ironic reinterpretation of Israel in which the nationalistic hopes of Acts 1:6 are fulfilled through the Christian mission to both Jews and gentiles, rather than being relegated to a vague future.[39] There is little doubt in the present author's mind that Jewish rejection of both the Christ and his apostolic envoys is a major theme in Luke-Acts, resulting in repeated Pauline pivots from the Jews to gentile mission.[40] It is, however, an entirely different matter to trace the lines of such turning and rejection and Deuteronomistic patterns forward into the eschaton and affirm that there are "no passages in Luke-Acts where any hint of Israel's future restoration is to be detected."[41]

If Luke's eschatological agenda were, in fact, as clear and as manifestly supersessionist as many posit, it must then be explained why the dialogues on the road to Emmaus in Luke 24:13–35 and that of the present pericope (Acts 1:6–8) resort to theological redirection rather than explicit refutation of the expressed socio-political expectations. The questions put to Jesus represent ideal narrative setups in which to clearly and categorically indicate the invalidity of such future hope. In Luke 24:25–26, Jesus instead emphasizes the fulfillment of Old Testament promise and the theological necessity

---

37. The "falling and rising" motion in the *Nunc Dimittis* echoes the inversion of Mary's *Magnificat*, although without the association of socio-economic or political language. Compare, for example, with Luke 1:52: "He has overthrown the lofty from their thrones and raised up the downtrodden" (καθεῖλεν δυνάστας ἀπὸ θρόνων καὶ ὕψωσεν ταπεινούς).

38. For a defense of this interpretation, see Tannehill "Tragic Story," 105–44, and "Story of Israel," 125–44.

39. For a defense of this argument, see Moessner, "Ironic Fulfillment," 35–50, and Brawley, *Centering on God*, 30.

40. See Acts 13:16–41 and 28:17–31. For further development, see Tannehill "Rejection and Turning," 145–65.

41. Carroll, *End of History*, 163.

(δεῖ) of his own suffering as the Christ.[42] As has been outlined above, in Acts 1:7–8, Jesus directs the apostles to focus on the task of being witnesses to the end of the earth, relegating socio-political expectations to the Father's authority.

It is for precisely this reason that the present author prefers not to attribute specific, closed ended eschatological conclusions to Luke. While all theological enterprise is conducted under the weight of presupposition and providing an adequate "solution to the puzzle" is a goal shared by all researchers, the present author hesitates to follow the lead of studies which aim to trace interpretive lines forward in order to make conclusions that the Lukan text seemingly forgoes opportunities to make for itself. It feels premature to attribute eschatological "punctuation" to Luke-Acts on this particular matter. The present author prefers to see Luke as leaving space for "more to be written" without attempting to deny patent socio-political challenges to the theological agenda presented, like the rejection of Jesus by Jewish leadership along with a significant portion of the people or the fact that Caesar's throne retained an iron grip on the Mediterranean while the "throne of David" remained little more than a vague hope.

A VISUAL METAPHOR: THE "TIGHTROPE" OF HUMAN RESPONSE TO DIVINE DIRECTIVE AND INCOMPREHENSIBILITY

The present author's understanding of the inherent tension between the divine attributes of knowability and incomprehensibility can be visually summarized in the following image, inspired by his experiences with Lisbon's 25th of April Bridge. In the spring and autumn, temperature differences between the land and the river result in thick fog, which frequently renders the opposite shore and its distinctive statue of *Cristo Rei* invisible through the mist. In this visual metaphor, knowability and incomprehensibility are expressed by degrees, as the further across the "bridge" of comprehensibility a particular concept comes, primarily as a result of the sensitive interpretation of divine revelation,[43] the more comprehensible and actionable it becomes. By contrast, the further a particular concept remains from the

---

42. The theological necessity of the Christ's sufferings, particularly as fulfillment of the Old Testament, is a repeated theme in Luke 24, in which three separate dialogues use δεῖ to make this point in Luke 24:6–7, 24:25–27, and 24:44–49.

43. The present author is a staunch defender of the creation of diverse, critical, and collaborative "reading cultures" in the spirit of Vanhoozer, *Mere Christian Hermeneutics*, 357–72.

"shore" of knowability, the more it is shrouded in mystery and, in a practical sense, the higher the risks of misinterpretation and misapplication.

Figure 3: A visual metaphor of human comprehension and divine incomprehensibility

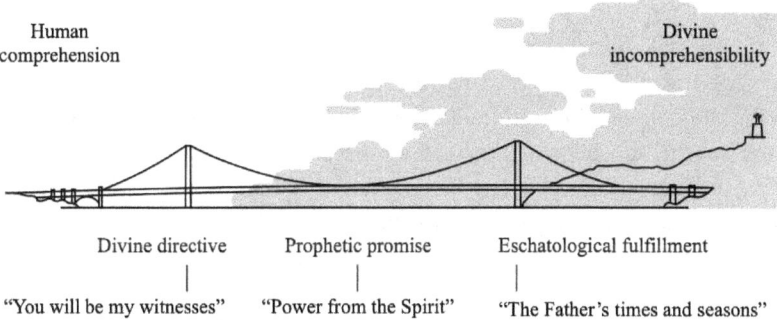

The visual metaphor above illustrates the author's understanding of the "push and pull" dynamic of divine incomprehensibility that is at play in Acts 1:6–8. Jesus's divine directive in Luke 1:8b pulls the Christian witness forward into the comprehensible and actionable "already" of human reality. The ability to execute this directive with impact depended on the enabling power of the Holy Spirit, a reality that still belonged to the realm of prophetic promise when Jesus uttered them in 1:8a. As Acts 2 and successive narratives show, the rapid fulfillment of this promise served as confirmation of God's plan at work in spite of Jesus's earthly absence. Acts 1:7, meanwhile, pushes the anxiously desired restoration of Jewish independence into the ambiguous distance of the eschatological "not yet." As has been defended above, the present author sees Luke's eschatology as being deliberately open ended on the subject of Israel's future.

While the figure above is based on a steel suspension bridge sturdy enough to support six lanes of traffic and two rail lines, the practical realities of doubt, uncertainty, and the incomprehensibility of God may in practice feel more like navigating a tightrope than crossing a bridge. Those who write or speak about the Scriptures with a voice of authority, especially to audiences beyond the theoretical playground of academia, should be aware that others on the tightrope may well be looking to their lead. Painting over degrees of textual ambiguity with a veneer of certainty or sowing doubt over technicalities among those looking for a simple but sure footing for their faith are simply some of the many ways that theological voices may make it harder for others to navigate the tightrope of divine directive and incomprehensibility.

It is for precisely this reason that the present author hesitates to trace theological paths from his own potentially fallible interpretation too far into the mists of promise and eschatological fulfillment. Curiosity and the desire for clarification, especially about the nature of God and his plans for the eschaton, are natural and can serve as a healthy stimulus to theological inquiry and discovery. It would perhaps, then, be wise for all who are engaged in the theological enterprise to maintain a clear notion of where biblical interpretation ends and their own presuppositions, systematization and speculation begin. It would be especially pertinent for all to refrain from excessively destabilizing the "ecclesiastical tightrope" on which no one treads alone, especially as a consequence of individual eagerness to peer deeper into the mists of that which "it simply may not be for you to know."

CONCLUSION: ACTS 1:6–8 AND A BIBLICAL THEOLOGY OF DIVINE INCOMPREHENSIBILITY

In spite of its brevity, Acts 1:6–8 brings the impossibility of total comprehension of God's plan, especially with regard to its eschatological timing, into striking tension with the necessity of human comprehension in order to relate to God and actively participate in the fulfillment of divine directive. The apostles' query in 1:6 served a double purpose, reviving unfulfilled expectations from the Lukan infancy narratives and highlighting the stakes of the author's rhetorical aim of helping the reader to "discern the certainty/steadfastness concerning the things you have been taught" (ἵνα ἐπιγνῷς περὶ ὧν κατηχήθης λόγων τὴν ἀσφάλειαν, Luke 1:4). Jesus's answer in 1:7–8 courts frustration from both the apostles and Luke's reader by relegating Jewish socio-political ambitions to the Father's purview. Rather than categorically refuting such hopes, however, Jesus redirects the apostles' focus to the imminent coming of the Spirit and to the missional commission that will orient the narratives that follow.

This chapter has sought to situate the text within both its Lukan context and the unresolvable tension between the incomprehensibility of God and the deeply human need to comprehend in order to act. Throughout Luke-Acts, God's plan provides clarity by transforming promises into fulfillments, bringing them forward from the mists of the eschaton into the realm of reality, often in an unexpected or unorthodox manner. Through John, Jesus, and the apostles, Luke reinforces how divine directives guide human comprehension of God's unfolding purpose through actionable participation. On the other hand, the mists of incomprehensibility do not fully dissipate, as the apostles' query strikingly demonstrates.

It is both remarkable and theologically significant that the incomprehensibility of God's plan in Acts 1:6–8 does not appear to result from the human inability to fathom a particular divine mystery. It is, rather, a result of the Father's decision to place the details of eschatological fulfillment "within his own peculiar authority." In what would appear to be an expression of divine wisdom, God keeps his people "in the know," albeit on a "need to know" basis. The narratives of Acts reveal that, with the guidance of the Holy Spirit and the strength and resolve of the missional community, the first-century apostles did, in fact, "know" all that was necessary to be effective witnesses in Jerusalem, all Judea and Samaria, and to the end of the earth. The same must be said of the twenty-first century disciple of Jesus, graced with the literary and theological records of the first generations of witnesses and nearly two thousand years of church history, replete with victories, failures, experiments, and tragedies from which to learn. They are also, it should be noted, empowered by the same Spirit.

In short, we "know" all that is necessary to be effective witnesses on our streets, in our neighborhoods, among our perceived rivals, and to the ends of the earth. It is both legitimate and beautiful when biblical ambiguity and theological curiosity spur the disciples of Jesus to study, inquiry, dialogue, debate, and even to appropriately cautious speculation. It is, however, profoundly unfortunate when curiosity, expectation, or anxious hope lead God's people to neglect divine directives in their eagerness to peer into the mists of incomprehensibility, searching for an interpretive certainty that may simply be beyond knowledge at this stage of revelation history. Luke narrates how early Christian communities sought to navigate the "already" and "not yet" tightrope of divine directive, prophetic promise, and various forms of divine incomprehensibility. It is the present author's hope that those who interpret these accounts are inspired to walk the same tightrope in a spirit of humility and the power of the spirit of Acts.

BIBLIOGRAPHY

Aland, B., et al., eds. *The Greek New Testament*. 5th revised ed. (UBS 5). Stuttgart: Deutsche Bibelgesellschaft, 2014.

Alexander, Loveday. *The Preface to Luke's Gospel: Literary Convention and Social Context in Luke 1:1–4 and Acts 1:1*. Society for New Testament Studies Monograph Series 78. Cambridge: Cambridge University Press, 1993.

Barrett, Charles K. *A Critical and Exegetical Commentary on the Acts of the Apostles, vol. 1: Preliminary Introduction and Commentary on Acts I–XIV.* International Critical Commentary. Edinburgh: T&T Clark, 1994.

Berkhof, Louis. *Systematic Theology.* 4th revised ed. Grand Rapids: Eerdmans, 1946.

Bock, Darrell L. *Acts.* Baker Exegetical Commentary on the New Testament. Grand Rapids: Baker Academic, 2007.

———. *Luke 1:1—9:50.* Baker Exegetical Commentary on the New Testament. Grand Rapids: Baker Academic, 1994.

———. *A Theology of Luke and Acts: God's Promised Program, Realized for All Nations.* Biblical Theology of the New Testament. Grand Rapids: Zondervan, 2012.

Bovon, François. *Luke 1: A Commentary on the Gospel of Luke 1:1—9:50.* Translated by Christine M. Thomas. Hermeneia Commentary Series, edited by Helmut Koester. Minneapolis, Minnesota: Fortress, 2002.

Brawley, Robert L. *Centering on God: Method and message in Luke-Acts.* Louisville, Kentucky: Westminster John Knox, 1990.

Brown, Raymond E. *The Birth of the Messiah: A Commentary on the Infancy Narratives in Matthew and Luke.* Garden City, New York: Doubleday & Company, 1977.

Broyles, Craig C. "Psalm 72's Contribution to the Messianic Ideal." In *Eschatology, Messianism, and the Dead Sea Scolls*, edited by Craig A. Evans and Peter W. Flint, 23–40. Grand Rapids, Michigan: Eerdmans, 1997.

Calvin, John. *The Acts of the Apostles, 1–13.* Translated by John W. Fraser and W. J. G. McDonald. Calvin's New Testament Commentaries, edited by Thomas F. Torrance and David W. Torrance. Edinburgh: Oliver & Boyd, 1965.

Carroll, John T. *Response to the End of History: Eschatology and Situation in Luke-Acts.* SBL Dissertation Series 92. Atlanta, Georgia: Scholars, 1988.

Danker, Frederick W. *Jesus and the New Age: A Commentary on St. Luke's Gospel.* Philadelphia, Pennsylvania: Fortress, 1988.

Fitzmyer, Joseph A. *The Gospel According to Luke I–IX.* The Anchor Bible Commentary. New York: Doubleday, 1981.

Green, Joel B. *The Gospel of Luke.* The New International Commentary on the New Testament. Grand Rapids: Eerdmans, 1997.

Grudem, Wayne A. *Systematic Theology.* Grand Rapids: Zondervan, 1994.

Jervell, Jacob. *Die Apostelgeschichte.* Kritisch-exegetischer Kommentar über das Neue Testament 3. Göttingen: Vandenhoeck & Ruprecht, 1998.

———. *The Theology of the Acts of the Apostles.* Cambridge: Cambridge University Press, 1996.

Kilpatrick, George D. "Laos at Luke 2:31 and Acts 4:25, 27." *Journal of Theological Studies* 16.1 (1965) 127.

Marshall, I. Howard. *The Gospel of Luke: A Commentary on the Greek Text.* New International Greek Testament Commentary. Grand Rapids, Michigan: Eerdmans, 1978.

Moessner, David. "The Ironic Fulfillment of Israel's Glory." In *Luke-Acts and the Jewish People; Eight Critical Perspectives*, edited by Joseph B. Tyson, 35–50. Minneapolis: Augsburg, 1988.

Runge, Steven E. *Discourse Grammar of the Greek New Testament: A Practical Introduction for Teaching and Exegesis.* Peabody, Massachusetts: Hendrickson, 2010.

Schneider, Gerhard. *Die Apostelgeschichte, Teil I: Einleitung, Kommentar Zu Kap. 1,1— 8,40*. Herders Theologischer Kommentar zum Neuen Testament 5.1. Freiburg im Breisgau: Herder, 1980.

Stott, John R. W. *The Message of Acts: To the Ends of the Earth*. Downers Grove, IL: InterVarsity, 1990.

Strauss, Mark L. *The Davidic Messiah in Luke-Acts: The Promise and its Fulfillment in Lukan Christology*. Sheffield: Sheffield Academic, 1995.

Tannehill, Robert C. "Israel in Luke-Acts: A Tragic Story." In *The Shape of Luke's Story: Essays on Luke-Acts*, 105–24. Eugene, OR: Cascade, 2005.

———. "Rejection by Jews and Turning to Gentiles: The Pattern of Paul's Mission in Acts." In *The Shape of Luke's Story: Essays on Luke-Acts*, 125–44. Eugene, OR: Cascade, 2005.

———. "The Story of Israel within the Lukan Narrative." In *The Shape of Luke's Story: Essays on Luke-Acts*, 125–44. Eugene, OR: Cascade, 2005.

———. "What Kind of King? What Kind of Kingdom?" In *The Shape of Luke's Story: Essays on Luke-Acts*, 48–55. Eugene, OR: Cascade, 2005.

Tiede, David L. *Luke*. Augsburg Commentaries on the New Testament. Minneapolis: Augsburg, 1988.

———. "Glory to Thy People Israel: Luke-Acts and the Jews." In *Luke-Acts and the Jewish People; Eight Critical Perspectives*, edited by Joseph B. Tyson, 21–34. Minneapolis: Augsburg, 1988.

Vanhoozer, Kevin J. *Mere Christian Hermeneutics: Transfiguring What It Means to Read the Bible Theologically*. Grand Rapids: Zondervan, 2024.

Witherington III, Ben. *The Acts of the Apostles: A Socio-Rhetorical Commentary*. Grand Rapids: Eerdmans, 1998.

Yamada, Kota. "The Preface to the Lukan Writings and Rhetorical Historiography." In *The Rhetorical Interpretation of Scripture: Essays from the 1996 Malibu Conference*, edited by Stanley E. Porter and Dennis L. Stamps, 154–72. Journal for the Study of the New Testament Supplement Series 180. Sheffield: Sheffield Academic, 1999.

Chapter 10

The Relation Between Spiritual Intelligence and Understanding God: Reading 1 Corinthians 2:6–16

—Elma M. Cornelius

    Research Focus Area: Ancient Texts: Text, Context, and Reception, Faculty of Theology, North-West University, Potchefstroom, South Africa

ABSTRACT

The NT claims that God is immortal, invisible, and that he lives in an unapproachable light, that he created all races from one human being, that he is Lord of heaven and earth and that he cannot be located as heaven is his throne and the earth is his footstool. Given the inability to understand this God with no limits, it may cause feelings of uneasiness, fear or even dread among believers. Apart from not understanding the unlimitedness of God, individual believers may also at times fail to appreciate God's hand at work in their personal lives. They often experience God's seeming absence during sickness, depression or when a loved one dies and may begin to question his divine actions, his apparent indifference and, ultimately, even his existence. Paul, however, praises God in Rom 11:33–36 for the greatness of his riches, wisdom, and knowledge, for God's decisions being unfathomable and his paths being impossible to understand. Paul thus praises God for being ultimately incomprehensible. Incomprehensibility is considered by theologians to be an attribute of God implying that God can never be fully understood by human beings. Paul acknowledges in 1 Cor 2:11 that only the Spirit of God can comprehend God's thoughts, that nobody understands the things of God except the Spirit of God, that the Spirit of God searches everything of God, including the deep things of God. Even so, in 1 Cor Paul shows how God has revealed these things to them through the Spirit, that they have "received the Spirit of God" and that they "have the mind of Christ." Does being spiritually intelligent—i.e., "receiving the Spirit," "having the mind of Christ," and "speaking God's wisdom"—guarantee the believer's comprehension of God? What is the relation between spiritual intelligence and understanding God's knowledge, wisdom, actions, thoughts, decisions or judgments, and his paths or ways? 1 Corinthians 2 is interpreted by focusing on the author, text and reader through a multidisciplinary approach. It is concluded that the reactions of believers to the incomprehensibility of God will vary according to different levels of spiritual intelligence. Spiritual intelligence nonetheless has the potential to bring the believer to a point of accepting the incomprehensibility of God as an indication of his almightiness, and trusting God even in times when his plans are not clear to the believer. The incomprehensibility of God will not discourage the mature Christian from seeking to know him, but rather humble Christians, persuade them of God's deity, and inspire them to worship him irrespective of an inability to fully appreciate his inexplicable vastness.

INTRODUCTION

Paul pronounces in 1 Tim 6:16 that God is immortal (ἔχων ἀθανασίαν), invisible (ὃν εἶδεν οὐδεὶς ἀνθρώπων οὐδὲ ἰδεῖν δύναται) and that he lives in an unapproachable light (φῶς οἰκῶν ἀπρόσιτον). From one human being God created all races (ἐποίησέν τε ἐξ ἑνὸς πᾶν ἔθνος ἀνθρώπων Acts 17:26), he is Lord of heaven and earth (οὗτος οὐρανοῦ καὶ γῆς ὑπάρχων κύριος Acts 17:24) and cannot be located as heaven is his throne and the earth his footstool (Ὁ οὐρανός μοι θρόνος, ἡ δὲ γῆ ὑποπόδιον τῶν ποδῶν μου Acts 7:49). James 1:17 refers to God as One being impervious to change. Some believers may experience feelings of uneasiness, fear or even dread for being unable to understand this God with no limits.[1]

Except for not understanding the power, boundlessness and unlimitedness of God, individual believers can at times not understand the workings of God's hands in their personal lives. Ballenger[2] writes, "Life is more than confusing . . . At times we wish we could fully understand what God is

---

1. Duquoc, "Who Is God?," 2–4.
2. Ballenger, *Why Can't We Understand?*

doing in our lives." Those believing in the possibility of God intervening in their lives are often surprised by God's silence and apparent inaction in their daily existence.[3] Believers often experience the absence and silence of God either in sickness,[4] or when oppressed,[5] or when they experience the death of a loved one.[6] Those trusting God may begin to question his divine actions or even his apparent indifference or seeming absence in their lives. Not fully understanding God's plans and actions brings frustration to many, and it sometimes causes believers to lose hope. This frustration can lead to doubt and disbelief. Van den Brink[7] rightly observes that humankind's experience of evil forces "forms a challenge to the doctrine of God's almightiness." This can ultimately result in the decision to altogether deny the existence of God.

Paul, however, praises God in Rom 11:33–36 for the greatness (βάθος) of his riches (πλούτου), wisdom (σοφίας), and knowledge (γνώσεως), for his judgments or decisions being unfathomable (ὡς ἀνεξεραύνητα τὰ κρίματα αὐτοῦ) and his paths being impossible to understand (ἀνεξιχνίαστοι αἱ ὁδοὶ αὐτοῦ). Paul thus praises God for being ultimately incomprehensible. Incomprehensibility is considered by theologians to be an attribute of God implying that God can never be fully or exhaustively understood by human beings.[8]

Paul acknowledges in 1 Cor 2:11 that only the Spirit of God can comprehend God's thoughts: "Nobody understands the things of God except the Spirit of God"[9] (τὰ τοῦ θεοῦ οὐδεὶς ἔγνωκεν εἰ μὴ τὸ πνεῦμα τοῦ θεοῦ). Paul explains in verse 10 that the Spirit of God searches everything of God, including the deep things of God (τὸ γὰρ πνεῦμα πάντα ἐραυνᾷ, καὶ τὰ βάθη τοῦ θεοῦ). In 2:10, however, Paul remarks how God has revealed "these things" to "us" (referring to Paul and the Corinthian believers) through the Spirit (ἡμῖν γὰρ ἀπεκάλυψεν ὁ θεὸς διὰ τοῦ πνεύματος). Paul considers himself and the Corinthians (as believers) to be different from those clinging on to the wisdom of the world, when he says that they have "received the Spirit of God" (ἐλάβομεν ἀλλὰ τὸ πνεῦμα τὸ ἐκ τοῦ θεοῦ 2:12) and that they "have the mind of Christ" (ἡμεῖς δὲ νοῦν Χριστοῦ ἔχομεν 2:16). Does "being spiritually intelligent"—that is "receiving the Spirit," "having the mind of Christ" and "speaking God's wisdom"—guarantee the believer's comprehension of

---

3. Larcher, "Divine Transcendence," 49.
4. Baum, "Sickness and the Silence," 23–26.
5. Richard, "Presence and Revelation," 27–37.
6. De Locht, "Death, the Ultimate Form," 48–56.
7. Van den Brink, *Almighty God*, 240.
8. Bavinck et al., *Reformed Dogmatics*, 27, 37.
9. Translation of Greek texts in this chapter has been done by the author.

God? What, in other words, is the relation between spiritual intelligence and understanding God's knowledge, wisdom, actions, thoughts, decisions or judgments, and his paths or ways?

The main goal of this chapter is to interpret 1 Cor 2:6–16 by focusing on the author, text and reader and the method of interpretation includes socio-historical, lexical-syntactical, literary, rhetorical, epistolographic and theological analyses.

SOCIO-HISTORICAL BACKGROUND TO 1 CORINTHIANS, RELEVANT FOR AN INTERPRETATION OF 1 CORINTHIANS 2:6–16

The author of the first letter to the Corinthians introduces himself in the letter-opening (1 Cor 1:1) as Paul, an apostle of God. It is believed that this letter was actually the second letter from Paul to the Corinthians, written from Ephesus during Paul's third missionary journey.[10] Witherington[11] reminds us that the Paul we meet in 1 Cor "has been a Christian for as long as twenty years," being a mature Christian and having been involved in missionary activities for more than ten years. This explains Paul's claims in 1 Cor 2:4 that his preaching and message demonstrated the power of the Spirit, in 2:6 that he brought a message of wisdom, in 2:12 that he received the spirit of God, and in 2:16 that he had the mind of Christ. Paul evidently enjoyed a close relationship with God.

Paul, as indicated, had an intimate relationship with God, even when he experienced abuse and opposition from the Corinthians. Acts 18:6 reports how Paul planned to leave the Corinthians because of the opposition directed toward him and the abuse he endured at their hands and in verse 9 it is reported how God spoke to him in a vision to calm him down, and to ensure him of his presence. God promised him safety and commanded him to stay there and preach: "So Paul stayed in Corinth for a year and a half, teaching them the word of God" (Acts 18:11).

Paul addresses his readers in the letter-opening (1 Cor 1:2) as "the church of God in Corinth," "sanctified in Christ Jesus," and "called to be holy." Corinth was one of the largest and most prosperous cities in the Roman world and Paul visited around the year 50 AD and stayed in Corinth

---

10. Gundry, *Survey of the New Testament*, 413.
11. Witherington, *Conflict and Community*, 5.

for more than a year.[12] Witherington[13] explains how a high social status and public recognition was important to the Corinthians as a person's worth was "based on recognition by others" and how a "ruthless competitive spirit" affected all. This explains the themes of boasting, preening, and false pride in this letter (1 Cor 1:29–31). The Corinthian church was thus still influenced by social values in Corinth. "Their faith appears not to have created any significant social and moral realignment of their lives," writes Garland.[14] In 1 Cor 3:1, Paul refers to the Corinthians as infants in Christ, making it clear that some were not yet mature in their faith. It seems fair to assume that the members of the Corinthian church showed different levels of maturity in faith.

Because of still being infants in faith, some Corinthian church members were still influenced by the values held in Corinth and this is why Paul refers to the wise man, the scholar and the philosopher who clung onto the wisdom of the world in 1 Cor 1:18–31. In chapter 2 of this letter, Paul teaches his readers about the opposite of worldly wisdom, namely the wisdom of God.

Paul's overall purpose with his letter was to address the problems in the Corinthian church[15] after being informed thereof by Chloe's people (1 Cor 1:11) and probably receiving a letter from them (1 Cor 7:1).[16] Snyman[17] points out that Paul was informed by these sources about divisions in Corinth, "which had implications for his apostolic authority." Snyman summarizes the rhetorical situation as Paul's attempt to persuade the Corinthians to accept his authority as apostle, to accept him preaching the truth and to follow his exhortations in living their new lives in Christ, which makes sense against the socio-historical background of the period in question.

THE PLACE OF VERSES 6–16 IN THE LETTER STRUCTURE OF 1 CORINTHIANS 2

The letter-opening of 1 Cor (1:1–9) contains the greeting (1:1–3) and a thanksgiving (1:4–9). The letter-closing (16:5–24) includes personal requests and final exhortations (16:5–18), secondary greetings (16:19–20), a

12. See Acts 18:11; Witherington, *Conflict and Community*, 5, 19; Gundry, *Survey of the New Testament*, 412.
13. Witherington, *Conflict and Community*, 6, 11, 23.
14. Garland, *1 Corinthians*, 27.
15. Witherington, *Conflict and Community*, 73.
16. Schüssler-Fiorenza, "Rhetorical Situation," 395.
17. Snyman, "1 Corinthians 1:18–31," 2.

note in Paul's own handwriting (16:21), a warning (16:22), and final blessings and greeting (16:23–24). In the letter-body in between (1:10–16:4),[18] Paul responds to the reports by the household of Chloe and the questions raised in a letter from the Corinthians. In his response to the problem of church division (1:10–4:21), Paul speaks on:

- The divisions in the church over leaders (1:10–17)
- Christ crucified is God's wisdom and power (1:18–31)
- The power of his preaching (2:1–5)
- *God's wisdom revealed by the Spirit (2:6–16)*
- The church and its leaders (3:1–23)
- The nature of true apostleship (4:1–13)
- His appeal and warning (4:14–21).

AN OUTLINE OF THE ARGUMENT IN 1 CORINTHIANS 2:1–16[19]

Because of their immaturity in faith, the Corinthians were "caught up in debates about wisdom,"[20] and rhetoric (or eloquence) was regarded as wisdom by the Corinthians. The church was divided on the issue of different leaders and that is why Paul speaks on the power of his preaching in 1 Cor 2:1–5, showing the Corinthians that he did not rely (solely) on rhetoric in his preaching. Paul makes three statements[21] to persuade the readers that his preaching was different from what the world expected: he did not come with excellence of word or wisdom (καθ' ὑπεροχὴν λόγου ἢ σοφίας) when he proclaimed the mystery of God (τὸ μαρτύριον τοῦ θεοῦ 2:1), because his focus was on Jesus Christ and him crucified (Ἰησοῦν Χριστὸν καὶ τοῦτον

---

18. Gundry, *Survey of the New Testament*, 415–16, regards 1 Cor 16:5–9 as part of the letter-body on the topic of collection for the church. Garland, *1 Corinthians*, 39, considers 16:1–12 as instructions for the collection and travel itineraries, as last part of the letter-body.

19. See Fitzmyer, *First Corinthians*, 169, for a discussion on the debate among some scholars on the different style of 2:6–16. In this chapter, the inclusion of 2:6–16 in the rest of the letter is not considered to be problematic.

20. Verbrugge, "1 Corinthians," II.A.2.c.

21. Fee, *First Epistle to the Corinthians*, 94, interprets these statements to pertain to the contents of his preaching (2:1–2), the form of his preaching (2:3–4) and the reason for both (2:5). The purpose statement in verse 5, however, rather seems to qualify only the statement in verse 4.

ἐσταυρωμένον 2:2); he came in weakness with fear and much trembling (ἐν ἀσθενείᾳ καὶ ἐν φόβῳ καὶ ἐν τρόμῳ πολλῷ 2:3); and his message and preaching demonstrated spirit and power (ἐν ἀποδείξει πνεύματος καὶ δυνάμεως 2:4). The purpose of this statement that his message demonstrated spirit and power, is so that their faith might not be in human wisdom, but in the power of God (ἵνα ἡ πίστις ὑμῶν μὴ ᾖ ἐν σοφίᾳ ἀνθρώπων ἀλλ' ἐν δυνάμει θεοῦ. 2:5).

In 1 Cor 2:6, Paul continues the theme of contrast between worldly wisdom and God's wisdom, between the believer and the unbeliever and he makes a statement that *they* (referring to Christians[22]) speak (λαλοῦμεν) a message of wisdom, which was different from the wisdom of the age or of the rulers of the age. In 2:7–16, he then elaborates on the wisdom Christians speak among the mature.

- The *origin of this wisdom* is God (θεοῦ σοφίαν 2:7a).

- The *nature of this wisdom* is that it is a mystery once hidden (ἐν μυστηρίῳ, τὴν ἀποκεκρυμμένην 2:7b), "that God destined for our glory" (ἣν προώρισεν ὁ θεός. . . εἰς δόξαν ἡμῶν 2:7c), and that it was never understood by the rulers of the age (ἣν οὐδεὶς τῶν ἀρχόντων τοῦ αἰῶνος τούτου ἔγνωκεν 2:8a) and which explains why they crucified Jesus (2:8b).

- The *means of revelation* of this mystery is that it was revealed by God's Spirit (ἀπεκάλυψεν ὁ θεὸς διὰ τοῦ πνεύματος 2:10a). The explanation of why the Spirit is the One, is because God's Spirit searches all things (τὸ γὰρ πνεῦμα πάντα ἐραυνᾷ 2:10b) and no one knows God's thoughts except the Spirit (τὰ τοῦ θεοῦ οὐδεὶς ἔγνωκεν εἰ μὴ τὸ πνεῦμα τοῦ θεοῦ 2:11). Verses 12 and 13 explain that "we have received the Spirit from God" (ἡμεῖς δὲ οὐ τὸ πνεῦμα τοῦ κόσμου ἐλάβομεν 2:12a) with the purpose of understanding what God has given us (ἵνα εἰδῶμεν τὰ ὑπὸ τοῦ θεοῦ χαρισθέντα ἡμῖν 2:12b). The implication of having the Spirit is to be able to speak words taught by the Spirit, explaining spiritual realities in spirit-taught words (ἃ καὶ λαλοῦμεν. . . ἐν διδακτοῖς πνεύματος, πνευματικοῖς πνευματικὰ συγκρίνοντες 2:13).

- The *receivers of God's revelation* are:

22. Scholars offer different opinions on the identity of the first-person plural of λαλοῦμεν. Fitzmyer, *First Corinthians*, 169, opines that it refers to Christians, and also refers to 1 Corinthians 1:23 where there is most probably also a general reference to Christians. Gardner and Arnold, *1 Corinthian*, 136, however, are of the opinion that Paul here refers to "all who preach the gospel." In this chapter the understanding is that the first-person plural refers to Christians, including Paul and the Corinthians (and likewise the other leaders among them).

- NOT those without the Spirit (Ψυχικὸς δὲ ἄνθρωπος οὐ δέχεται τὰ τοῦ πνεύματος τοῦ θεοῦ 2:14a), because they consider the things of the Spirit as foolishness (μωρία γὰρ αὐτῷ ἐστίν 2:14b) and they cannot understand the things of the Spirit (καὶ οὐ δύναται γνῶναι 2:14c). The reason behind it all is because these things are discerned spiritually (ὅτι πνευματικῶς ἀνακρίνεται 2:14d)

- ONLY those with the Spirit (ὁ δὲ πνευματικὸς 2:15), as declared by Paul: "we have the mind of Christ" (ἡμεῖς δὲ νοῦν Χριστοῦ ἔχομεν. 2:16b)

Paul makes it clear in 2:6–16 that Christians preach the wisdom of God (θεοῦ σοφίαν)—a mystery once hidden (ἐν μυστηρίῳ, τὴν ἀποκεκρυμμένην)—and destined for the "glory" (εἰς δόξαν) of only those with the Spirit (ὁ δὲ πνευματικὸς). This mystery is a "truth revealed by God."[23] Paul could tell the people of Jesus and Jesus's crucifixion, as it was revealed in the time of fulfilment,[24] written and reported by many. This wisdom of God—the gospel preached, "what God had prepared for those who love him,"[25] and the message of the cross—is juxtaposed with the wisdom of the world.

THE POWER OF CONTRAST IN 1 CORINTHIANS 2:6—3:4

Paul uses the rhetorical device of contrast extensively in 1 Cor 2:1-16, namely:

- The wisdom of this age (σοφίαν δὲ οὐ τοῦ αἰῶνος τούτου 2:6) versus God's wisdom (θεοῦ σοφίαν 2:7)
- The spirit of the world (τὸ πνεῦμα τοῦ κόσμου 2:12) versus God's Spirit (τὸ πνεῦμα τὸ ἐκ τοῦ θεοῦ 2:12)
- Speaking in words taught by human wisdom (ἐν διδακτοῖς ἀνθρωπίνης σοφίας λόγοις 2:13) versus speaking in words taught by the Spirit (ἐν διδακτοῖς πνεύματος 2:13)
- The unspiritual (Ψυχικός 2:14) versus the spiritual (ὁ δὲ πνευματικὸς 2:15).

The main contrast in this passage seems to be between the Ψυχικὸς and the πνευματικὸς. The Ψυχικὸς who will never receive the things of the Spirit of God (οὐ δέχεται τὰ τοῦ πνεύματος τοῦ θεοῦ) is a worldly person whose

---

23. Garland, *1 Corinthians*, 85.
24. Garland, *1 Corinthians*, 86.
25. Fitzmyer, *First Corinthians*, 179.

behaviour is at odds with "that which is under the control of God's Spirit,"[26] while the πνευματικὸς—the receiver of the revelation of the mystery of God—is a spiritual person who acts in a spiritual manner,[27] meaning that this person's life is controlled by the Spirit of God.[28] The contrast between Ψυχικὸς and πνευματικὸς is thus an important marker:

Table 8: The contrast between Ψυχικὸς and πνευματικὸς

Ψυχικὸς (1 Cor 2:14)	πνευματικὸς (1 Cor 2:12, 13, 15)
Does not accept the things coming from the Spirit of God (οὐ δέχεται τὰ τοῦ πνεύματος τοῦ θεοῦ)	Understands what God has revealed (ἵνα εἰδῶμεν τὰ ὑπὸ τοῦ θεοῦ χαρισθέντα ἡμῖν)
Considers the things of God to be foolishness (μωρία γὰρ αὐτῷ ἐστίν)	Speaks in words taught by the Spirit (λαλοῦμεν...ἐν διδακτοῖς πνεύματος)
Cannot understand the things of God (καὶ οὐ δύναται γνῶναι)	Makes accurate judgments (ἀνακρίνει τὰ πάντα)
Cannot be Spiritually discerned (ὅτι πνευματικῶς ἀνακρίνεται)	

It seems as if the key difference between the Ψυχικὸς and the πνευματικὸς is the response to the revelation of God.[29] One also recognizes this difference in response in 1 Cor 1:18 where Paul indicates that the one party (this will be the Ψυχικὸς) responds by regarding the message of the cross as foolishness, while the other party (this will be the πνευματικὸς) responds by regarding the message of the cross to be the power of God. First Corinthians 1:18, however, not only differentiates between these two opposing responses, but also the difference in outcome—the one is perishing (τοῖς μὲν ἀπολλυμένοις) while the other is being saved (τοῖς δὲ σῳζομένοις).

A question that invariably comes to mind, involves the contrast between the Ψυχικὸς and the πνευματικὸς in 1 Corinthians 2:6–16 and whether it resembles the contrast between the πνευματικοῖς and the σαρκίνοις in 1 Cor 3:1. Louw and Nida give two translation possibilities for the use of σαρκίνοις in 1 Cor 3:1, namely: "ordinary human beings" with human behaviour,[30] or "worldly people" with behaviour typical of their human nature.[31] In 1 Cor 3:1, Paul says οὐκ ἠδυνήθην λαλῆσαι ὑμῖν ὡς πνευματικοῖς ἀλλ'

26. Louw and Nida, *Greek-English Lexicon*, 509, 695.
27. Louw and Nida, *Greek-English Lexicon*, 323–24.
28. Louw and Nida, *Greek-English Lexicon*, 509.
29. Verbrugge, "1 Corinthians," II.A.2.d; Blomberg, *1 Corinthians*, 14d.
30. Louw and Nida, *Greek-English Lexicon*, 694–95.
31. Louw and Nida, *Greek-English Lexicon*, 509.

ὡς σαρκίνοις, ὡς νηπίοις ἐν Χριστῷ (I could not address you as "spiritual," but as "wordly"—as infants in Christ). Focussing on Paul's addition of ὡς νηπίοις in this verse, one can agree with Blomberg[32] that the contrast is not between believer and unbeliever, but rather between the "spiritual Christian" (the spiritual) and the "worldly Christian" (the carnal)—those *having* the Spirt versus those being *controlled by* the Spirit.[33] Fitzmyer[34] agrees that these verses describe two types of Christians. Even here among the Corinthians one can already discern the inclination to group Christians into categories. Some of them succeeded in being open to the Spirit's control, while others were still controlled by the values prevailing in the ancient Roman culture. Verbrugge[35] summarizes the difference between the unspiritual and the spiritual as that the Ψυχικὸς (like the σαρκίνος) clearly does not understand God's acts in human history, while the πνευματικὸς is able to put the things of God's revelation into a comprehensive life-changing perspective.

This issue brings one back to 1 Cor 2:6 where Paul states that they speak a message of wisdom to the "mature" (ἐν τοῖς τελείοις) which also seems to be a category of Christians. In 1 Cor 14:20, Paul admonishes the Corinthians to not be "children" in the way they think (μὴ παιδία γίνεσθε ταῖς φρεσίν,), but to be "adults" in the way they think (ταῖς δὲ φρεσὶν τέλειοι γίνεσθε). In 1 Cor 3:1, Paul expands on what he means by σαρκίνοις, namely that they are like "infants in Christ" (ὡς νηπίοις ἐν Χριστῷ). The contrast between being mature in one's spiritual intelligence versus being an infant in one's spiritual intelligence is thus present in this letter. Garland[36] is of the opinion that Paul makes some kind of distinction in 1 Cor between "those in whom the Spirit has really become a fundamental power of life" and the "weak" Christians—those "who are spiritual, but live as if they did not have the Spirit," those "not yet been freed from the normative practices of the world," those adhering "to secular attitudes and values" and being cut off "from the transforming power of the cross."

One finds another contrast in Paul's metaphor in 1 Cor 3:2 where he states that he gave these infants in Christ milk (γάλα) instead of solid food (βρῶμα). Is this a contrast between providing the weak Christian with "rudimentary teaching" instead of "advanced teaching?"[37] The emphasis in this

32. Blomberg, *1 Corinthians*, 14k, 14m.
33. Blomberg, *1 Corinthians*, 16c.
34. Fitzmyer, *First Corinthians*, 184.
35. Verbrugge, "1 Corinthians," IIA2d.
36. Garland, *1 Corinthians*, 102.
37. See Garland, *1 Corinthians*, 103.

metaphor is probably not on the "food" suitable for an infant,[38] but rather on the contrast between how an infant is fed and how an adult is fed. One can thus agree with Garland[39] that Paul provided these different groups with the same preaching content. The difference was most probably in how the message was brought to the Christians on different levels. One can imagine how much patience and time went into teaching the infant, while the mature Christians could easily grasp the intended message and show insight.

Paul makes it clear that the rulers of the age never understood God (2:8), while God's mystery was revealed to them (2:10). In 1 Cor 2:9, connecting vv. 8 and 10, Paul quotes from Isaiah[40] to highlight the contrast between those not knowing the wisdom of God and "us" to whom it has been revealed.[41] The quote communicates that God's things are beyond everything.

The purpose of these contrasts seems to be to downplay human wisdom that was very important to ancient societies, and to persuade the Corinthians of God's wisdom instead.

PERSUASION STRATEGIES IN 1 CORINTHIANS 2:1–16

It was shown that in his response to the problem of church division (1:10—4:21), Paul speaks in 2:1–5 on the power of his preaching, namely that he proclaimed the mystery of God, that his focus was on Jesus Christ, that he came in weakness, and that his preaching demonstrated spirit and power. Paul's dominant rhetorical strategy in these verses is to persuade the Corinthians of the power of his preaching because he has the power of the Spirit. With the expression ἐν ἀποδείξει πνεύματος καὶ δυνάμεως in 1 Cor 2:4, Paul introduces the theme of the Spirit.

To communicate effectively in these verses, Paul makes use of the persuasion strategies of *ethos*, *pathos* and *logos*. In defense of the character of his preaching, one notes the use of *ethos*,[42] where Paul makes statements about himself as a manner to render himself worthy of confidence in a situation where the Corinthians were divided on the matter of their spiritual

---

38. As claimed by Louw and Nida, *Greek-English Lexicon*, 5.

39. Garland, *1 Corinthians*, 103.

40. Fitzmyer, *First Corinthians*, 177, discusses how the quote does not correspond to a single passage, but how different Isaiah passages can be seen in this quote—64:3, 52:15, 65:16e. Fitzmyer even refers to possible passages from Jeremiah. However, most scholars agree that Paul quoted form Isaiah in this case.

41. Garland, *1 Corinthians*, 96.

42. Aristotle, *Ars Rhetorica* I:ii, 4.

leaders. Paul proves himself to have authority and to be trustworthy as an evangelist, due to his relationship with God, while having access to God's wisdom. Paul's preaching is different in the sense that he relied on God's wisdom and power instead of human wisdom and power. This makes an appeal to the emotions of the readers and can be considered to be the use of the strategy of *pathos*.[43] Paul attempts to persuade the readers by affecting them emotionally to place their trust in him. The rhetorical strategy in this passage is to persuade the Corinthians of Paul's maturity as a Christian—he speaks God's wisdom, he accepted it and made it part of his life; the death of Jesus thus gave Paul a new birth in Christ.[44] It also aims at persuading the Corinthians to follow his example in following Christ instead of the values of the culture of their time.

To communicate effectively in these verses, Paul makes use of the persuasion strategies of *ethos*, *pathos* and *logos*. In defense of the character of his preaching, one notes the use of *ethos*,[45] where Paul makes statements about himself as a manner to render himself worthy of confidence in a situation where the Corinthians were divided on the matter of their spiritual leaders. Paul proves himself to have authority and to be trustworthy as an evangelist, due to his relationship with God, while having access to God's wisdom. Paul's preaching is different in the sense that he relied on God's wisdom and power instead of human wisdom and power. This makes an appeal to the emotions of the readers and can be considered to be the use of the strategy of *pathos*.[46] Paul attempts to persuade the readers by affecting them emotionally to place their trust in him. The rhetorical strategy in this passage is to persuade the Corinthians of Paul's maturity as a Christian—he speaks God's wisdom, he accepted it and made it part of his life; the death of Jesus thus gave Paul a new birth in Christ.[47] It also aims at persuading the Corinthians to follow his example in following Christ instead of the values of the culture of their time.

In 1 Cor 2:6–16, Paul switches from the first-person singular (in 2:1–5) to the first-person plural, introducing a shift from himself to Christians in general, when he states that Christians speak wisdom and he then proceeds with a discussion of this wisdom and elaborates on the role of the Spirt in all of this, making it necessary to be spiritual (πνευματικὸς 2:15). The use of

---

43. Aristotle, *Ars Rhetorica* I:ii, 5.

44. Christ's salvation affected the person of Paul in all respects so that Paul even rejoiced in the incomprehensibility of God, as stated in Rom 11:33–36.

45. Aristotle, *Ars Rhetorica* I:ii, 4.

46. Aristotle, *Ars Rhetorica* I:ii, 5.

47. Christ's salvation affected the person of Paul in all respects so that Paul even rejoiced in the incomprehensibility of God, as stated in Rom 11:33–36.

contrast plays a major role in these strategies as Paul shows his readers the differences between human wisdom and God's wisdom, between the Spirit of this world and the Spirit of God, between the unspiritual person and the spiritual person.

The use of contrast plays a major role in these strategies as Paul shows his readers the differences between human wisdom and God's wisdom, between the Spirit of this world and the Spirit of God, between the unspiritual person and the spiritual person.

The rhetorical strategy in vv. 6–16 is to affect the Corinthians emotionally when he switches to the first-person plural, showing them that he identifies with them, that they are allies, and that they are different—with the aim to persuade them to live out their differentness. The implied rhetorical strategy is to persuade the Corinthians of the importance of one's relationship with the Spirit of God, in understanding God's plans.

The persuasion strategy of *logos*[48] dominates in 2:7–16 where Paul uses logical reasoning to persuade the readers of the following:

- That God's wisdom was once hidden but is now revealed (2:7);
- That God's wisdom was destined for the glory of the believer (2:7);
- That worldly people do not understand God's wisdom (2:8);
- That God's wisdom is meant for those who love him (2:9);
- That God's wisdom is revealed by his Spirit (2:10);
- That only the Spirit knows the thoughts of God (2:10b–11);
- That the spiritual received the Spirit of God in order to understand God and to speak words taught by the Spirit and that such a person can judge things (2:12–13, 15); and
- that the unspiritual person does not accept or understand God (2:14).

In his logical reasoning, Paul quotes Scriptural passages (in 2:9[49] and 2:16) to strengthen his argument on how incomprehensible God is: *nobody has conceived God* and *who has known the mind of the Lord?* In 2:16, as Verbrugge[50] points out, Paul uses rhetorical questions from Isaiah 40:13 to show "how much more majestic and powerful God is than any human being." That is

---

48. Aristotle, *Ars Rhetorica* I:ii, 8.

49. Verbrugge, "1 Corinthians," IIA2d, is of the opinion that the quote in 2:9 can come from Isa 64:4, Isa 52:15, the Apocalypse of Elijah, some unknown apocalyptic writing, perhaps a loose quote form Isaiah 64:4 and 52:15, or from "a series of texts already linked together in Hellenistic Judaism."

50. Verbrugge, "1 Corinthians," IIA2d.

perhaps the reason why Garland[51] says Paul's intention with these verses is to "place the things of God squarely outside the limits of human knowing." Although this theme is definitely present here, Paul's main rhetorical strategy in 2:6-16 rather seems to be to persuade the Corinthians that it is within their grasp to live good lives, as the Spirit who knows everything about God, is guiding the believer in behavior and thoughts. This does not mean Christians will know everything about God, but it means Christians have the most powerful, incomprehensible, almighty God at their side.

The persuasion strategy of *logos* is used in this passage to remind the Corinthians of the role of the Spirit in God's outreach to humankind and in effect exhort them to be spiritually mature. The rhetorical strategy of *pathos* is also used to affect the readers emotionally—to persuade them of the benefits of being spiritual: to be able to see salvation through Christ as wisdom, to be able to understand what really affords status, to be able to make judgments (1 Cor 2:15), not to judge other Christians based on which leader they follow, they will be able to say with Paul, and this is the essence, that "we have the mind of Christ."[52]

When Paul concludes this section with the statement that "we have the mind of Christ" (ἡμεῖς δὲ νοῦν Χριστοῦ ἔχομεν. 2:16b), he uses the conjunction δὲ to highlight the contrast between worldly individuals and believers. This aims at affecting the readers emotionally (by using *pathos*) in such a way as to motivate them to distinguish themselves from others by being mature in their faith in order to have the mind of Christ. The Corinthians are persuaded that an advantage of having the Spirit is that one can know, understand and evaluate what comes from God, but also that one can only know *what God graciously reveals*.[53]

Paul redefines the Corinthians' understanding of wisdom already in chapter 1. In chapter 2 he persuades them of the role of the spirit in having God's wisdom as Christians, as they need to be spiritually mature in order to navigate the problems among them.

THEOLOGICAL ANALYSIS

What is being communicated about God in 1 Cor 2:6-16? It is clear that a loving and gracious God revealed to humankind his loving act of salvation which was to the glory of humankind. It is made clear in this passage that the Spirit has an active role to play in God's mysteries. Not only is the Spirit

---

51. Garland, *1 Corinthians*, 97.
52. Gardner and Arnold, *1 Corinthian*, 147-49.
53. Gardner and Arnold, *1 Corinthian*, 145.

the only One to know and understand and reveal God's plans, but it is also through the Spirit that the believer can know what God revealed. While the worldly do not have the Spirit, they do not share in the advantages of this new identity and new life in Christ.

The Nature of God's Wisdom

In 2:7, Paul declares that he speaks God's wisdom, and he describes God's wisdom (σοφίαν) in three expressions:

- in a mystery (ἐν μυστηρίῳ[54])
- hidden (τὴν ἀποκεκρυμμένην)
- preordained by God for our glory (ἣν προώρισεν ὁ θεὸς . . . εἰς δόξαν ἡμῶν).

When Paul says λαλοῦμεν θεοῦ σοφίαν ἐν μυστηρίῳ, the question is whether the prepositional phrase ἐν μυστηρίῳ has an adverbial function to describe the verb λαλοῦμεν or an adjectival function to describe the noun σοφίαν.[55] In other words, does Paul say "we speak in a mystery" or "we speak the wisdom (being) in a mystery" When one considers Paul's statement in 1 Cor 15:51 that he tells them a mystery (μυστήριον ὑμῖν λέγω) when he speaks about the resurrection, it makes sense to interpret the prepositional phrase as describing "wisdom."

Paul makes a connection between "wisdom" and "mystery," perhaps because in ancient mystery religions, well known in those areas, each religion had a μυστήριον only known to the initiated members.[56] Louw and Nida[57] translate μυστήριον as "that which was not known before," with the implication of its being revealed at least to some persons. Strong's Concordance adds that it is a mystery or secret, "now revealed in the gospel *or some fact thereof.*" Barnett[58] remarks that the wisdom "turned out to be something utterly unexpected," namely the crucifixion of Jesus. God preordained (προώρισεν[59]) this wisdom, meaning that he decided ahead of time (πρὸ τῶν

---

54. Funk, *Greek Grammar*, 118, translates this prepositional phrase as "in the form of a mystery."
55. Ciampa and Rosner, *First Letter to the Corinthians*, 125.
56. Barnett, *1 Corinthians*, 42.
57. Louw and Nida, *Greek-English Lexicon*, 345.
58. Barnett, *1 Corinthians*, 48.
59. Louw and Nida, *Greek-English Lexicon*, 360–61, list the following possible meanings: "to come to a decision beforehand, to decide beforehand, to determine ahead of time, to decide upon ahead of time."

αἰώνων) and the purpose was the "glory" (εἰς δόξαν[60] ἡμῶν) of the believer. God's plans for humankind in the crucifixion of Christ was thus for the benefit of the believer.

God's wisdom, referred to as a mystery, refers to the deep things of God, including the "full meaning of Christ," the "purpose of His coming," "salvation," and "gifts."[61] In 1 Cor 2:2, Paul admits that his focus was "Jesus Christ and him crucified." Verbrugge[62] reminds us that the verb ἐσταυρωμένον is in the perfect form, with the implication that Paul not only proclaimed the historical event of the crucifixion, but also the long-term effects of this event for believers. The kind of wisdom Paul thus spreads to others, was that God's act in Jesus changes how things are for believers.

The quote from Isaiah in 1 Cor 2:9 is seen by Fitzmyer[63] to summarize the content of the hidden mystery. The passage quoted is about the uniqueness of God's plan of salvation, which remains hidden. Ciampa and Rosner[64] note how Paul, through this citation, shows that the wisdom they preach is the fullness of God's plan of salvation. Witherington[65] says this wisdom refers to "the divine truth of Christ crucified and its ramifications."

Who Has Access to the Wisdom of God and How and Why Was It Revealed?

First Corinthians 2:11 makes it clear that only the Spirit of God has *complete access* to the thoughts of God. First Corinthians 2:6–16 communicates that God's wisdom—the revealed divine truth of Christ crucified—is only available to those who believe in God. Verbrugge[66] observes that the mystery "has only been revealed to those who are in tune with God's Spirit." Paul says in 2:6 that they speak God's wisdom "among the mature" (ἐν τοῖς τελείοις). This maturity implies maturity in thought and behavior.[67] Ciampa and Rosner[68] note that this maturity is about behaviour in line with one's identity in Christ. This maturity needs also to be understood in contrast

---

60. This "glory" is defined by Louw and Nida, *Greek-English Lexicon*, 736, as a state of being great and wonderful.
61. Verbrugge, "1 Corinthians," II.A.2.d.
62. Verbrugge, "1 Corinthians," II.A.2.c.
63. Fitzmyer, *First Corinthians*, 179.
64. Ciampa and Rosner, *First Letter to the Corinthians*, 126.
65. Witherington, *Conflict and Community*, 123.
66. Verbrugge, "1 Corinthians," IIA2d.
67. Louw and Nida, *Greek-English Lexicon*, 753–54.
68. Ciampa and Rosner, *First Letter*, 123.

with Paul's reference to "babies" (νηπίοις) in 3:1. One who is immature in Christ, is the opposite of one living by the Spirit, being worldly and a baby in Christ. In chapter 2, Paul addresses the Corinthians as Christians who do have the Spirit of God when he uses the pronoun "we" in "we have the mind of Christ" and "we have the spirit of God" in vv. 12 and 16. Paul considers himself and the Corinthians to be different from those clinging on to the wisdom of the world, when he says that they have "received the Spirit of God" (ἐλάβομεν ἀλλὰ τὸ πνεῦμα τὸ ἐκ τοῦ θεοῦ 2:12) and that they "have the mind of Christ" (ἡμεῖς δὲ νοῦν Χριστοῦ ἔχομεν 2:16). Only the spiritual person has access to the wisdom of God. Garland[69] regards spiritual persons to be believers "in whom the Spirit has really become the fundamental power of life." Gaffin[70] adds hereto that they are "indwelt, renewed, enlightened, and directed by the Spirit." That is why Paul concludes in 2:16 with "we have the mind of Christ," meaning that they have a "clearer insight into the mind of God."[71]

In 2:14, Paul makes it clear that the man without the Spirit, the non-Christian, cannot understand spiritual matters. This person cannot understand spiritual matters because they regard it as mere foolishness.

Witherington[72] sums it up by remarking that "the link between God and Christians is the Spirit." Paul states in 1 Cor 2:12 that we can know God by virtue of all of what God might reveal is available to be fully received and understood for any Christian, through the Spirit. We can have the mind of Christ and share in his thoughts and perspective, but only through the Spirit who reveals God's wisdom to us. Not only, then, do we need the Spirit to guide and teach us (John 16:13), but we also need God's grace and power to transform our minds.

The Gospel of John (20:31) states that the purpose of God's revelation in the Gospel of John is so that people would believe and that by believing they may have life in his name. Paul says in 1 Cor 2:7 that God revealed his wisdom εἰς δόξαν ἡμῶν ("for our glory"). Ciampa and Rosner[73] interpret this verse to mean that "the goal of God's plan was the ultimate good of believers."

For Christians it is enough to know God's plans for our salvation, but this knowledge affords us but a glimpse of who God really is. The Spirit only

---

69. Garland, *1 Corinthians*, 97.
70. Gaffin, "Some Epistemological Reflections," 144.
71. Dunn, *Theology of Paul*, 250.
72. Witherington, *Conflict and Community*, 126.
73. Ciampa and Rosner, *First Letter to the Corinthians*, 126.

reveals the essence of God—but there is more to God than what is revealed to us.

What Does God's Incomprehensibility Communicate About the Nature of God?

Although Paul claims to have the mind of Christ, it is not a claim of being "all-knowing."[74] The Spirit of God reveals only the essence of God and for the believer it is enough to know God for his salvation of humankind in Christ. However, what is revealed, is but only a taste of God's wisdom. As only the Spirit has full access to God's plans and thoughts, it means that believers will unquestionably experience God's incomprehensibility.

Bavinck, Bolt and Vriend[75] are of the opinion that God will not fully reveal himself to creatures who are not divine. That is why Bloom[76] says God is merciful not to tell us everything. There is some comfort for the believer in not comprehending God.[77] God will not reveal anything that could place humankind in danger, stress, fear, or anxiety, as it will not be to our glory.

If God was not incomprehensible, in other words, if we could understand all his actions and thoughts, it would mean that he is not divine, that he is not the almighty God, that he is not truly God, that his wisdom, power and love are limited and equal to ours. What makes God *God* is the fact that no one can understand him exhaustively—no one can fully grasp, gauge nor understand the true and full extent of God.

God will always be infinite, always be beyond the human ability to know him comprehensively. God is greater than our understanding. But still, we can know God even if we do not understand him completely. Rosmarin, Pargament and Mahoney[78] consider faith to be believing that God has constant regard for all worldly affairs, that he has absolute knowledge of what is in people's best interests, that no power is greater than God, that God must be involved for anything to occur, that God is merciful and generous, and that God is righteous in judgment. Faith also includes an acceptance that God is incomprehensible at times, resulting in completely trusting God even when one's expectations are violated.

---

74. Barnett, *1 Corinthians*, 50.
75. Bavinck et al., *Reformed Dogmatics Vol. 1*, 29.
76. Bloom, *God Is Merciful*.
77. Ballenger, *Why Can't We Understand?*
78. Rosmarin et al., "Role of Religiousness."

CONCLUSION: WHAT IS THE RELATION BETWEEN SPIRITUAL INTELLIGENCE AND UNDERSTANDING GOD?

Does "being spiritually intelligent,"—i.e., "receiving the Spirit," "having the mind of Christ," and "speaking God's wisdom"—guarantee the believer's comprehension of God? What is the relation between spiritual intelligence and understanding God's knowledge, wisdom, actions, thoughts, decisions or judgments, and his paths or ways?

Uddin and Khan[79] summarize different scholars' definitions of spiritual intelligence. Spiritual intelligence can be defined as "the ability to apply, manifest and embody Spiritual resources, values, and qualities for enhancing daily functioning and well-being," and it is about "an awareness of divine presence and existential questioning." Spiritual intelligence "implies an awareness of our relationship to the divine."[80] It is "the belief that one is embedded in something greater than oneself." Christian spiritual intelligence starts with the recognition of the existence of God, then reaching out to Christianity for resources to get to know God[81] in order to live a good life in honor of God, guided by the Spirit. Through the Spirit of God, the believer shares in the wisdom of God. Only the spiritual intelligent person can *begin* to understand God.

One cannot, however, ignore "individual variation in beliefs, behaviors, bonding, and belonging."[82] From the socio-historical background on Paul and from what he says in 1 Corinthians about himself and the Corinthians, it seems fair to assume that the members of the Corinthian church showed different levels of maturity in faith. Paul refers to the Corinthians as *infants* in Christ (1 Cor 3:1), making it clear that some were not yet *mature* in their faith. Keeping in mind that Paul was a Christian for twenty years and involved in missionary work for more than ten years, it is clear that Paul's maturity as a Christian was on an altogether different level. This is why he claims in this letter that his preaching and message demonstrated the power of the Spirit, that he preached a message of wisdom, that he received the spirit of God, and that he had the mind of Christ. One can thus speak of different levels of spiritual intelligence. Blomberg[83] contends that the believer might move from being spiritual the one moment to being

---

79. Uddin and Khan, "Spiritual Intelligence," 170–71.
80. Sadiku and Musa, *Primer on Multiple Intelligences*, 55.
81. Cornelius, "Spiritual Intelligence," 4.
82. Hook et al., "Trust in God," 1.
83. Blomberg, *1 Corinthians*, 16j.

carnal the next moment and vice versa. Being a mature Christian, then, might mean the believer experiences intermittent periods of being carnal.

Blomberg[84] explains that Paul communicates that all Christians are "potentially" mature. It is important to realize that spiritual intelligence implies a cognitive choice to believe in God, but it also implies a process of transformation by God's Spirit. Spiritual intelligence can reach different levels: an awareness of a divine power, personal Bible study, church attendance, developing a relationship with God and placing one's trust in God. The question is, how the different levels of spiritual intelligence relate to different levels of understanding God. Once the Spirit is the believer's power in life, once one is "indwelt, renewed, enlightened and directed"[85] by the Spirit, one can achieve and develop a clearer insight into the mind of God.[86]

Templeton and Eccles[87] write that "personal meaning making is at the core of mature personal spiritual identities." They refer to Corbett[88] who suggests that whenever religious beliefs no longer comfort the believer from suffering and no longer provide reasons for injustice in this world, it becomes an opportunity to develop a more mature spirituality. This process of spiritual growth, according to Templeton and Eccles,[89] usually develops in private. The individual thus moves closer to God in order to better understand the incomprehensibility of God's actions.

Being indwelt by the Spirit means that it is accepted in faith that God is at times incomprehensible, and it guarantees that God's incomprehensibility is not confusing to the believer. The higher the level of spiritual intelligence, being a πνευματικὸς, the more the believer will be able to put those aspects of God's revelation into a comprehensive life-changing perspective and to understand God's acts in human history.[90]

The reactions of believers to the incomprehensibility of God will vary according to the different levels of spiritual intelligence. Spiritual intelligence has the potential to bring the believer to a point of accepting the incomprehensibility of God as an indication of his almightiness, and to a point of trusting God in times when his plans are not clear to the believer. The incomprehensibility of God will not discourage the mature Christian from seeking to know him, but rather humble Christians, persuade them

---

84. Blomberg, *1 Corinthians*, 14m.
85. Gaffin, "Some Epistemological Reflections," 144.
86. Dunn, *Theology of Paul*, 250.
87. Templeton and Eccles, "Relation Between Spiritual Development," 255.
88. Corbett, "Depth Psychological Approach."
89. Templeton and Eccles, "Relation Between Spiritual Development," 255.
90. Verbrugge, "1 Corinthians," IIA2d.

of God's deity, and inspire them to worship unreservedly irrespective of the inexplicable vastness that is God.

The spiritual intelligent person can grow into:

- the new identity in Christ,
- having God's wisdom to put the things of God's revelation into a comprehensive life-changing perspective,
- improving the quality of life and wellbeing,
- trusting God, even in difficult circumstances, and
- praising God for being incomprehensible!

BIBLIOGRAPHY

Aristotle. *Ars Rhetorica*. Loeb Classical Library. London: William Heinemann, 1947.

Ballenger, Mark. "Why Can't We Understand God Completely? The Comfort of Not Comprehending." Apply God's Word, November 12, 2016. https://applygodsword.com/why-cant-we-understand-god-completely/.

Barnett, Paul. *1 Corinthians. Holiness and Hope of a Rescued People*. Scotland: Christian Focus, 2011.

Baum, G. "Sickness and the Silence of God." In *Where is God? A Cry of Human Distress*, edited by Christian Duquoc and Casiano Floristan, 23–26. London: SCM, 1992.

Bavinck, Herman J., et al. *Reformed Dogmatics Vol. 1: God and Creation*. Grand Rapids: Baker Academic, 2004.

Blomberg, Craig L. *1 Corinthians*. The NIV Application Commentary. Grand Rapids: Zondervan, 1995.

Bloom, Jon. "God is Merciful Not to Tell Us Everything." Desiring God, November 7, 2014. https://www.desiringgod.org/articles/god-is-merciful-not-to-tell-us-everything.

Ciampa, Roy E., and Rosner, Brian S. *The First Letter to the Corinthians*. Pillar New Testament Commentary. Grand Rapids: Eerdmans, 2010.

Corbett, Lionel. "A Depth Psychological Approach to the Sacred." In *Depth Psychology: Meditations in the Field*, edited by Dennis P. Slattery and Lionel Corbett, 73–86. Carpinteria, CA: Pacifica Gradiate Institute, 2000.

Cornelius, Elma M. "Spiritual Intelligence Can Heal this World and Christianity Has a major role to play." *In die Skriflig* 54 (2020) a2546. https://doi.org/10.4102/ids.v54i2.2546

De Locht, P. "Death, The Ultimate Form of God's Silence." In *Where is God? A Cry of Human Distress*, edited by Christian Duquoc and Casiano Floristan, 48–56. London: SCM, 1992.

Dunn, James D. G. *The Theology of Paul the apostle*. Grand Rapids: Eerdmans, 1998.

Duquoc, Christian, and Casiano Floristan, eds. *Where Is God? A Cry of Human Distress*. London: SCM, 1992.

Duquoc, Christian. "'Who Is God?' Becomes 'Where Is God?' The Shift in a Question." In *Where is God? A Cry of Human Distress*, edited by Christian Duquoc and Casiano Floristan, 1–10. London: SCM, 1992.

Fee, Gordon D. *The First Epistle to the Corinthians*. Rev. ed. Grand Rapids: Eerdmans, 2014.

Fitzmyer, Joseph A. *First Corinthians: A New Translation with Introduction and Commentary*. Anchor Yale Bible Commentaries Series 32. New Haven: Yale University Press, 2008.

Funk, Robert. *A Greek Grammar of the New Testament and Other Early Christian Literature*. Translated and revised by F. Blass and A. Debrunner. Notes by A. Debrunner. Chicago: University of Chicago Press, 1961.

Gaffin, Richard B. "Some Epistemological Reflections on 1 Cor 2:6–16." *Westminster Theological Journal* 57 (1995) 103–24.

Garland, David E. *1 Corinthians*. Baker Exegetical Commentary on the New Testament. Grand Rapids: Baker Academic, 2003.

Gardner, Paul D., and Clinton E. Arnold. *1 Corinthians*. Zondervan Exegetical Commentary on the New Testament. New York: HarperCollins Christian, 2018.

Gundry, Robert H. *A Survey of the New Testament*. 5th ed. Grand Rapids: Zondervan, 2012.

Hook, Joshua N., et al. "Trust in God: An Evaluative Review of the Literature and Research Proposal." *Mental Health, Religion and Culture* 24 (2021) 1–19.

Larcher, C. "Divine Transcendence As Another Reason for God's Absence." In *The Presence of God*, edited by Pierre Benoit et al., 49–64. Concilium Theology in the Age of Renewal, vol. 50. New York: Paulist, 1969.

Louw, Johannes P., and Eugene A. Nida. *Greek-English Lexicon of the New Testament Based on Semantic Domains*. New York: United Bible Societies, 1988.

Richard, P. "The Presence and Revelation of God in the World of the Oppressed." In *Where is God? A Cry of Human Distress*, edited by Christian Duquoc and Casiano Floristan, 27–37. London: SCM, 1992.

Rosmarin, David H., et al. "The Role of Religiousness in Anxiety, Depression, and Happiness in a Jewish Community Sample: A Preliminary Investigation." *Mental Health, Religion and Culture*, 12 (2009) 97–113.

Sadiku, Matthew N. O., and Sarhan M. Musa. *A Primer on Multiple Intelligences*. Springer: Cham, 2021.

Schüssler-Fiorenza, Elisabeth. "Rhetorical Situation and Historical Reconstruction in 1 Corinthians." *New Testament Studies* 33 (1987) 386–403.

Snyman, Andries H. "1 Corinthians 1:18–31 from a Rhetorical Perspective." *Acta Theologica* 29.1 (2009) 1–8.

Strong's Concordance. Bible Hub. https://www.biblehub.com/greek/3466.htm.

Templeton, J. L., and J. S. Eccles. "The Relation Between Spiritual Development and Identity Processes." In *The Handbook of Spiritual Development in Childhood and Adolescence*, edited by E. C. Roehlkepartain et al., 252–65. Thousand Oaks, CA: Sage, 2006.

Uddin, Faheem, and Khan, Muhammad J. "Spiritual Intelligence, Resilience, Life Satisfaction and Bonding to God: Towards a Psych Spiritual Eclectic Model." *Journal of Academic Research for Humanities* 3.4 (2023) 169–81.

Van den Brink, Gijsbert. *Almighty God: A Study of the Doctrine of Divine Omnipotence*. Kampen: Kok, 1993.

Verbrugge, Verlyn. "1 Corinthians." In *1 and 2 Corinthians*, edited by Verlyn Verbrugge and Murray, J. Harris. The Expositor's Bible Commentary. Grand Rapids: Zondervan Academic, 2008.

Witherington, Ben, III. *Conflict and Community in Corinth*. A Socio-Rhetorical Commentary on 1 and 2 Corinthians. Grand Rapids: Eerdmans, 1995.

www.ingramcontent.com/pod-product-compliance
Lightning Source LLC
Chambersburg PA
CBHW070317230426
43663CB00011B/2160